The Formation and Development of Small Business

This book brings together thirty years of original empirical research on key aspects of the formation and development of small firms from selected articles authored or co-authored by Peter Johnson. Complete with a comprehensive introduction from the author placing the work in relation to the contemporary debates on the subject and providing a cohesive overview, these essays provide an excellent historical context for current research in this area.

Many of the studies in this book emphasise the interrelatedness of economic activity and decisions, an emphasis that serves as an important reminder of the complex business environments in which small firms operate. The book is divided into five sections. The first part focuses on the process of business formation. In part two, the role of new firms in regional development is considered. The third section deals with employment issues, whilst part four looks at various aspects of growth and development. Finally, the book concludes with two articles on policy.

This collection is a valuable source of reference and ideas for students and researchers working in the area of small firms and particularly in the analysis of their formation and development.

Peter Johnson is Emeritus Professor of Business Economics at Durham Business School.

Routledge Studies in Small Business

Edited by David J. Storey,
Centre for Small and Medium Sized Enterprises, Warwick Business School, UK

The Formation and Development of Small Business

Issues and evidence

Peter Johnson

Routledge
Taylor & Francis Group

LONDON AND NEW YORK

First published 2008 by Routledge
2 Park Square, Milton Park, Abingdon, Oxon OX14 4RN
711 Third Avenue, New York, NY 10017, USA

Routledge is an imprint of the Taylor & Francis Group, an informa business

First issued in paperback 2016

Typeset in Times New Roman by
RefineCatch Limited, Bungay, Suffolk

British Library Cataloguing in Publication Data
A catalogue record for this book is available from the British Library

Library of Congress Cataloging in Publication Data
Johnson, P.S.
   The formation and development of small business : issues and
evidence / Peter Johnson.
      p. cm. – (Routledge studies in small business ; 12)
   Includes bibliographical references and index.

ISBN 978-0-415-39409-3 (hbk)
ISBN 978-1-138-97453-1 (pbk)

1. Small business.   2. New business enterprises.   I. Title.
   HD2341.J643 2008
   338.6′42–dc22   2007044177

Contents

Preface

This book brings together a number of the journal articles that I have written, either as a sole author or in collaboration with others, on new and small firms. The articles cover the period 1979 to 2005. An exercise of this kind is a risky one and may be regarded by some as no more than self-indulgence by an ageing academic. I believe however that the book helps to highlight some important themes and issues in small business research, not least the complex business environment in which small firms and their owners operate. The last chapter provides some support for this belief. I also hope that in some modest way, the collection, with its variety of data sources and methodologies, will be a helpful source of reference and ideas for researchers, and enhance the historical context for current research in a number of important areas of small business activity and policy.

I have resisted the temptation to rewrite the articles. Apart from one or two minor changes (usually introduced to correct very obvious errors) they are as they were originally published. I have however taken the opportunity that reproduction provides to standardise some headings and the font and to convert all notes to endnotes. However, referencing methods were very varied and I have largely left these unchanged.

My decision not to engage in substantive rewriting means that very occasionally there is some duplication of material. For example, the same data sources are sometimes used in more than one paper and are necessarily described in each. In a few cases, where it seems appropriate and straightforward, I have been able to replace some of the duplicated material with a cross reference to another chapter. Such changes are indicated in italics within square brackets. There are also occasionally some words – e.g. 'forthcoming' or 'recent' – that now look rather dated. Again, I have not sought to edit out these words, on the grounds that it would be difficult to know where to stop an updating process once it has started. Thus the articles are virtually as they originally appeared.

Acknowledgements

In collecting these papers together, I have become very much aware of the many colleagues who have played a key part over the years in developing my interest in new and small firms and in helping me in my research in this area. I am particularly grateful to past and present colleagues at Durham University, where I have spent most of my career. It makes a world of difference to have colleagues working in the same or closely related areas in the same institution. It has also been a privilege to get to know numerous fellow researchers in other universities in both the United Kingdom and overseas. To all these colleagues, I say a heartfelt thank-you.

I am especially grateful to those individuals who, in one way or another, are associated with this volume. My particular thanks go to the co-authors of the papers included here: Professor John Ashworth, Professor John Creedy, Geoff Cathcart, Cheryl Conway, Dr Paul Kattuman, Professor Simon Parker and Dr Barry Thomas. Working with such colleagues has been a great privilege and a source of much enjoyment and learning. None of these colleagues of course bears any responsibility for the additional material I have written for this volume.

I should also like to thank Professors Colin Mason and David Storey for their support in the early stages of the book. And at Routledge, Terry Clague, Sarah Hastings and their colleagues have been most helpful.

A number of publishers have kindly allowed me to reprint (with alterations) papers which first appeared in their journals. The full details are set out below.

The following are reprinted with the kind permission of Taylor and Francis Ltd (http:/www.informaworld.com):

J. Creedy and P.S. Johnson, 'Firm formation in manufacturing industry', *Applied Economics*, 1983, 15 (2), 177–185.

Peter Johnson, 'Employment change in the small establishment sector in UK manufacturing', *Applied Economics*, 1989, 21 (2), 251–260.

P.S. Johnson and D.G. Cathcart, 'New manufacturing firms and regional development: some evidence from the Northern region', *Regional Studies*, 1979, 13 (3), 269–280.

Peter Johnson and Simon Parker, 'Spatial variations in the determinants and effects of firm births and deaths', *Regional Studies*, 1996, 30 (7), 679–688.

The following are reproduced with kind permission of the publisher, Blackwell Publishing:

P.S. Johnson and D.G. Cathcart, 'The founders of new manufacturing firms: a note on the size of their "incubator" plants', *Journal of Industrial Economics*, 1979, 28 (2), 219–224.

Peter Johnson, 'Differences in regional firm formation rates: a decomposition analysis', *Entrepreneurship Theory and Practice*, 2004, 28 (5), 431–445.

Peter Johnson, 'Unemployment and self-employment: a survey', *Industrial Relations Journal*, 1981, 12 (5), 5–15.

P.S. Johnson and R.B. Thomas, 'Government policies towards business formation: an economic appraisal of a training scheme', *Scottish Journal of Political Economy*, 1984, 31 (2), 131–146.

The following is reproduced with kind permission of John Wiley & Sons Limited:

P.S. Johnson and R.B. Thomas, 'New firms and employment creation', *Managerial and Decision Economics*, 1982, 3 (4), 218–224 (copyright: John Wiley & Sons Limited).

The following are reproduced with kind permission of Springer Science and Business Media:

Peter Johnson and Cheryl Conway, 'How good are the UK VAT registration data at measuring firm births?', *Small Business Economics*, 1997, 9 (5), 403–409.

John Ashworth, Peter Johnson and Cheryl Conway, 'How good are small firms at predicting employment ?', *Small Business Economics*, 1998, 10 (4), 379–387.

Peter Johnson, Cheryl Conway and Paul Kattuman, 'Small business growth in the short run', *Small Business Economics*, 1999, 12 (2), 103–112.

Peter Johnson, 'Targeting firm births and economic regeneration in a lagging region', *Small Business Economics*, 2005, 24 (5), 451–464.

The following is reproduced by kind permission of IP Publishing Ltd:

Peter Johnson, 'The size–age–growth relationship in not-for-profit tourist attractions: evidence from UK museums', *Tourism Economics*, 2000, 6 (3), 221–232 (copyright, ©. 2000, IP Publishing Ltd).

I am also grateful to the Thomson Corporation for permission to use data from their Social Sciences Citation Index® in Table 1.1.

For the last five or six years I have been based at Durham Business School, in the Centre for Entrepreneurship. This has been a great place to be. I should like to thank Professor Tony Antoniou (former Dean of the School) and Professor Simon Parker (former Director of the Centre) for providing such a congenial environment for research and writing.

Peter Johnson
March 2008

1 Introduction

Some background

The last 30 years or so have been a good time in the UK to be involved in research into new and small business and entrepreneurial activity. During this period, research in these areas developed rapidly across the world: see Landström (2005: chs 4 and 5) for a comprehensive survey.

This development has expressed itself in numerous ways: for example, through the establishment of many chairs and research centres and through high profile annual conferences, such as those of the Institute for Small Business and Entrepreneurship in the UK and Babson College in the US. Numerous specialist journals have also been launched including the *Journal of Small Business Management* (1964); *Entrepreneurship Theory and Practice* (1976); *International Small Business Journal* (1982); *Journal of Business Venturing* (1986); *Entrepreneurship and Regional Development* (1989) and *Small Business Economics* (1989). By the end of 1999, there were 44 English language refereed journals operating or announced on entrepreneurship or small business (Katz 2003).

All this has provided a supportive environment for researchers in the UK, where several factors have favoured entrepreneurship and small firms research.[1] A key one has been a policy environment that became much more supportive after the publication, in 1971, of the report by the Committee of Inquiry into Small Firms (Bolton Committee 1971).

The Committee's report had at least four features that encouraged research. First, it was widely regarded as a very thorough analysis. It thus provided a robust starting point and framework for further investigation of the small firms sector. Second, it pursued its own extensive research programme, using where appropriate outside investigators, under the able guidance of Graham Bannock, the Committee's Research Director. Much of the research was published through eighteen separate reports. This demonstrated a substantive commitment to the contribution that research could make to the analysis and understanding of small firms.

Third, against a background of long-run substantial decline in the relative share of small firms in economic activity, the Committee very effectively highlighted the important economic functions attributable to small firms, particularly in manufacturing (p. 343). It took the view that some of these functions were absolutely central to the preservation of the economy's dynamism. For example, it saw the small firms sector as '. . . the traditional breeding ground for new industries – that is for innovation writ large.' Even more importantly, the committee argued – in words strongly reminiscent of Alfred Marshall[2] – that '. . . small firms provide the means of entry into business for new entrepreneurial talent and the seedbed from which new large companies will grow to challenge and stimulate the existing leaders of industry' (p. 343). Such public commitment to the economic importance of small firms inevitably enhanced the attractiveness of research in the area. It also served as a counterbalance to the widespread view, especially dominant in the 1960s, that larger size, particularly in manufacturing, was likely to be a key source of additional efficiency.

Finally, the Committee itself underlined the scope for more research: 'The field offers enormous scope for further research: our own work and that of our commissioned researchers has suggested many avenues that could be fruitfully pursued and which lack of time alone has prevented us from attempting' (p. 353).

Since Bolton, other inquiries have served to maintain the public policy profile of small firms. For example, the Committee to Review the Functioning of Financial Institutions (Wilson Committee 1979) devoted significant attention to the financing of smaller firms. In more recent years the Bank of England has published a series of Annual Reports on the Financing of Small Firms.[3] In addition, it has also published studies on particular aspects of small firm financing, including technology-based small firms, ethnic minority businesses and social enterprises.[4]

At government level, the Bolton Committee report led to the establishment of a specialist unit, responsible for small firms policy and advocacy. This unit is now contained within the Department for Business, Enterprise and Regulatory Reform. In terms of industrial policy pronouncements, 'enterprise', 'enterprise society', 'enterprising behaviour' or 'enterprise culture' have been popular terms in recent years: see for example HM Treasury (2002). The nature of 'enterprise' and its relationship with small or new firms or indeed with entrepreneurship are never fully spelt out, although it is clear that small scale enterprise and business formation figure very prominently in policymakers' deliberations. All these developments have provided a very supportive policy environment for small firms research in the UK in recent decades. (It remains to be seen however whether the downgrading in 2006 of the government's small firms unit, in terms of its staffing, budget and status, represents any weakening of that policy commitment.)

Another factor that has been encouraging for UK small firms research has been the availability of databases. These databases, often refined and developed by researchers, have enabled various aspects of the dynamics of the small firms sector to be studied in some depth. Establishment-based

Factory Inspectorate data was widely used in the early days (see e.g. Gudgin 1974). Firn and Swales (1978) were able to utilise data from the Employers Register. Creedy and Johnson (1983) (see Chapter 3) utilised data from the (then) Department of Industry on openings in manufacturing industry. Following the pathbreaking study by Birch (1979) in the US (see below) based on Dunn and Bradstreet records, Gallagher and colleagues put this same database to good effect in their analysis of job change in the UK (Gallagher and Stewart 1986, Daly et al. 1991). Perhaps the most widely used data set in recent years has been that based on VAT registrations and deregistrations, e.g. in Ganguly (1985); Keeble and Walker (1994); Black et al. (1996); Robson (1996a and b); and chapters 6, 7 and 15 in this volume. Some use has also been made of company data (Johnson and Cathcart 1979a and b: see chapters 2 and 5; and Johnson 2003), the Census of Employment (Hart 2007) and the Inter-Departmental Business Register (Hijzen et al. 2007).

As is well known, each of these data sources has limitations, in terms of coverage and the range, reliability and suitability of the information provided. They are not set up with specific research uses in mind. They have nevertheless proved a valuable facilitator of empirical work. In addition some researchers have of course developed their own data sets through survey work or have obtained special tabulations of official data. An example of the latter is given in chapter 10. Perhaps the most exciting recent development in terms of data has been the Global Entrepreneurship Monitor (GEM), a very substantial international comparative exercise in the measurement of early stage entrepreneurial activity. In the latest report that uses these data (Bosma and Harding 2007), 42 countries were included.

A final development that has favoured small firms research in the UK in recent decades may be mentioned. It is the *recovery* in the relative importance of small firms. As Storey (1994: 25–34) has shown, both the share of small firms in manufacturing employment and the percentage of the labour force who are self-employed bottomed out in the mid 1960s, after which both measures started to rise again (see also Stanworth and Gray 1991). This reversal of decline meant an increased profile for small firms as an economic force and a consequent increased interest in their management and role.

Against this background it is hardly surprising to find a very substantial increase in academic articles in the area. Table 1.1, which is based on the Social Sciences Citation Index® (SSCI®), provides a very crude measure of publishing trends since the 1960s. These data must be used very cautiously. An important obvious limitation is that the number of journals included in the SSCI changes over time. It also takes time for a new journal to get onto the books.

Inevitably the particular words used for the search have an arbitrariness about them; no doubt other possibilities might have been used. Nevertheless the table does have some interesting insights to offer. Column 1 suggests that small firm(s)/business(es) publications grew very significantly from the 1960s, but that they might have peaked in the 1990s. *New* firm(s)/business(es)

Table 1.1 Data from Social Science Citation Index®: articles on new and small firms and entrepreneurship

	1	2	3	4	5	6	7
	Titles of journal articles with the following words:						
	"small firm" OR "small business" OR "small firms" OR "small businesses"	"new firm" OR "new business" OR "new firms" OR "new businesses"	"entrepreneur*"[2]	"firm" OR "firms" OR "business" OR "businesses"	Col 1 per hundred articles in Col 4	Col 2 per hundred articles in Col 4	Col 3 per hundred articles in Col 4
1960–1969	141.0	15.0	223.0	4010.0	3.5	0.4	5.6
1970–1979	209.0	44.0	435.0	6610.0	3.2	0.7	6.6
1980–1989	490.0	69.0	913.0	8916.0	5.5	0.8	10.2
1990–1999	809.0	115.0	1441.0	12045.0	6.7	1.0	12.0
2000–2010 est[1]	698.6	138.6	2302.9	14491.4	4.8	1.0	15.9

Notes
1 Data are not of course available for all years in this decade. The figures have therefore been scaled up on a *pro rata* basis.
2 *Indicates that the word may have alternative endings.

Source: Web of Knowledge: Social Science Citation Index®, by kind permission of the Thomson Corporation.

publications (column 2), although on a much lower absolute level, have continued to grow throughout the period and there is no sign yet of any decline in absolute numbers.

In columns 5 and 6 an attempt to normalise the data is made by relating the small/new firm(s)/business(es) data to more general mentions of firm(s) and business(es). Column 5 suggests that in fact the 1970s was relatively less productive than the preceding decade but that since then the 'share' of small firm(s)/business(es) articles continued to increase up to the 1990s. It has since substantially fallen back. Column 6 shows that there has been no corresponding decline in the relative importance of titles with *new* firm(s) /business(es), although there may have been some levelling-out in recent years.

The most striking feature of Table 1.1 however relates to articles with the broader concept of 'entrepreneur . . .' in the title: see columns 3 and 7. Column 3 shows that the numbers of articles meeting this criterion has continued to grow strongly over the decades. Furthermore, the relative importance of these articles (column 7) has increased very rapidly. It now substantially outstrips that based on titles which utilise new/small firm(s)/ business(es) words. Supporting evidence for this trend may be found in Ireland et al. (2005), who looked at the publication of entrepreneurship articles published in the *Academy of Management Journal*.

The broad trends suggested in Table 1.1 accord with what appears to be happening on the ground. For example there can be little doubt that entrepreneurship has come much more to the fore in recent years, partly as a result of the emphasis on nascent entrepreneurship (see Johnson et al. 2006) and partly because entrepreneurship has become much more closely associated with business formation. Indeed some influential researchers have linked entrepreneurship exclusively with new venture creation (Gartner 1988; Low and MacMillan 1988; Parker and Gartner 2004); it has also become much more closely associated with small business in recent years. The downside of such linkage of course is that it detracts attention from the question of what might be the optimal *mix* (in any given sectoral or geographical context) of new and old, small and large, businesses in the delivery of those functions that historically have been associated with entrepreneurship, such as risk-taking and innovation.

The focus of this volume

The papers in this volume focus on five areas that have been extensively researched in the UK: business formation; regional issues; employment; growth and development; and policy. Each is examined in turn.

Business formation

The term 'formation' is used here to describe the setting up of an entirely new independent business. The establishment of a new subsidiary is thus excluded.

It is fair to say that up to the early 1970s, relatively little had been written on such formation activity. There was of course an established literature on entry and the barriers faced by entrants, stimulated by the path-breaking work of Joe Bain (1956). This literature did in fact make a distinction between (what was termed) 'de novo' entry, i.e. the formation of firms from scratch, and cross entry, i.e. established firms moving across industrial boundaries (see Hines 1957 and Brunner 1961), but little attention was paid to the actual processes and scale of the former type of entry. However from the mid 1970s, some detailed empirical work on studies on formation – usually in the context of wider studies of the dynamics of industrial change – had begun to appear (e.g. Gudgin 1974, 1978; Firn and Swales 1978; Cross 1981; Storey 1982). In 1984, *Regional Studies* published a special issue on small firms in regional development in which several articles, using a variety of sources, look at regional variations in formation rates. Then in the 1990s, a number of studies utilising VAT registration data appeared (see the references above).

Many of the papers in this volume deal in one way or another with formation. However those in Part I are focused on aspects of the actual process of formation itself. The first paper (Chapter 2) provides some evidence – for manufacturing – on the 'fertility' of 'incubator' plants in different size bands in generating firm founders. 'Fertility' is measured here as the proportion of employees, in any given time period, who leave to set up their own businesses. In terms of *a priori* arguments, it is unclear whether or not smaller or larger plants are more conducive to higher rates of fertility (see Beesley 1955 and Cooper 1973). In the study reported in Chapter 2, however, the evidence suggests that fertility tends to be greater in smaller plants. The study raises at least three issues. First, how should the findings be interpreted? Might it be the case that would-be founders *pre-select* a period in a small plant in order to gain relevant experience of small-scale operations before setting up themselves? Second, how far is the *plant*, as opposed to the *business*, the appropriate incubator unit to study? Third, what other factors affect plant fertility? Incubator size is likely to be only one influence.

Since this study was published a number of empirical studies of cross-region differences in formation (e.g. Keeble and Walker 1994 and Chapter 6) have included a variable, e.g. the percentage of output produced in small plants/firms, designed to capture the impact of the size of incubator plant. The problem with this approach of course is that such a variable may be picking up other effects apart from the influence of incubator size. It may, for example, be indicating how favourable the economic environment is to small firm activity.

In Chapter 3, the formation decision itself is considered. A simple model of this decision is presented and tested against cross-section data from UK manufacturing. The model is straightforward: it views the potential founder as comparing two income streams, one from self-employment (self-employment is used here as shorthand for any own account activity), and the other from paid employment. When the former exceeds the latter by enough to cover the costs of transition into self-employment, formation will occur. It is not difficult to think of ways in which such a model could have been made more sophisticated, for example by incorporating non-monetary factors. The study did however serve to highlight further the difference between 'push' and 'pull' factors in the formation decision, a distinction that is embedded in various ways in a good deal of empirical work on formation and which has been expressed most recently in the GEM data categorisation of 'necessity-based' and 'opportunity-based' entrepreneurship (Minniti et al. 2006).

The possibility of a 'push' factor at work in the formation decision lies behind the considerable interest researchers have shown in the effects of unemployment on births: see Storey (1991). The empirical results on this topic are somewhat mixed, a reflection perhaps of the difficulties of disentangling empirically the effects of actual or expected unemployment on perceived paid employment prospects – and hence on the attractiveness of self-employment – and on the perceived self-employment returns themselves. Higher unemployment could thus have both positive and negative effects on births.

Another implication of the presence of a push factor is that it emphasises the importance, in both research and policy terms, of looking at business formation in the context of the alternatives. *Ceteris paribus*, an improvement in paid employment prospects will lower the birth rate.

The subject matter of the last paper in this Part – reproduced in Chapter 4 – is of a rather different kind and is primarily concerned with the quality of VAT registration data as an indicator of the extent of formation activity. Clearly, there are considerable limitations to these data, not least the fact that they are generated by a legal requirement rather than by a research need. Keeble and Walker (1994) however pointed out in the mid 1990s that the data are probably the best available and this picture has not really changed since.

Two features of this paper are worth noting. First, just over a quarter of registrations involved the purchase of an existing business ('purchase entry') as opposed to setting up from scratch ('formation entry'). This finding raises the interesting question of why different approaches to moving into business might be adopted. Second, the paper looks at the relationship between the start of trading – one, but not the only, way of defining the date of birth of a business – and registration and shows that the latter is often a poor guide to the former. The date of a business birth is not an unambiguously defined event. It is particularly important to be aware of this problem when looking at trends in births.

Regional issues

The papers in Part II are all about the regional dimension of formation activity and in one case, of business deaths. The spatial distribution of formation activity has attracted widespread attention over the years. This has covered work on both regions within a country (e.g. Barkham 1992; Keeble and Walker 1994; and the papers in this Part), and cross-national comparisons (e.g. Reynolds et al. 2007, a reprint of a paper first published in 1994).

The first of these papers, in Chapter 5, examines the role of new firms in assisting development in an economically disadvantaged region, in this case, the Northern Region (as it was known at the time of the study). The study relies for its empirical base on data on newly incorporated businesses whose registered offices were in the region. The paper demonstrates the dangers both of relying too heavily on business formation as a means of regional recovery and of looking at formation activity in isolation from the industrial structure of the region as a whole. New firms cannot simply be parachuted in as a 'free-standing' means of industrial recovery. It is interesting that these same issues are directly relevant to more recent debates: see Chapter 15.

In Chapter 6, the paper by Johnson and Parker (1996) utilises VAT registration and deregistration data at UK county level to look not only at some of the underlying determinants of births and deaths but also at the interrelationships between them. Another feature of the study is its treatment of economic variables as endogenous, i.e. subject to influence by births and deaths. As the paper shows, interdependence between births and deaths is a complex matter. It is not difficult to think of ways in which births in one period might affect births in subsequent periods, either positively or negatively. Similarly, deaths in one period may have an impact on deaths in later periods, again in either a positive or negative way. And in addition, births may affect deaths, and deaths, births.

The results reported in the paper pick up a number of interdependencies although surprisingly perhaps, relatively little direct birth–death interdependence was identified, apart from a negative effect of lagged births on deaths. The study did however find that net housing wealth – used in other studies (e.g. Black et al. 1996) as a proxy for the availability of collateral for new business founders and thus having a positive effect on formation – had a negative association with births.

The paper reprinted as Chapter 7 adopts an accounting approach to differences in regional formation rates, again using VAT data. The paper makes a distinction between structural and formation effects. The former effect examines the impact of industrial structure on the formation rate, given that the birth rate tends to vary across sectors; the latter effect captures the impact of birth rate variations across regions in the same sector. The same kind of approach was used earlier in Johnson (1983) and Storey and Johnson (1987). Such an approach has the obvious limitation that it does not provide an *explanation* of regional differences except in a narrow accounting sense. It can nevertheless provide initial pointers to possible influences. For example, the study suggests that in the North East, the relatively low formation rate overall reflects the fact that, *sector by sector*, the formation rate tends to be lower in this region than elsewhere. This in turn raises fundamental questions about why this should be so.

Employment

Part III includes three papers on employment in new and small firms, a topic that attracted enormous research and policy interest following the publication, at the end of the 1970s, of David Birch's path breaking study of employment change in the US (Birch 1979).[5] Perhaps the finding that made the biggest impact was Birch's estimate that two-thirds of net job generation (i.e. gross job gains minus gross job losses) occurred in firms of under 20 employees. This is the size category that is most densely populated by *new* firms. Birch's work was matched by Fothergill and Gudgin's (1979) study in the UK. Cross (1981) followed shortly afterwards. Since then there have been numerous studies of job accounting in the UK.[6] Most of these studies show that both job generation and destruction are relatively higher in the smaller size bands, reflecting the greater 'churn' in these bands, and that births play a key role in gross job generation. The picture on *net* job generation by size band is however a little less clear.

Birch's work was criticised on a number of counts, not least on the grounds that the net job generation figure may be an invalid measure where the net change, either overall or in particular size bands, is negative (Storey 1982: 18–19). Subsequently, Davis et al. (1996) and Okolie (2004) have argued that whether firms are classified to a size band on the basis of their base or end year size may have an important effect on the results. There are also the issues of the sensitivity of the results to the precise size bands used and of the extent of the employment 'knock-on' effects of jobs in different size bands. There is some evidence that employees in large firms are paid more than their small firm counterparts (Brown et al. 1990: 42; see also the studies quoted in Dennis 2000). This in turn is likely to mean that, *ceteris paribus*, the economic impact of the former, once the effects of their higher spending are taken into account, is greater.

Even when these 'technical' issues are left aside, there is the question of what the figures *mean*. It may for example be argued that job accounting exercises do not tell us very much about the underlying causes of job generation (Johnson 2007: 90–91). Furthermore, they say little about the inter-relationships between firms in different size bands.

It is against this general background that the papers reproduced in Part III were written. The first of these (in Chapter 8), surveys the evidence (up to 1981) on the movement of unemployed workers into self- employment. This movement took on particular significance in the early 1980s because of rapidly rising unemployment rates. The underlying question was: How far could self-employment provide an outlet for those who were actually or likely to become unemployed? Or to put the question another way: How strong was the 'push' factor? The survey found that published studies suggested that no more than 5 per cent of people affected by redundancy became self-employed. This may however be an underestimate in a twenty-first century context because of the much higher profile that self-employment now has. It is also important to note that the published studies reviewed concentrated primarily on manual workers; the rate is likely to be higher for non-manual workers.

The paper reproduced as Chapter 9 uses some basic micro-economic analysis to examine the net employment effects of new firm formation. The key issue here is the impact firm formation may have on *existing* firms. This impact will be affected by a whole range of factors, including the competitive advantage of the new firm, in terms of both costs and innovativeness. Where a formation offers little that is new and enters an established, highly competitive market, its net impact may be virtually zero. It will simply lead to the overall market being spread more thinly over the firms supplying that market. The paper presents some evidence to suggest that many, perhaps most, new firms do not have anything very new to offer.

The last paper in this Part (Chapter 10) draws on special tabulations from official Census of Production statistics to examine the movement of establishments between size bands in manufacturing over the period 1975–1983 (see also Johnson 1989). Because of data restrictions it was possible to divide establishments into two basic size bands only: 'small', under 200 employees, and 'large', the rest. *Within* the small size band, however, some data were available for a finer size breakdown. The analysis shows, *inter alia*, that although the employment share of the small establishment sector increased over the period, this share was enhanced by small establishments being less able to grow out of their size band and by large establishments becoming smaller. This finding highlights the need for caution when interpreting trends in small-scale activity. It is important to note that *establishments* rather than *firms* are the subject of this paper. The former embraces both the single establishment firm and the establishment owned by a multi-establishment business. These different types of establishment may behave differently and be subject to different constraints.

Growth and development

The topic in Part IV is small-firm development and growth. There is of course a very substantial literature in this area, a literature that has been reviewed in a number of surveys: e.g. Storey (1994: ch 5); Barkham et al. (1996: ch 2); Davidsson (2006); and, specifically in relation to *measures* of growth, Delmar (2006). Much attention has been paid to trying to explain small-firm growth. Unfortunately, the results of these studies are often not easy to reconcile. This in part reflects the 'inherent complexity' of the topic (Davidsson 2006), one element of which may be that the factors affecting the growth of a particular firm or a cohort of firms may well change significantly through time. In addition, variations in how growth is defined[7] and measured, the choice and specification of the dependent variables, the time period chosen and the geographical and sectoral coverage, make direct comparisons problematic. It is also worth noting that by definition, those firms that fail are not included in growth studies. Notwithstanding these challenges, some broad generalisations are possible (Storey 1994: ch 6; Davidsson 2006: 370–373). Not surprisingly, owner motivation and strategy and the availability of skills and resources have a key role to play. Although a good deal more is now known about small-firm growth, it is still not possible to forecast with any accuracy *future* growth on the basis of *current* firm, ownership, market or strategy characteristics.

Alongside the studies devoted to small-firm growth is a very considerable literature on firm growth in more general terms. Much of this has focused on the relationship between growth, size and age.[8] Economists particularly have been interested in the size–growth relationship, and especially with testing 'Gibrat's Law' (Gibrat 1931) or, as it is more widely known, the Law of Proportionate Effect, which postulates that firm growth is a stochastic phenomenon that favours no particular size of firm. Thus if the Law holds it would be expected, *inter alia*, that the average rate of growth and the variance of that growth would be the same in all size bands. The empirical evidence is mixed, although overall, the weight of the evidence suggests that the Law does not hold, with a number of studies showing that small firms tend to grow faster and to have higher variances of growth than their larger counterparts. For a good survey, see Dunne and Hughes (1994).

Another relevant strand of interest of development is the 'stages of growth' or 'life cycle' literature, which goes back to a paper of Churchill and Lewis (1983), but developed since by others (e.g. Scott and Bruce 1987; Burns 2007: 218–219). This literature has endeavoured to identify various stages through which the life cycle of the firm goes. A key limitation of this approach is that the various stages are not particularly well defined. It also remains unclear precisely what a firm must do to move from one stage to another. (For a useful review of stage models, see O'Farrell and Hitchens 1988.)

The first paper in this Part (Chapter 11) examines how good very small firms are at predicting their future growth. The measure of growth used, employment, was determined by the availability of data. The study found that these 'micro' firms tended systematically to overestimate their employment prospects, with the overestimation, not surprisingly, being higher the longer the period examined. The study raises the important policy challenge about what, if anything, can be done to make firms more realistic in their forecasts and thereby to avoid at least some of the costs that arise from over-optimism.

The second paper reports on a preliminary study of the growth of (mainly) micro businesses in the short run, i.e. twelve months. Perhaps the most interesting implication of the study is the tentative suggestion that there might be more than one optimal size for such businesses. For example, there is some evidence that for the kind of service businesses covered in this study, the optimum might be achieved at *either* about 2 employees *or* about 17 employees. Thus the widely accepted notion, implicit in the way most economics textbook writers draw the long run average cost curve, that there might be just one optimal size, is open to question. Another implication is that a growing firm that wants to remain competitive may find itself with the challenge of having to jump quite rapidly from a very small size to a significantly bigger scale of operation.

At first sight the topic of the paper that forms Chapter 13 – museums and the relationship between their size, age and growth – has little to do with small, or indeed large, firms. However it is included in order to give some focus to the not-for-profit sector and for a reason that goes beyond its particular findings. It is fair to say that most work to date on entrepreneurship and new and small-scale operations has focused on commercial businesses and probably rightly so. There is however a rapidly growing literature on social and public entrepreneurship (e.g. Haugh 2006: 401–436), which is essentially about the recognition and development of new opportunities to increase *social* well-being.

Some researchers have restricted their notion of entrepreneurship to the discovery and exploitation of *profitable* opportunities (Shane and Venkataraman 2000[9]) or to the creation of new commercial organisations (see above), but this focus seems unnecessarily restrictive. Given that the contribution of the not-for-profit sector to human well-being is being increasingly recognised – in the UK, an Office of the Third Sector, with its own government minister, was set up in the Cabinet Office in 2006 – the understanding of the way in which this sector develops and grows is likely to take on greater significance.

Although museums face a number of constraints and opportunities as a result of their (mainly) public sector status, their growth is nevertheless, like that of their private sector counterparts, subject to a wide range of influences. The evidence presented in this paper nevertheless suggests little support for the Law of Proportionate Effect in museum growth.

Policy

The final part of the book is about policy issues. Again, there is now a very substantial literature on the analysis and evaluation of various aspects of small firms policy. In addition, many papers, including most in this volume, that deal in one way or another with small firms, discuss – to varying degrees – the potential policy implications of their findings. Interest in this area ranges from an analysis of the relevance for small firms of macroeconomic policy instruments, such as tax rates (e.g. Parker and Robson 2004) to some form of assessment of particular policy measures (e.g. Bennett and Robson 1999, Bennett et al. 2001; see also Chapter 14).

When it comes to the assessment of particular policy initiatives, most of the focus has been on the efficiency or effectiveness of the measures, rather than on a full-blown cost benefit assessment which addresses the key issue of whether or not a policy is worthwhile in a social welfare sense. One of the reasons for this gap in the literature is that the data demands for such evaluations are very considerable, not least in the assessment of the counterfactual: what the picture would be like in the absence of the policy.[10]

It is against this background that the study in Chapter 14 examines some key social costs and benefits of a training programme for would-be business owners. The estimation of the counterfactual was based primarily on interviews with the trainees. While this approach was not ideal, a number of factors (spelt out in the paper) suggest it was a robust one.

The study found a relatively high rate of return from the training, a return that was generated by a range of factors, including confidence building, as well as help on technical aspects of running a business. Perhaps the most interesting finding however was the estimate that 70 per cent of the return was generated by just two businesses (out of a total of 15). This finding in turn raises the critical question of whether such high fliers could have been identified *prior* to the course, in which case substantial cost savings could have been made by eliminating the 'low fliers'. If not, then one of the inevitable costs of training the high fliers is that trainees with less or no potential to benefit are also trained. This issue underpins the debate on whether targeted or blanket policy assistance should be given to small firms. Of course it may be possible successfully to identify high fliers *ex ante*, but only at a substantial cost. If so, then the debate should revolve round a comparison of the additional costs incurred in such identification compared with the costs saved as a result of the non recruitment of the low fliers.

The final paper is a case study of a policy target set in the context of regional regeneration. The specific target examined is the raising of the birth rate to match that of other regions. The paper shows that the precise way in which such a target is defined has big implications for policy. It also raises questions about the appropriateness of seeking 'parity' with other regions, whose economic structure and context may be very different and who may themselves be seeking to influence their own birth rate. To an important extent of course, a region's birth rate – and indeed its death rate – reflects underlying supply and demand characteristics and there is likely to be only limited scope to raise the birth rate without at the same time tackling some economic fundamentals.[11]

A concluding comment

As Table 1.1 suggests, research into entrepreneurship and new and small firms is dynamic. Interests, emphases, data sources and methodological approaches change, and that is how it should be, particularly in an area which is flourishing and developing. It is therefore important to remember that the papers in this volume were written in a specific research context and their contents reflect the nature of that context. It is also true to say that although the five areas covered in this volume have received substantial attention from researchers, there are other important topics, notably finance and management, that are not given any substantive coverage. Furthermore, the papers reproduced here inevitably constitute only a tiny contribution to the literature in the relevant areas. Notwithstanding these limitations, the papers nevertheless serve to demonstrate the long-standing nature of some of the issues and challenges that researchers face. Some of these are briefly highlighted in the reflections at the end of this volume.

Notes

1 The study of entrepreneurship is not of course new; indeed the serious analysis of this function extends back at least to the early eighteenth century: see Johnson (2007: ch 3).
2 See Marshall (1920: 263).
3 For each year between 1994 and 2004. See for example Bank of England (2004).
4 See, for example, Bank of England (1996, 1999, 2000, 2001, and 2003).
5 In his detailed and comprehensive review of entrepreneurship and small business research, Landström has argued (2005: 160) that 'It was Birch's systematic studies and empirical results that gave small business a place on the research map.'
6 Studies include Gallagher and Stewart (1986); Daly et al. (1991); Hart and Hanvey (1995); Blanchflower and Burgess (1996); Barnes and Haskel (2002); Hart (2007); Hijzen et al. (2007).
7 Davidsson (2006: 362–363) has made a helpful distinction between growth as an increase in amount (e.g. sales, employment) and growth as a *process* of development.
8 There are a few studies that have looked at these relationships in the context of small firms only: see e.g. Dobson and Gerrard (1989) and Reid (1993).
9 These authors define the field of entrepreneurship as 'the scholarly examination of how, by whom, and with what effects opportunities to create future goods and services are discovered, evaluated and exploited'. No explicit mention is made in this definition of profitability. It is clear however from the rest of the article that it is *profitable* opportunities that the authors have in mind.
10 This is of course a problem in any form of evaluation, not only in social cost benefit analysis.
11 Chapter 5 also provides some supporting evidence on this issue.

References

Bain, J. S. (1956) *Barriers to New Competition: their Character and Consequences in Manufacturing Industries*, Cambridge, Mass: Harvard University Press.
Bank of England (1996) *The Financing of Technology-Based Small Firms*, London: Bank of England.
Bank of England (1999) *The Financing of Ethnic Minority Businesses in the United Kingdom*, London: Bank of England.
Bank of England (2000) *Finance for Small Business in Deprived Areas*, London: Bank of England.
Bank of England (2001) *The Financing of Technology-Based Small Firms*, London: Bank of England.
Bank of England (2003) *The Financing of Social Enterprises: A Special Report by the Bank of England*, London: Bank of England.
Bank of England (2004) *Finance for Small Firms – An Eleventh Report*, London: Bank of England.

Barkham, R. (1992) 'Regional variations in entrepreneurship: some evidence from the United Kingdom', *Entrepreneurship and Regional Development*, 4: 225–244.

Barkham, R., Gudgin, G., Hart, M. and Hanvey, E (1996) *The Determinants of Small Firm Growth. An Inter-Regional Study in the United Kingdom 1986–1990*, Regional Studies Association, Regional Policy and Development series, no 12, London: Jessica Kingsley Publishers.

Barnes, M. and Haskel, J. (2002) *Job Creation, Job Destruction and the Contribution of Small Businesses: Evidence for UK Manufacturing*, Working Paper No 461, London: Queen Mary College.

Beesley, M. (1955) 'The birth and death of industrial establishments: experience in the West Midlands conurbation', *Journal of Industrial Economics*, 4: 45–61.

Bennett, R. and Robson, P. (1999) 'Business Link: use, satisfaction and comparison with Business Shop and Business Connect', *Policy Studies*, 20: 107–131.

Bennett, R. J., Robson, P. J. A. and Bratton, W. J. A. (2001) 'Government advice networks for SMEs: an assessment of the influence of local context on Business Link use, impact and satisfaction', *Applied Economics*, 33: 871–885.

Birch, D. (1979) *The Job Generation Process*, Cambridge, Mass: MIT Program on Neighborhood and Regional Change, no. 14.

Black, J., de Meza, D. and Jeffreys, D. (1996) 'House prices, the supply of collateral and the enterprise economy', *Economic Journal*, 106: 60–75.

Blanchflower, D. and Burgess, S. (1996) 'Job creation and destruction in Great Britain in the 1980s', *Industrial and Labor Relations Review* 50: 97–109.

Bolton Committee (1971) *Report of the Committee of Inquiry on Small Firms*, Cmnd 4811, HMSO: London.

Bosma, N. and Harding R. (2007) *Global Entrepreneurship Monitor Summary Results 2006*, Babson Park, Mass: Babson College and London: London Business School.

Brown, C., Hamilton, J. and Medoff, J. (1990) *Employers Large and Small*, Cambridge, Mass: Harvard University Press.

Brunner, E. (1961) 'A note on potential competition', *Journal of Industrial Economics*, 9: 248–251.

Burns, P. (2007) *Entrepreneurship and Small Business*, 2nd edn. Basingstoke: Palgrave.

Churchill, N. C. and Lewis, V. L. (1983) 'The five stages of small business growth', *Harvard Business Review*, 61: 30–50.

Cooper A. C. (1973) 'Technical entrepreneurship: what do we know?', *R&D Management*, 3: 59–64.

Creedy, J. and Johnson, P. S. (1983) 'Firm formation in manufacturing', *Applied Economics*, 15: 177–185.

Cross, M. (1981) *New Firm Formation and Regional Development*, Farnborough: Gower.

Daly, M., Campbell, M., Robson, G. and Gallagher, G. (1991) 'Job creation 1987–9: the contributions of small and large firms', *Employment Gazette*, 99: 589–596.

Davidsson, P. (2006) 'What do we know about firm growth?' in S. Parker, ed., *The Life Cycle of Entrepreneurial Ventures*, International Handbook Series on Entrepreneurship, vol 3, New York: Springer, 361–398.

Davis, S. J., Haltiwanger, J. and Schuh, S. (1996) 'Small business and job creation: dissecting the myth and reassessing the facts', *Small Business Economics*, 8: 297–315.

Delmar, F. (2006) 'Measuring growth: methodological considerations and empirical results', in P. Davidsson, F. Delmar and W. Wiklund, *Entrepreneurship and the Growth of Firms*, Cheltenham: Edward Elgar, 62–84.

Dennis, W. J. (2000) 'Wages, health insurance and pension plans: the relationship between employee compensation and small business owner income', *Small Business Economics*, 15: 247–263.

Dobson, S. and Gerrard, B. (1989) 'Growth and profitability in the Leeds engineering sector', *Scottish Journal of Political Economy*, 36: 334–351.

Dunne, P. and Hughes, A. (1994) 'Age, size, growth and survival: UK companies in the 1980s', *Journal of Industrial Economics*, 42: 115–140.

Firn, J. R. and Swales, J. K. (1978) 'The formation of new manufacturing establishments in the Central Clydeside and West Midlands conurbations 1963–1972: a comparative analysis', *Regional Studies*, 12: 199–213.

Fothergill, S. and Gudgin, G. (1979) *The Job Generation Process in Britain*, Research Series 32, London: Centre for Environmental Studies.

Gallagher, C. and Stewart, H. (1986) 'Jobs and the business life-cycle in the UK', *Applied Economics*, 18: 875–900.

Ganguly, P. (1985) *UK Small Business Statistics and International Comparisons*, edited by Graham Bannock, published on behalf of the Small Business Research Trust, London: Harper and Row.

Gartner, W. B. (1988) ' "Who is an entrepreneur?" is the wrong question', *American Small Business Journal*, 12: 11–31.

Gibrat, R. (1931) *Les Inégalités Économiques*, Paris: Sirey.

Gudgin, G. (1974) *Industrial Location Processes, the East Midlands in the Postwar Period*, unpublished PhD thesis, Leicester University.

Gudgin, G. (1978) *Industrial Location Processes and Regional Employment Growth*, Farnborough: Saxon House.

Hart, M. (2007) *Job Generation in Northern Ireland: the Relative Contributions of New and Existing Small Firms, 1993–2005*, Enterprise Research Programme, Working Note 2, Belfast: Economic Research Institute of Northern Ireland.

Hart, M. and Hanvey, E. (1995) 'Job generation in new and small firms: some evidence from the late 1980s', *Small Business Economics*, 7: 97–109.

Haugh, H. (2006) 'Nonprofit social entrepreneurship', in S. Parker, ed., *The Life Cycle of Entrepreneurial Ventures*, International Handbook Series on Entrepreneurship, vol. 3, New York: Springer, 401–436.

Hijzen, A., Upward, R. and Wright, P. (2007) *Job Creation, Job Destruction and the Role of Small Firms: Firm Level Evidence for the UK*, Research Paper 2007/01, Nottingham: Leverhulme Centre for Globalisation and Economic Policy.

Hines, H. H. (1957) 'Effectiveness of "entry" by already established firms', *Quarterly Journal of Economics*, 21: 132–150.

HM Treasury and Small Business Service (2002) *Enterprise Britain: A Modern Approach to Meeting the Enterprise Challenge*, London: HMSO.

Ireland, R. D., Reutzel, C. R. and Webb, J. W. (2005) 'Entrepreneurship research in AMJ: what has been published and what might the future hold?', *Academy of Management Journal*, 48: 556–564.

Johnson, P. S. (1983) 'New manufacturing firms in the UK regions', *Scottish Journal of Political Economy*, 30: 75–79.

Johnson, P. S. (1989) 'Employment change in the UK small business sector: evidence from five manufacturing industries', *Small Business Economics*, 11: 315–323.

Johnson, P. S. (2003) 'A note on the interregional movement of new companies', *Applied Economics Letters*, 10: 463–466.

Johnson, P. S. (2007) *The Economics of Small Firms: An Introduction*, London: Routledge.

Johnson, P. S. and Cathcart, D. G. (1979a) 'New manufacturing firms and regional development: some evidence from the Northern Region', *Regional Studies*, 13: 269–280.

Johnson, P. S. and Cathcart, D. G. (1979b) 'The founders of new manufacturing firms: A note on the size of their incubator plants', *Journal of Industrial Economics*, 28: 219–224.

Johnson, P. S. and Parker, S. (1996) 'Spatial variations in the determinants and effects of firm births and deaths', *Regional Studies*, 30: 679–688.

Johnson, P. S., Parker, S. C. and Wijbenga, F. (2006) 'Nascent entrepreneurship research: achievements and opportunities', *Small Business Economics*, 27: 1–4.

Katz, J. A. (2003) 'The chronology and intellectual trajectory of American Entrepreneurship education 1876–1999', *Journal of Business Venturing*, 18: 283–300.

Keeble, D. and Walker, S. (1994) 'New firms, small firms and dead firms: spatial patterns and determinants in the United Kingdom', *Regional Studies*, 28: 411–427.

Landström, H. (2005) *Pioneers in Entrepreneurship and Small Business Research*, New York: Springer Science and Business Media.

Low, M. B. and MacMillan, I. C. (1988) 'Entrepreneurship – past research and future challenges', *Journal of Management*, 14: 139–161.

Marshall, A. (1920) *Principles of Economics*, 8th edn, reset 1949, London: Macmillan.

Minniti, M. with Bygrave, W. D. and Autio, E. (2006) *Global Entrepreneurship Monitor. 2005 Executive Report*, Babson Park, Mass: Babson College and London: London Business School.

O'Farrell, P. N. and Hitchens, D. M. W. N (1988) 'Alternative theories of small-firm growth: a critical review', *Environment and Planning A*, 20: 1365–1383.

Okolie, C. (2004) 'Why size class methodology matters in analyses of net and gross job flows', *Monthly Labor Review*, 127: 3–12.

Parker, S. C. and Gartner, W. B. (2004) 'Introduction to the special issue on entrepreneurship and new venture creation', *Entrepreneurship Theory and Practice*, 28: 413.

Parker, S. C. and Robson, M. T. (2004) 'Explaining international variations in self-employment: evidence from a panel of OECD countries, *Southern Economic Journal*, 71: 287–301.

Reid, G. C. (1993) *Small Business Enterprise. An Economic Analysis*. London: Routledge.

Reynolds, P., Storey, D. and Westhead, P. (2007) 'Cross-national comparisons of the variation in new firm formation rates', *Regional Studies*, 41: S123–S136.

Robson, M. T. (1996a) 'Housing wealth, business creation and dissolution, in the U.K. regions', *Small Business Economics*, 8: 39–48.

Robson, M. T. (1996b) 'Macroeconomic factors in the birth and death of UK firms: evidence from quarterly VAT registrations', *Manchester School*, 43: 170–188.

Scott, M. and Bruce, R. (1987) 'Five stages of growth in small business', *Long Range Planning*, 20: 45–52.

Shane, S. and Venkataraman, S. (2000) 'The promise of entrepreneurship as a field of research', *Academy of Management Review*, 25: 217–226.

Stanworth, J. and Gray, C. (1991) *Bolton 20 Years on: the Small Firm in the 1990s*, London: Paul Chapman Publishing.

Storey, D. (1982) *Entrepreneurship and the New Firm*, London: Croom Helm.

Storey, D. (1991) 'The birth of new firms – does unemployment matter? A review of the evidence', *Small Business Economics*, 3: 167–178.

Storey, D. (1994) *Understanding the Small Business Sector*, London: Routledge.

Storey, D. and Johnson, S. (1987) 'Regional variations in entrepreneurship in the UK', *Scottish Journal of Political Economy*, 34: 161–173.

Wilson Committee (1979) *The Financing of Small Firms. Interim Report of the Committee to Review the Functioning of Financial Institutions*, Cmnd 7503, HMSO: London.

Part I
Business formation

2　The founders of new manufacturing firms

A note on the size of their 'incubator' plants[1]

P. S. Johnson and D. G. Cathcart

Source: *Journal of Industrial Economics*, 1979, 28 (2), 219–224.

In an article in this *Journal* in 1955 Beesley [2] put forward the proposition that larger plants may provide better incubator environments than smaller ones for stimulating the growth of entrepreneurial aspirations in their work forces. Employees of such plants would thus be more likely to set up in business on their own account. In comparing the north-west and south-west zones of the West Midlands, he suggested that the higher rate of formation in the metal industries in the former might have been attributable in part to the fact that they had relatively more larger plants; this 'may have given the zone as a whole more experience of management techniques'.[2] On the other hand, however, other writers (e.g. Cooper [3]) have suggested that there are good grounds for holding the opposite view. It is, for example, more likely that employees of smaller plants will have greater contact with individuals who have themselves set up in business. They will gain greater familiarity with the types of market that could be served by a new business, which in the early years at least is almost inevitably going to be small. They are also likely to obtain greater all-round experience in the running of a business. While these arguments in favour of the small unit as an incubator have been put forward mainly in the context of technological spin-off, i.e. the formation of new enterprises in science-based industries, they are not specific to it and could have more general applicability.

The effect of plant size on fertility in terms of new business formation is not of academic interest only. The absolute size of plants has been increasing in the UK over a fairly long period (Prais [9, pp. 51–4]) and it would be useful to know whether this trend is likely to have any effect on the rate of new firm formation. This rate is of industrial significance since there is a good deal of evidence – based largely on case studies – to suggest that new firms have often played an important part in introducing innovations and stimulating competition; see for example Freeman [4, p. 14].[3]

This note provides some evidence on variations in fertility across different sizes of incubator plant in the Northern Region of the UK. Although there are considerable differences between the industrial structure of the Northern Region and that in other parts of the UK, there are no grounds for supposing that plants of *a given size* in this region differ markedly in their characteristics from those of plants elsewhere. In the first section we outline the sources of our data, and in the second we present some results.

I. Sources of data

This study covers the incubator plants of the founders of 74 manufacturing firms formed in the Northern Region in recent years. 'New' was interpreted in a fairly strict way – only businesses, none of whose principal founders was a sole proprietor, partner or major shareholder in any other business at the time of formation were included. (A 'principal founder' was one without whom the business would not have been formed. Many new businesses had several such founders.) Thus we concentrated very much on the business starting up from scratch.

The main source of information used to identify the relevant businesses was a regional newspaper which regularly publishes details of all new incorporations where the registered office and/or the address of at least one of the directors was in the Northern Region.[4] All incorporations occurring in 1971, 1972 and 1973 were scrutinized and those which appeared likely, on the basis of the published information, to be in manufacturing were contacted for further information. This led to the exclusion of a number of businesses on the grounds either that they were not in manufacturing or that they were not 'new' in the sense defined above. The 74 businesses were established by 115 principal founders.

The data have obvious limitations. For example, unincorporated businesses are excluded, as are companies which did not give the relevant addresses at the date of incorporation. However they were the best available and from the limited cross-checking we were able to do with other sources, it does appear that the final list is not seriously deficient. All the companies were 'live'; attempts to trace dead businesses proved abortive.

Information on the size of the incubator plant (at the time the founder left) was sought through interview and correspondence with each company. In most cases the information was checked through correspondence with the incubator itself. 18 per cent of the incubators were in non-manufacturing and 10 per cent were located outside the region.

II. Some results

Table 2.1 summarizes the data on fertility by incubator plant size. The data cover only those incubators which are both in manufacturing and in the Region. The measure of fertility used is the number of new business equivalents (NBEs) per thousand employees. The NBE of any given founder is the reciprocal of the number of principal founders involved in establishing

The founders of new manufacturing firms   23

Table 2.1 Fertility of Northern Region manufacturing incubators by employment size

Size of plant (No. of employees)	No. of employees (000s) in the Northern Region (1972)	No. of founders	No. of NBEs	No. of NBEs per 1000 employees
1–10	8.8ᵃ	7	5.0	0.57
11–99	55.7	20	16.0	0.29
100–499	128.2	24	13.5	0.11
500 or over	274.4	19	9.7	0.04
Sub-total	467.1	70	44.2	0.09
Incubator size unknown		10	7.0	
Total		80	51.2	

Source: Authors' data, Business Monitor PA1001, HMSO, London, 1972, and Business Statistics Office.

Note
a This figure was supplied separately to the authors by the BSO. There are considerable problems of data collection at this size level and the figure must be seen as subject to a margin of error.

the relevant business (for example if a firm has two such founders, then the NBE of each founder is a half).[5] Thus each founder is weighted by a rough measure of his contribution to the formation of a new business. (Previous studies of founders have implied equal weights for all founders.) Using the chi-square goodness of fit test with two degrees of freedom – the two smallest size categories had to be amalgamated – we may reject, at the 1 per cent significance level, the null hypothesis that the number of NBEs in each size band is proportionate to the number of employees in that size band i.e. that there is no difference in fertility across the bands. Although the limitations of the data must be borne firmly in mind, it appears from the table that fertility declines with plant size.

It should be noted too that the number of principal founders per new business also appears to decline with increases in incubator plant size. The seven founders (4.5 NBEs) who moved from manufacturing incubators *outside* the region and for whom we have data, all came from plants of 200 employees or less.

The results obtained from Table 2.1 may disguise an industry effect. Some industries may be more fertile than others because, for example, their growth rate is relatively slow and employees are therefore searching more intensely for outlets in other forms of employment. Again, some industries may have an occupational structure that is more conducive to spin-off. For example, employees in industries which emphasize marketing functions may be more aware of possible opportunities for self-employment. If the industries which are fertile for these reasons also have a relatively greater number of smaller plants then the results in Table 2.1 would follow. Unfortunately our data base is not sufficiently large for us to disaggregate in any extensive way. However we are able to provide some limited data on incubators in Mechanical Engineering (Order VII) This is given in Table 2.2 below.

To apply the chi-square test to these data we were forced to reduce the size bands to two only; below and above 500 employees. We were able to reject at the 5 per cent level the null hypothesis that the number of NBEs in both size bands was proportionate to the number of employees in that band. It seems from the sample data in the table that once more fertility declines with plant size although the absence of any spin-off in the smallest size band should be noted.

It may of course be argued that although the fertility rate in the larger plants appears to be lower, the new businesses that are formed by founders from these plants are likely to be more successful on the grounds that the founders concerned will have been able to draw on more sophisticated managerial experience in their approach to their new ventures, and will thus have been able to identify more accurately their potential markets. 'Success' can be interpreted in several ways. In this study the only satisfactory measure we have been able to adopt is the business's total employment in the fifth year after formation. Using the Kruskal–Wallis test, we are able to find support (at the 5 per cent level) for the hypothesis that employment in this year is unrelated to incubator size. (The employment figure was weighted by the number of founders involved in each business.) Unfortunately we were unable to disaggregate the data.

Table 2.2 Fertility of Northern Region mechanical engineering incubator plants by employment size

Size of plant (No. of employees)	No. of employees (000s) in the Northern Region (1972)	No. of founders	No. of NBEs	No. of NBEs per 1000 employees
1–10	1.4[a]	—	—	—
11–99	8.4	6	4.5	0.54
100–499	19.1	11	7.0	0.37
500 or over	34.9	11	4.33	0.12
Sub-total	63.8	28	15.83	0.25
Incubator size unknown		3	2.0	

Source: Authors' data, Business Monitor PA1001, HMSO, London, 1972, and Business Statistics Office.

Note
a See the similar note to Table 2.1. Because of the level of disaggregation involved in the above table, the reservation applies with even greater force.

III. Conclusions

This note offers some support for the hypothesis that business fertility – measured in terms of the number of new business founders per thousand employees – tends to be greater amongst smaller plants, at least over the size ranges examined. We have not found support for the proposition that the businesses formed by the founders from the bigger plants are likely to grow more rapidly in employment terms, at least in their early years.

The evidence presented is consistent with some preselection by potential founders: they may deliberately seek employment in small plants before setting up in order to gain relevant experience. Conversely, the less entrepreneurially minded may tend to go for the larger plant which provides a more secure environment. Closures among bigger plants is also less common; thus smaller plant employees are more likely to face actual or potential redundancy. This threat may make self-employment a more attractive proposition (Oxenfeldt [8]). The results are also consistent with the findings of Mansfield for the US [7] and Gudgin for the East Midlands [5] on inter-industry differences in formation rates. Mansfield showed that his measure of barriers to entry – the capital investment required to establish a firm of minimum efficient size – had a significant negative effect on entry rates. Gudgin found that variations in the percentage of employment in small plants had a significant positive effect on variations in formations across industries. Both were attempting to capture some measure of the ease with which founders could enter a given industry. (The measure used by Mansfield is almost certainly highly (negatively) correlated with the type of measure used by Gudgin.) However, given the level of aggregation at which both studies were made, the majority of founders involved probably also worked as employees in the *same* industry in which they founded their new businesses, i.e. the destination and source industries of the founders were the same (see note 2). Thus the measures used may also reflect differences in the capacity of the industries concerned to generate new founders. Both results are therefore consistent with the hypothesis that the larger the employment in smaller plants the higher the level of fertility.

Notes

1 The research on which this note is based was financed by the Nuffield Foundation and the SSRC. The help of both are gratefully acknowledged. We would also like to thank Adrian Darnell for his helpful comments on an earlier draft.
2 It is worth noting that Beesley implicitly assumes that the high rate of formation in a given industry may in part be attributable to favourable incubator characteristics within the *same* industry. The obvious implication of this view is that the founders were previously employed in that industry. He thus ignores the possibility that founders may *cross* industrial boundaries when setting up in business. We have shown [6] that almost one-third of the founders covered in our study – see section I in the text – moved out of the industrial order in which they were previously employed when setting up. (At MLH level the movement was understandably much higher.) However as mentioned in the conclusion to this note, the fact that the

majority of founders stayed within the same order has implication for the way in which studies on inter-industry differences in new business formation may be interpreted.

3 G. C. Allen writing in 1961 [1] claimed that such firms 'have been responsible for a considerable part of the industrial expansion of the last fifty years' (p. 28).

4 The information is supplied to the newspaper by a London agent. Correspondence with the newspaper and the agent confirmed that within the stated criteria, the lists were comprehensive. It is perhaps worth noting that the date of incorporation was not treated in the study as synonymous with that of formation. The latter was defined as the year in which the first full-time employee was taken on. For a fuller discussion of the data see Johnson and Cathcart [6].

5 The founders of any given firm may not of course have come from the same incubator or indeed from incubators which are in the same size band.

References

[1] ALLEN, G.C., *The Structure of Industry in Britain* (Longmans, London, 1961).

[2] BEESLEY, M.E., 'The Birth and Death of Industrial Establishments: Experience in the West Midlands Conurbation', *Journal of Industrial Economics*, **4** (1) (October 1955), pp. 45–61.

[3] COOPER, A.C., 'Technical Entrepreneurship: What Do We Know?', *R&D Management*, **3** (2) (February 1973), pp. 59–64.

[4] FREEMAN, C., *The Role of Small Firms in Innovation in the United Kingdom Since 1945*, Committee of Inquiry on Small Firms, Research Report No. 6 (HMSO, London, 1971).

[5] GUDGIN, G., *The East Midlands in the Post-War Period*, Ph.D. submitted to Leicester University (1974).

[6] JOHNSON, P. S. and CATHCART D. G., 'New Manufacturing Firms and Regional Development: Some Evidence from the Northern Region', *Regional Studies*, **13** (3) (June 1979).

[7] MANSFIELD, E., 'Entry, Gibrat's Law, Innovation and the Growth of Firms', *American Economic Review*, **52** (5) (December 1962), pp. 1023–51.

[8] OXENFELDT, A.R., *New Firms and Free Enterprise* (American Council on Public Affairs, Washington, 1943).

[9] PRAIS, S., *The Evolution of Giant Firms in Britain* (Cambridge University Press, Cambridge, 1976).

3 Firm formation in manufacturing industry [1]

J. Creedy and P.S. Johnson

Source: *Applied Economics*, 1983, 15 (2), 177–185.

I. Introduction

In 1971 the Bolton Committee of Inquiry on Small Firms attributed a vital economic function to new businesses. They stated that

> We believe that the health of the economy requires the birth of new enterprises in substantial number and the growth of some to a position from which they are able to challenge and supplant the existing leaders of industry.

(HMSO, 1971, p. 85)

This view, which does of course have strong overtones of Marshall's 'trees of the forest' analogy,[2] was backed by little supporting evidence.[3] Yet it served to increase both policy interest and research in the economic role of new firms. The present government now sees the encouragement of such enterprises as an important part of its industrial policy not least because they are regarded as a significant source of new jobs. On the research side, several studies have now been undertaken on new firms.[4] As a result of these studies the availability of data on the extent and nature of formation activity in particular regions and areas of the UK is now much improved. There has also been a very considerable increase in the management literature on new and small firms. However, relatively little attention has been given to the formal modelling of the formation decision (although there is no shortage of suggestions about why people form businesses). This paper represents an attempt to provide a step towards filling this gap. Section I outlines a very simple model of the formation decision which may be used in empirical work.[5] In Section II the model is applied to cross section data for manufacturing industry in the UK.

It is important to stress that the concern of this paper is with the formation of entirely new businesses and not with those formed as a result of diversification by existing businesses. Because of the paucity of data in this area, the approach must necessarily be rather basic, and the results regarded as suggestive rather than conclusive.

II. A framework of analysis

The first basic element of the present approach is the argument that the formation of a new business involves the transfer, for the founder of the business, from the status of being an *employee* to being *self-employed*. The framework does not therefore apply to individuals who remain in employment while devoting their 'spare time' to a small business; such cases would be unlikely to employ other individuals (or be recorded in official data).

The potential founder may therefore be viewed as comparing his expected income from remaining an employee with his expected income which may result from setting up his own business.[6] While the comparison between employment and self-employment income is fundamental to the present analysis, and may indeed seem to be an obvious component of a model of firm formation, it is surprising that in the literature on both barriers to entry and the nature of the firm, areas in which new firm formation is central to the analysis, there is little explicit treatment of the earnings that the potential founder may obtain in paid employment.[7] For present purposes it is assumed that potential founders consider only prospective incomes within the industry in which they are currently employed. This assumption is not entirely unrealistic, since the majority of founders are likely to consider manufacturing possibilities only within the range of their own experience.

It is therefore suggested that the proportion of employees in an industry who successfully form a new business depends on the proportion for whom the expected income from self-employment exceeds the expected income from employment by a minimum amount. This minimum, or 'threshold', level depends on a number of factors, including barriers to entry within the industry. There are differences between individuals in their perceived prospects from employment and self-employment, and the distribution of the ratio of the latter to the former may be expected to follow a unimodal distribution which is positively skewed. It is clear that not all of those who would like to form a new business will succeed in doing so, or will manage to survive for a sufficient length of time, or grow to a sufficient size, to be included in official statistics. It is important to stress at this stage that the formation of new firms necessarily represents a *process* of adjustment, and the analysis is not concerned directly with the question of the equilibrium number of firms in an industry. Such an analysis would require a much more extensive model, and considerably more data.

The above arguments suggest therefore that the 'formation rate' (the number of new firms recorded over a specified period as a ratio of the number of employees) in an industry is proportional to the percentage of individuals for whom expected self-employment income exceeds expected employment earnings by the minimum (threshold) amount. Further empirical content must of course be added to this simple statement, and it is first useful to examine the ways in which the framework may deal with a number of elements which are commonly associated with firm formation.

Comparison of prospects in self-employment with those of employment in an industry may well be influenced by a number of non-monetary considerations. Such factors have long been acknowledged, and several authors have stressed considerations such as independence, prestige and power in self-employment.[8] These factors are of course notoriously difficult to measure quantitatively, though their importance is shown by questionnaire results. However, in the context of cross-section analysis it may reasonably be supposed that non-pecuniary factors are associated with the status of self-employment itself, and are not industry specific. They may therefore be excluded from the statistical analysis.

It is often suggested that unemployment in an industry may stimulate firm formation, and there is some evidence from questionnaires that the threat of unemployment may sometimes affect the formation decision.[9] In the present framework the extent of unemployment in an industry may therefore be used in the construction of measures of expected earnings. There is the further point that the chances of survival in an industry (for sufficiently long to be recorded in official data) may also be related to unemployment. The present framework also allows for this kind of effect to be included in the specification.

It may also be thought that the structure of the industry in which an individual is employed has some effect on the formation decision. For example, there is some evidence which suggests that proportionately more founders come from smaller plants.[10] To the extent that earnings from employment and profits are affected by the size of firm, the structure of the industry will be reflected in the form of the distribution of the ratio of expected self-employment income to employment income. In this case the structure of the industry does not need to be introduced explicitly into the model. However, it may be argued that barriers to entry vary across industries. The approach taken here is to use a direct measure of the difficulty of forming an entirely new firm in an industry; namely the capital expenditure required.

III. Empirical results

The data

The very basic approach outlined in the previous section may in principle, after the addition of sufficient empirical content, be applied to single industries over a period of time, or to a cross-section of industries. However, time series data are not available, so that the results presented here apply to a cross-section. As with all cross-section analyses it is necessary to assume that the basic parameters of the model are the same in each industry.

The detailed specification of the model for empirical purposes is necessarily severely restricted by the available data. Indeed, very few data on formations by industry are available for the UK; for example, company and business name registrations are not broken down by industry. The formation data used in this paper are derived from the Department of Industry's monitoring of openings and closures in the U.K. regions. One of the categories used by the Department is that of 'Enterprise New to Manufacturing' (ENMs).[11] This category covers openings of establishments which do not have a manufacturing parent. Here attention is restricted further to ENMs without origin (ENMWOs), by excluding the opening of an establishment with any parent. Such ENMWOs come fairly close to the definition of the new firm used in this paper. The ENMWOs are allocated to orders under the 1968 Standard Industrial Classification. Unfortunately, the monitoring of ENMWOs is not entirely consistent in its coverage; while in most of the U.K., ENMWOs which reach 11 employees are included, the minima in the Greater London Council and the West Midlands Metropolitan County are 20 and 50 respectively. These two areas have, therefore, been excluded from consideration in this paper.

It is important to stress that only firms which reach 11 employees and which were in existence in 1977 are included in the analysis, so that the expression 'survival' (used in Section II) should be interpreted to mean 'grow to at least 11 employees and survive to 1977'. These formation data are available for the twelve-year period 1966 to 1977; the annual average value in each industry has been used here.[12] In calculating the formation rate the denominator is measured by the average number of full-time male employees in each industry over the period 1966–1977.[13] These data are published in the Department of Employment *Gazette*. The formation rate is measured as an annual average rate of formation per 1000 male employees.

It is shown in the Appendix that the framework outlined in Section II, combined with a number of convenient simplifications, suggests that the formation rate is given as follows:

$$R = \beta_0 + \beta_1 \log \Pi - \beta_2 \log Y - \beta_3 \log C + u \tag{1}$$

In Equation 1 R is the formation rate, Π is the geometric mean of expected income from self-employment, Y is the geometric mean of expected earnings from employment, and C is the capital expenditure required to start a new firm in the industry. The term u is a stochastic term which is assumed to satisfy the usual conditions required for Ordinary Least Squares.

The measurement of the independent variables does of course present serious difficulties. For example, an ideal measure of Π would be the geometric mean of the distribution of discounted expected self-employment income resulting from founding a firm; where the distribution included *all* employees, not just those who became founders. The model of course explicitly allows for the fact that some individuals who expect less than average profits will become founders, depending on their expected employment income. Such an ideal measure cannot possibly be obtained, and this paper measures Π using data on the actual annual profits of firms in the smallest size category (1–99 employees), from the Census of Production. In fact only arithmetic means are available and suitable data are only provided for the years 1970–73 and 1975. Gross profits per enterprise (before depreciation and interest) were obtained as the difference between total Gross Value Added and Wages and Salaries in the smallest size group, divided by the number of enterprises in that group.[14] All values were converted into 1975 prices, and the average was calculated over the five years for which comparable data were available. All the usual problems associated with the use of *ex post* data will obviously apply, and the skewness of the distributions also means that arithmetic and geometric means are unequal.

Similarly the geometric mean of expected employment income in each industry was measured by the annual average value of the median earnings of full-time males (unaffected by absence), expressed in 1975 prices. Data were taken from the *New Earnings Survey* for years comparable with profits data; that is, 1970–75 inclusive.

Finally, Census of Production data provide information about the net capital expenditure in firms of 1–99 employees. The annual average, in 1975 prices, of the net capital expenditure per enterprise in this smallest group was therefore used as the measure of C for each industry.

Cross-section results

The data described above for 16 industries were then used to carry out an ordinary least squares regression based on Equation 1. The results are shown below, where t-values are given in parentheses immediately underneath parameter estimates.

$$R = 5.235 + 0.079 \log \Pi - 0.647 \log Y - 0.092 \log C + u \qquad (2)$$
$$(4.202) \quad (2.135) \qquad (-4.973) \qquad (-3.917)$$

$$R^2 = 0.791$$

All of the coefficients are highly significantly different from zero, and the goodness of fit is very good. The regression 'explains' almost 80 per cent of the variation in formation rates across industries. The coefficients have the appropriate signs, but the significant difference between the coefficients on $\log \Pi$ and $\log Y$ requires further comment. The framework developed earlier suggests that the formation of entirely new firms is related to expected profits and expected earnings from employment in a symmetric manner, but this is not supported by the results shown in Equation 2. Thus the elasticities of R with respect to Π and Y are 1.13 and −9.25 respectively where these are calculated at the average value of R of 0.0699 (thus on average over the period there were approximately 7 new firms formed each year, per 100,000 employees, of which each grew to employ at least 11 individuals and survived to 1977).

The use of a measure of realised profits of existing firms does not, as already noted, allow in any way for the expectations of those who do not form firms, and furthermore does not allow for optimism or pessimism. The 'error' in the measurement of Π is expected to be much greater than in the measurement of anticipated earnings, Y, and individuals generally have relatively much more information about earnings from employment and their distribution.[15] Also, the measure of profits does not allow for depreciation and interest, and these may be systematically related to gross profits (but if the relationship were proportional, and the same in each firm and industry, the effect would be to alter the constant term rather than the coefficient on $\log \Pi$).

A further possibility is that there may be other significant barriers to entry which face the new firm and whose omission affects the regression results. It is also worth repeating that the cross-section application of the specification in Equation 1 assumes that the parameters of the model are the same for each industry. Bearing all these points in mind, the performance of the model as reflected in Equation 2 may perhaps be regarded as encouraging. The results suggest that the application of the general framework to improved data would be a useful exercise.

IV. Conclusions

The purpose of this paper has been to suggest a framework for the empirical analysis of the formation of entirely new firms in manufacturing industry. The formation decision was assumed to depend on a comparison of prospects in employment and in self-employment, and the capital expenditure required to form a new business was regarded as a major barrier to entry. The functional relationship (a semi-logarithmic form) between the relevant variables was derived explicitly from the model, and applied to cross-section data relating to U.K. manufacturing industry. Although the data have many acknowledged shortcomings, the empirical results are sufficiently encouraging to suggest that the model provides a useful basis for further analysis. Further refinements, such as more detailed specification of the chances of survival in an industry, and the inclusion of further barriers to entry, could be made once additional data become available.

Appendix

Further simplifications

In Section II it was suggested that the formation rate, R, is proportional to the proportion of employees for whom the expected self-employment income, π, exceeds expected employment income, y, by a sufficient amount, called the threshold, t. Thus

$$R = \theta [1 - F(t)] \tag{A1}$$

Where θ is a parameter and F is the distribution function of the ratio of π to y. The first stage in the simplification of Equation A1 is the specification of the form of F. It is assumed that a suitable functional form to describe both the distribution of π and of y is the lognormal distribution, which has been widely used in analyses of earnings and profits. The distributions may therefore be written as

$$\pi \text{ is } \Lambda(\pi|\mu_\pi, \sigma_\pi^2) \text{ and } y \text{ is } \Lambda(y|\mu_y, \sigma_y^2) \tag{A2}$$

where Λ denotes the lognormal distribution function, and μ_π and σ_π^2 are the mean and the variance respectively of the logarithms of anticipated profits. Similar definitions apply to μ_y and σ_y^2.

The lognormal distribution has the convenient property that the ratio of lognormal variables is also lognormally distributed (see Aitchison and Brown, 1957, p. 11), so that

$$F(\pi/y) \text{ is } \Lambda(\pi/y|\mu_\pi - \mu_y, \sigma_\pi^2 + \sigma_y^2). \tag{A3}$$

From the definition of the lognormal, it can be seen that

$$F(t) = N([\log t - \mu_\pi + \mu_y]/v|0,1) \tag{A4}$$

where N denotes the Normal distribution function and $v = (\sigma_\pi^2 + \sigma_y^2)^{1/2}$.

As this integral cannot be evaluated explicitly it is convenient for present purposes to use a linear approximation over the relevant range; that is, to write the function $N(x|0, 1)$ simply as $N(x|0, 1) = a + bx$. This approximation is perhaps reasonable, given the quality of the available data and the range of magnitudes involved. Thus

$$1 - F(t) = 1 - a + (b/v)(\mu_\pi - \mu_y - \log t). \tag{A5}$$

It is also suggested that the threshold t is proportional to the amount of capital expenditure required to form a new firm, C. Thus

$$t = kC. \tag{A6}$$

Now define Π and Y as the geometric means of anticipated self-employment and employment income respectively. Then by definition $\mu_\pi = \log \Pi$ and $\mu_y = \log Y$. Substitution of Equations A5 and A6 into the basic Equation A1 gives

$$R = \beta_0 + \beta_1 \log \Pi - \beta_2 \log Y - \beta_3 \log C \tag{A7}$$

Where, $\beta_0 = \theta[1 - a - (b/v) \log k]$, etc. It can also be seen that $\beta_1 = \beta_2 = \beta_3$.

Notes

1 We are grateful to S. Nunn for kindly providing the data on firm formations which are used in this paper and for helpful discussions. We have also benefited from discussions with our colleagues in Durham.

2 It is interesting to note that in the sixth and following editions of his *Principles* Marshall admitted that the advent of the joint stock company might have modified the applicability of the analogy by increasing the adaptability of the established business which is challenged by younger rivals. Such a company 'often stagnate(s) but do(es) not readily die' (1920, p. 263). At the same time, it is still likely 'to have lost so much of its elasticity and progressive force, that the advantages are no longer exclusively on its side in its competition with younger and smaller rivals' (p. 264).

3 It is perhaps surprising that although the committee stressed the lack of availability of satisfactory data on firm births (HMSO 1971, pp. 72–73) and attached considerable economic importance to births, none of its commissioned research reports was specifically concerned with the formation process.

4 A number of studies of particular areas have been make, including Beesley (1955), Firn and Swales (1978), Gudgin (1978), Fothergill and Gudgin (1979), Johnson and Cathcart (1979a), Robinson and Storey (1981) and Cross (1981).

5 A general equilibrium analysis of firm formation is given by Kihlstrom and Laffont (1979).

6 Knight (1921, p. 271) refers to the former as contractual income and the latter as residual income, but these terms are not used here.

7 This is true of Bain (1952), Coase (1937), Alchian and Demsetz (1972) and Williamson (1975).

8 See the survey by Parnes (1970), McClelland (1961, p. 52), Boswell (1971, p. 55), Golby and Johns (1971, p. 59), Roberts and Wainer (1971) and Scott (1978).

9 See Schumpeter (1939, p. 94, fn.), Oxenfeldt (1943, pp. 120–3) and Steindl (1945, p. 61).

10 See Johnson and Cathcart (1979b) and Cross (1981, pp. 220–2).

11 The Department's monitoring system does not, however, define a change of ownership *alone* as the formation of an ENM. A change in both ownership and activity is required. Thus, a new business that takes over existing premises and makes no change in that premises' activities is not classified as an ENM, although it comes within the definition given at the beginning of the paper. However, the number of cases involving such take-overs is likely to be small.

12 The age distribution of firms which do *not* survive to 1977 is not, unfortunately, known. The firms included in R obviously vary in their ages. Also order IV (coal and petroleum products) was excluded from the analysis as no formations occurred over the period.

13 Females account for a very small minority of founders in manufacturing. For example, there was only one female founder from 74 new businesses formed in the Northern Region; see Johnson and Cathcart (1979a).

14 Gross Value Added (GVA) is derived by subtracting from the traditional Net Output measure (NO) the cost of certain services. Unfortunately the GVA measure is not available for all five years. The GVA/NO ratio for 1971 was therefore applied to NO figures in each year to provide an estimate of GVA.

15 The measure of earnings for each industry was adjusted for the unemployment rate in the industry, but this did not improve the results.

References

Aitchison, J. and Brown, J. A. C. (1957) *The Lognormal Distribution*, Cambridge University Press, Cambridge.

Alchian, A. and Demsetz, H. (1972) Production, Information Costs and Economic Organisation, *American Economic Review*, **62**, 777–95.

Bain, J. S. (1952) *Barriers to New Competition*, Harvard University Press, Cambridge, Massachusetts.

Beesley, M. (1955) The Birth and Death of Industrial Establishments: Experience in the West Midlands Conurbation, *Journal of Industrial Economics*, **4**, 45–61.

Boswell, J. L. (1973) *The Rise and Decline of the Small Firm*, Allen and Unwin, London.

Coase, R. H. (1937) The Nature of the Firm, *Economica*, **4**, 386–405.

Cross, M. (1981) *New Firm Formation and Regional Development*, Gower, Farnborough.

Firn, J. and Swales, K. (1978) The Formation of New Manufacturing Establishments in the Central Clydeside and West Midlands Conurbations, *Regional Studies*, **12**, 199–213.

Fothergill, S. and Gudgin, G. (1979) *The Job Generation Process in Britain*, Centre for Environmental Studies, Research Series No 32, CES, London.

Golby, C.W. and Johns, G. (1971) *Attitude and Motivation*, Committee of Inquiry on Small Firms, Research Report No 7, HMSO, London.

Gudgin, G. (1987) *Industrial Location Processes and Regional Employment*, Saxon House, Farnborough.

HMSO (1971) *Report of the Committee on Inquiry on Small Firms* (The Bolton Report), Cmnd 4811, HMSO, London.

Johnson, P. S. and Cathcart, D. G. (1979a) New Manufacturing Firms and Regional Development, *Regional Studies*, **13**, 269–80.

Johnson, P. S. and Cathcart, D. G. (1979b) The Founders of New Manufacturing Firms: A Note on the Size of their Incubator Plants, *Journal of Industrial Economics*, **28**, 219–24.

Kihlstrom, R. E. and Laffont, J. J. (1979) A General Equilibrium Entrepreneurial Theory of Firm Formation, *Journal of Political Economy*, **87**, 719–48.

Knight, F. H. (1921) *Risk Uncertainty and Profit*, Houghton Mifflin, Boston.

Marshall, A. (1920) *Principles of Economics*, 8th edn, Macmillan, London.

McClelland, D. C. (1961) *The Achieving Society*, Van Nostrand, Princeton.

Nunn, S. (1980) *The Opening and Closure of Manufacturing Industry 1966–75*, Department of Industry, London, mimeo.

Oxenfeldt, A. R. (1943) *New Firms and Free Enterprise*, American Council on Public Affairs, Washington.

Parnes, H. S. (1970) Labour Force Participation and Labour Mobility, *Review of Industrial Relations Research*, **1**, 1–78.

Roberts, E. B. and Wainer, H. A. (1971) Some Characteristics of Technical Entrepreneurs, *IEEE Transactions on Engineering Management* EM-18 **3**, 100–109.

Robinson, J. F. F. and Storey, D. J. (1981) Employment Change in Manufacturing Industry in Cleveland, 1965–76, *Regional Studies*, **15**, 161–72.

Schumpeter, J. (1939) *Business Cycles*, Vol. 1, McGraw-Hill, New York,

Scott, M. (1978) Independence and the Flight from Large Scale: Sociological Factors in the Founding Process. Paper given to the Smaller Business Research Conference, Durham University Business School (November).

Steindl, J. (1945) *Small and Big Business*, Oxford Institute of Statistics Monograph No. 1, Blackwell, Oxford.

Storey, D. (1980) *Job Generation and Small Firm Policy*, Centre for Environmental Studies Policy Series 11, CES London.

Williamson, O. E. (1975) *Markets and Hierarchies*, Free Press, New York.

4 How good are the U.K. VAT registration data at measuring firm births?[1]

Peter Johnson and Cheryl Conway

Source: *Small Business Economics*, 1997, 9 (5), 403–409.

This paper utilises some data from a survey of recent VAT registrations in the North of England to examine two issues: first, the extent to which registrants are involved in setting up entirely new businesses; and second, the relationship between the date of registration and the start of trading. The paper suggests that some caution should be exercised in the use of VAT registration statistics in the analysis of firm births.

I. Introduction

Over the past decade or so numerous studies have examined the determinants of variations in U.K. firm birth rates across geographical areas, industrial sectors and over time. (For a good review of these studies and for recent empirical work, see Keeble *et al.*, 1993; see also Storey, 1994, pp. 49–77.) Work is now also being done on the *effects* of firm births on employment and other economic indicators (e.g. Ashcroft and Love, 1994; Johnson and Parker, 1994, 1996).

An increasingly utilised data source on firm births in the U.K. is now the VAT registration data produced by Customs and Excise and analysed by the Department of Trade and Industry.[2] Recent time series analyses of these data include those by Black *et al.* (1992), Keeble *et al.* (1993), and Robson (1994). Spatial variations in VAT registrations have been examined by Ashcroft *et al.* (1991), Westhead and Moyes (1992), Keeble *et al.* (1993), Hart and Gudgin (1994), and Johnson and Parker (1994, 1996). These registration data have the advantage that they are readily available and provide comprehensive spatial and industrial coverage of registrations. Consistent data are available back to 1980.[3]

The disadvantages of VAT registration statistics – which result from a taxation requirement imposed on businesses rather than from the needs of applied economic research – as a measure of firm births are well rehearsed (see for example Daley, 1990; Storey, 1994, pp. 50–51). Firms are not required to register, although they may do so, until they reach the threshold level of annual turnover, currently £46,000. Thus many very small firms are excluded from the VAT data: Bannock and Partners (1989) estimated that in 1986, only 60 per cent of all firms were registered for VAT. The VAT threshold has changed over time, although during the 1980s, it moved broadly in line with inflation.[4] Registration may sometimes result from a business reorganisation or change of ownership. For all these reasons, Storey has rightly concluded (1994, p. 51) that 'In only the broadest sense . . . can the number of businesses which are newly registered for VAT . . . be regarded as an indicator of the number of new business starts in any particular year'. Nevertheless, Keeble and Walker (1994) have argued that, at least in respect of spatial analyses, the data '. . . represents the most up-to-date, comprehensive, reasonably long term and spatially disaggregated data source currently available . . .'.

Investigators using the VAT registration data have usually been careful to point out their limitations, but have been unable to indicate how serious they are. To do so would require direct contact with the registrants involved. Such contact is extremely costly in terms of research resources.

This paper sheds further light on the data by utilising some data derived from a survey of VAT registrations carried out by the authors in the North of England. It focuses on two related issues. The first concerns the extent to which registrants are involved in the setting up of entirely new businesses. Such 'firm entry' represents a gross addition to the number of firms and is clearly the relevant concept for firm birth. Whether a *net* change ultimately results from firm entry will of course depend on the existence of positive or negative 'knock-on' effects of the entrant on existing firms (Johnson and Parker, 1994), and indeed on potential entrants (a firm birth may encourage or discourage others from entering). An alternative form of entry in which registrants may be involved may be termed 'purchase entry'. In these cases the registrant buys an existing business, and there is no immediate change in the number of firms (although, again, positive or negative knock-on effects may have an impact on the number of firms in the longer term). Purchase entry may range from the complete acquisition of a business to the buying of (say) a franchise or the tenancy of a business premises, where the individual concerned maintains an independent legal status. A new registration may not always occur when a change in business ownership occurs, but it will often be necessary or desirable. The VAT statistics do not distinguish between registrations on the basis of the type of entry in which the registrant is involved.

The possibility that some registrations may not involve an entirely new start-up but may simply mark a change of ownership clearly has important implications for the use of the VAT data in the analysis of firm births. A birth and a change of ownership are likely to be subject to rather different economic determinants, and to have difference economic impacts.

The second issue concerns the relationship between the date of registration and the date trading starts. The underlying question here is the precise time at which birth occurs. When birth is defined to occur is often critical for empirical studies, particularly those of a time series nature. A number of authors (e.g. Mason, 1983; Johnson, 1986) have pointed out that firm birth is not a well defined event. It may be seen as stretching back to the first consideration of the business idea by the founder(s), and forward to the point where the firm becomes fully established in the market place. VAT registration and the start of trading are just two important events in this process. (Other obvious landmarks in the birth process include the time at which the founder starts working full-time for the business or takes on the first employee.) VAT registration represents an important administrative and legal milestone, but has less economic significance than the start of trading. It is the latter that is used here to define the date of birth.

The two issues outlined above are of course interrelated, since where VAT registrants are involved in taking over existing businesses, it is likely that those businesses will have been trading for some time.

In the next section of this paper, the authors' data source is briefly discussed. Section III presents some data from the study, and Section IV offers a concluding discussion.

II. Data sources

The tables in the next section are based on a sample of VAT registrations made in the North of England[5] in March and April 1993. For legal reasons, Customs and Excise were unable to divulge the names and addresses of the 1,014 registrants (excluding those associated with registrations arising from business reorganisation) covered by this period, but they kindly agreed to send out a letter from the authors asking the registrants to contact the authors direct. A stamped addressed envelope and response form was enclosed for this purpose. In all 305 responded. Of this number, 89 indicated they did not wish to cooperate and 47 were excluded on the grounds that they were located outside the geographical boundaries within which the intended interview programme was to be conducted, and/or that they were not classified as private sector firms. It is the remaining 169 firms on which the following section is based. (Three of these firms had ceased business by the time their owners were interviewed, but can be included for the purposes of this exercise.) These 169 firms represent a response rate of 16.7 which compares very favourably with the response rate of 13 and 7 per cent for postal surveys of rural and urban small firms respectively, reported in Keeble *et al.* (1992), and with the 10 per cent response rate – again in a postal survey of small firms – reported in Mason and Harrison (1993).[6]

The broad industrial breakdown of the sample mirrors fairly closely that of the population from which the sample was drawn.[7] Unfortunately it is not possible to say whether the sample is similarly representative in relation to the characteristics of the businesses and respondents involved. For example, are more successful registrants more likely to respond positively or negatively to a request for assistance? The *a priori* arguments are fairly evenly balanced here, and there are no obvious grounds for supposing that the sample is seriously biased in these respects. In this context, it is worth noting that the deregistration rate among the sample firms is very similar to that for all U.K. registrations.[8]

III. Some findings

The two issues raised in Section II are considered in turn below.

The type of entry

The distinction between setting up an entirely new business and purchasing an existing one is not always clear cut. For example, a few of the businesses in the sample resulted from the break-up of an existing partnership, with the registrant launching out on his/her own and taking a share of the business. Inevitably therefore, at the margin, judgement over classification had to be exercised. The basic rule applied was that only businesses which experienced no immediate significant change in their organisation and/or operations at the time the new owner took over were classified as having been purchased. Table 4.1 provides the necessary data. About 27 per cent of registrations involved the purchase of an existing business, ie purchase entry. Retailing, unlike any of the other sectors, had more registrations involving purchase than those relating to the setting up of entirely new businesses. Other Services also had a high proportion of registrations resulting from business purchase. If Manufacturing and Services (Wholesaling, Retailing and Other Services) are compared, the null hypothesis that there is no difference in the breakdown of registrations by type of entry may be rejected at the 2 per cent level ($\chi^2 = 5.53$; critical value with one degree of freedom: 5.41).[9]

Table 4.1 raises at least two issues for further research which have not so far been addressed in the literature. First, it would be interesting to know why

Table 4.1 The nature of registration

Industrial/Com-mercial sector	Registrations involving entirely new businesses		Registrations involving purchase of businesses	
	Number	% of all businesses in sector	Number	% of all businesses in sector
Manufacturing	18	90.0	2	10.0
Construction	20	100.0	–	–
Transport	9	100.0	–	–
Wholesaling	8	100.0	–	–
Retailing	13	40.6	19	59.4
Other services	55	68.8	25	31.3
Total	123	72.8	46	27.2

those entering business choose one channel rather than another to effect their entry. A transactions cost perspective may be of value here in identifying the relative costs – for different owner and business characteristics – of the two channels. In some cases however, legal or institutional barriers may result in would-be entrants having no effective choice in respect of entry mechanism. For example, planning restrictions over the permissible number of shops in an area may mean that firm entry into retailing in that area is not possible. Second, it would be worthwhile investigating whether the balance between the two types of entry changes with the economic cycle. On the one hand it might be argued that as economic activity increases and resources come under pressure, the purchase of an existing business, with its established labour force and physical assets becomes a more attractive proposition; on the other hand, firms are likely to be doing well, and hence will be reluctant to sell. It is not clear what the net effect of these opposing forces is likely to be. Whatever the answers to these questions, it is evident that the VAT registration data include a significant proportion of cases that cannot be classified as firm births.

Registration and the start of trading

Table 4.2 compares the date of registration with the start of trading for the 169 firms. For registration involving the purchase of an existing business both the start of trading by the registrant (second row) and the start of trading of the business (third row) are given. (In three cases the date of the start of trading of the business was not known by the current owner.)

A number of features relevant to the interpretation of VAT statistics stand out from this table. First, for entry involving the setting up of an entirely new business, just over 12 per cent of the businesses concerned had been trading for over twelve months prior to registration; and a further 15 per cent had not started trading at registration. 45 per cent started trading in the month of registration. Second, where entry occurred by the purchase of an existing business, 72 per cent of the registrants started trading in the month of registration. This is hardly surprising given that in these cases the registrant is taking over a ready made business. Finally, however, the third row shows that 95 per cent of the *businesses* had been trading for more than three years. It is clear from table 4.2 that the registration date will often be only a poor guide to the date at which trading starts. The use of *quarterly* data on VAT registration (Keeble *et al.*, 1993) is particularly problematic.

IV. Discussion

Limitations of the registration data

This paper has provided some empirical insight into two of the limitations of the VAT registration data as a statistical source on firm births. First, it shows that in a substantial minority of cases, registration marks the purchase

Table 4.2 VAT registration and the start of trading

Type of entry by registrant	Started trading: months before registration							Started trading after month of registration	Total
	More than 36	25–36	13–24	7–12	4–6	1–3	0		
	No (%)	No (%)	No (%)	No (%)	No (%)	No (%)	No (%)	No (%)	No (%)
Entirely new business	5 (4.1)	2 (1.6)	8 (6.5)	8 (6.5)	10 (8.1)	17 (13.8)	55[a] (44.7)	17[b] (13.8)	123[c] (100)
Existing business {Registrant	4 (8.7)	– (–)	1[d] (2.2)	2 (4.3)	2 (4.3)	3 (6.5)	33 (71.7)	1[e] (2.2)	46 (100)
purchased [Business	41[d] (95.3)	1 (2.3)	– (–)	1 (2.3)	– (–)	– (–)	– (–)	– (–)	43[f] (100)

Notes

a Includes two businesses no longer trading.
b Sixteen of these businesses started trading within three months of registration, and one started trading in the fourth month after registration.
c Includes one business that has not yet started trading.
d Includes a business no longer trading.
e This business started trading in the eighth month after registration.
f In three of the cases where the registrant purchased a business, the date at which the business started trading was unknown.

of an existing business rather than the setting up of an entirely new one. This finding in turn highlights the general distinction between formation activity and movement into business. The former is focused on *institutions* – firms – while the latter is concerned with *individuals*, who may or may not become founders when they move into business. This distinction is not always acknowledged in the literature. A number of studies of *firm* formation (e.g. Creedy and Johnson, 1983; Storey and Jones, 1987; Beesley and Hamilton, 1994) utilise – to a greater or lesser degree – a theoretical framework in which *individuals* considering entering business are viewed as comparing the potential returns from self employment – a term used here to embrace all 'own account' activity – with those from alternative uses of their labour. Such individuals may however decide to enter through the purchase of a going concern, an event which will not be covered by data on entirely new formations.[10] The VAT registration data are of course picking up both types of entry mechanism, but it is because of this inclusiveness, that their use as a statistical source on firm births is open to some debate.

The key question in this debate is whether the inclusion of purchase entry in the registration data generates any systematic bias. Table 4.1 suggests that there may be some cause for concern on this score, since as indicated earlier, purchase entry is relatively much more common in Retailing and Other Services, than it is in Manufacturing. These sectoral differences have implications for the use of registration data in the time series analysis of the aggregate number of births, since sectors have had very difference registration growth rates. For example, between 1980 and 1991 annual VAT registrations in the U.K. grew by 29 per cent in 'Production' which includes Manufacturing) while the corresponding figures for 'Retailing' and 'Finance' were −14 and 109 per cent respectively (DTI, 1993, p. 13). Analyses of spatial variations in total numbers of births are also likely to be affected by sectoral differences in the breakdown between firm and purchase entry, as regions vary significantly in the sectoral distribution of registrations. For example, between 1980 and 1991, registrations in Retailing accounted for 13 per cent of all registrations in the South-East whereas the corresponding percentage for the North was 22. The implications of such sectoral bias require further consideration.

The second potential problem with the VAT data – highlighted by Table 4.2 – is that the date of registration may in some cases bear little relation to the date at which the business started trading. Not surprisingly, this is particularly true where the registrant purchases a going concern. There is of course no reason why the determinants and effects of the time path of registrations per se should not be studied. However, it is not at all clear what economic or business significance is associated with the registration event.

Adjusting the data

A clearer idea of the usefulness of VAT registration statistics in firm formation studies may be obtained by comparing – over time, and across industries and regions – the published registration data, with adjusted figures which exclude purchase entry, and which use the date at which trading started rather than the registration date.

Unfortunately the data provided here are insufficiently robust for extensive comparisons of this kind. However, for the purposes of illustration, Table 4.3 compares published (unadjusted) and adjusted data – for the Northern Region of the U.K. only – for 1981–87, the longest period for which the comparisons can currently be made. The unadjusted series is for all VAT registrations, excluding those in agriculture. The adjusted series is derived as follows. First, purchase entry is removed from each year's registrations. This is done by applying the coefficients derived from the second column of Table 4.1 and assumed not to change over the period, on a sector by sector basis. For this exercise it was necessary to group some of the sectors for which registration data are separately available.

The resulting firm entry registration figures are then converted to a start of trading basis using data summarised in the first row of Table 4.2.[11] For this conversion procedure, it was assumed, because of data limitations, that registrations in any given year are evenly distributed across the months of that year, and that the relationship between the date of registration and the date at which trading starts is the same in all sectors and in all years.

In view of the assumptions needed to construct Table 4.3, the figures must be treated cautiously, and as illustrative only. They do however serve to emphasise the wide divergence, in terms of absolute numbers, between the two series. Of more concern for the analysis of births over time are the noticeable differences in the annual growth rates. A more detailed investigation of registrations which enabled some of the assumptions underlying the calculations presented here to be relaxed and which extended the exercise beyond the Northern Region would be valuable.

Table 4.3 implies that the registration data significantly overstate births. It should be remembered however that very many entirely new businesses do

Table 4.3 Unadjusted and adjusted VAT registration data: Northern Region, 1981–1987

Year	Unadjusted registrations	Adjusted registrations	Adjusted registrations as % of unadjusted registrations	Annual growth (%)	
				Unadjusted registrations	Adjusted registrations
1981	5497	3860	70.2	–	–
1982	5791	4135	71.4	5.4	7.1
1983	6305	4448	70.5	8.9	7.6
1984	6331	4462	70.5	0.4	0.3
1985	6228	4458	71.6	–1.6	–0.1
1986	6543	4697	71.8	5.1	5.4
1987	7060	5114	72.4	7.9	8.9

not register for VAT because they are too small. Some of these businesses may eventually become registered as they grow, but others will either die before they reach the threshold, or remain below it. The absence of these firms means that there is also an important source of *under*statement of births in the VAT registration figures. Indeed it is likely that this understatement significantly exceeds the overstatement addressed in this paper,[12] although without further research on the non-registrants, the resultant net bias in the registration data is difficult to establish.

V. Conclusion

The VAT data are likely to remain a key statistical source in the analysis of new and small business. Their relative comprehensiveness, their 'official' status, and the regularity with which they are collected, give them a powerful advantage, despite their limitations, over other sources. Nevertheless some caution should be exercised in their use in the analysis of births. Their value to researchers undertaking such analyses would be greatly enhanced if the registration process could be used to collect, via a few additional questions on the relevant forms, data on the type of entry and on the date at which trading started. A study which examined the relationship between VAT registrations and the formation of firms which do not register for VAT would also yield important benefits.

Notes

1 This paper is based on research financed by the ESRC (ref R000234670). The support of the ESRC is gratefully acknowledged. Thanks are also due to Simon Parker and an anonymous referee who provided helpful comments. All errors and omissions however remain the sole responsibility of the authors.
2 The analysis was previously undertaken by the Department of Employment.
3 Data are in fact available back to the introduction of VAT in 1973. However the current published series only goes back to 1980.
4 In 1991 there was a very significant rise in the real value of the threshold. 'Adjusted' 1991 data which take account of this rise are however available. These data are comparable with those for the 1980s. Because of additional changes in 1992, a new series was started in that year. It should be noted however that even a threshold which is constant in real terms does not allow for any increases in business productivity. Such increases would mean that a firm reaching the threshold in a particular year might require a larger labour force than is implied by the same (real) threshold five years later. Thus the VAT data would be capturing progressively smaller firms in employment terms.
5 Specifically, those businesses coming within the areas covered by the Carlisle, Middlesbrough, Newcastle and Washington offices.
6 It is likely that a significant proportion of those who did not respond in any way at all to the authors' letter were ineligible anyway for inclusion in the study. Of the 305 who did in fact respond, 47 (15.4 per cent) were excluded as being ineligible for one reason or another (see text). If a similar proportion of the total of 1014 registrations was also ineligible, the total number of eligible registrations would be $1014 \times (1.00 - 0.154) = 858$. When the 169 firms included in this study are

expressed as a proportion of this total, the response rate rises to 19.7 per cent. This calculation is of course critically dependent on the assumption that the proportion of respondents who were ineligible for inclusion in this study is the same as that in the population as a whole.

7 The breakdown, by industrial sector, of all 1,014 registrations occurring during March/April 1993 and of the 169 registrations in the sample is as follows.

	1014 %	169 %
Manufacturing	6.6	11.8
Construction	11.5	11.8
Transport	4.8	5.3
Wholesale	7.8	4.7
Retail	17.9	18.9
Other services	51.4	47.3
Total	100.0	100.0

Using the chi-square goodness-of-fit-test, the null hypothesis that the 169 firms in the sample have the same sectoral distribution as the 1014 cannot be rejected at the 5 per cent level ($\chi^2 = 9.82$; critical value, with five degrees of freedom: 11.07).

8 Over the one and three quarter years that the sample firms have been monitored, 24 have deregistered, a loss rate of 14 per cent. The VAT data analysed by Ganguly (1985, p. 140) suggest that during the years 1973 to 1981, the percentage of registrants deregistering within two years was between 14 and 22. The loss rate for the sample registrations adjusted for a two year period on a pro rata basis, was 16 per cent.

9 Removal of Wholesaling would of course make the difference even more robust.

10 It is interesting to note that Beesley and Hamilton (1994) regard the inclusion of entry involving 'mere' ownership change as a weakness in their 'openings' data, even though they are 'seeking to explain the propensity with which individuals enter self-employment . . .'. Of course some changes of ownership will simply involve diversification of other businesses, but some will also relate to first time entry.

11 A full data set is available from the authors.

12 Earlier in the paper, it was suggested that about 60 per cent of businesses are not registered for VAT. The proportion of entirely *new* businesses not doing so is likely to be at least as high. Table 4.1 suggested that about 27 per cent of those businesses registering for VAT are not births of new firms.

References

Ashcroft, B., J. Love and E. Malloy, 1991, 'New Firm Formation in the British Counties, with Special Reference to Scotland', *Regional Studies* 25(5), 395–409.

Ashcroft, B. and J. Love, 1994, 'Employment Change and New Firm Formation in GB Counties', Paper presented at the ESRC Urban and Regional Economics Seminar Group, Craigie College, Ayr.

Bannock, G. and Partners, 1989, *Small Business Statistics: A Feasibility Study Prepared for the Department of Employment*, London: Graham Bannock and Partners.

Beesley, M. E. and R. T. Hamilton, 1994, 'Entry propensity, the Supply of Entrants and the Spatial Distribution of Business Units', *Regional Studies* **28**(3), 233–239.

Black, J., D. de Meza and D. Jeffreys, 1992, 'House Prices, the Supply of Collateral and the Enterprise Economy', Paper given at the Centre for Economic Performance, 5 June.

Creedy, J. and P. S. Johnson, 1983, 'Firm Formation in Manufacturing Industry', *Applied Economics* **15**(2), 177–187.

Daley, M., 1990, 'The 1980s – a Decade of Growth in Enterprise,' *Employment Gazette* **98**, 553–565.

DTI, 1993, *VAT Registrations and Deregistrations in the U.K. (1980–1991)*, Sheffield: DTI.

Ganguly, P., 1985, *U.K. Small Business Statistics and International Comparisons*, London: Harper and Row.

Hart, M. and G. Gudgin, 1994, 'Spatial Variations in New Firm Formation in the Republic of Ireland, 1980–1990', *Regional Studies* **28**(4), 367–380.

Johnson, P. S., 1986, *New Firms: An Economic Perspective* London: Unwin Hyman.

Johnson, P. S. and S. Parker, 1994, 'The Interrelationships between Births and Deaths', *Small Business Economics* **6**(4), 283–290.

Johnson, P. S. and S. Parker, 1996, 'Spatial Variations in the Determinants and Effects of Firm Births and Deaths', *Regional Studies*, forthcoming.

Keeble, D., P. Tyler, G. Broom and J. Lewis, 1992, *Business Success in the Countryside*, London: Department of the Environment.

Keeble, D. and S. Walker, 1994, 'New Firms, Small Firms and Dead Firms: Spatial Patterns and Determinants in the United Kingdom', *Regional Studies* **28**(4), 411–427.

Keeble, D., S. Walker and M. Robson, 1993, *New Firm Formation and Small Business Growth in the United Kingdom: Spatial and Temporal Variations and Determinants*, Research Series No. 15, London: Employment Department.

Mason, C., 1983, 'Some Definitional Difficulties in New Firms Research', *Area* **15**(1), 53–60.

Mason, C. and R. Harrison, 1993, 'Spatial variations in the role of equity investment in the financing of SMEs', in J. Curran and D. Storey, *Small Firms in Urban and Rural Locations*, London: Routledge.

Robson, M., 1994, 'Housing Wealth, Business Creation and Dissolution in the U.K. Regions', Department of Economics, Newcastle upon Tyne, mimeo.

Storey, D. J., 1994, *Understanding the Small Business Sector*, London: Routledge.

Storey, D. J. and A. M. Jones, 1987, 'New Firm Formation – A Labour Market Approach to Industrial Entry', *Scottish Journal of Political Economy* **34**(1), 37–51.

Westhead, P. and A. Moyes, 1992, 'Reflections on Thatcher's Britain: Evidence for New Production Firm Registrations 1980–88', *Entrepreneurship and Regional Development* **4**(1), 21–56.

Part II

Regional issues

5 New manufacturing firms and regional development

Some evidence from the Northern Region [1]

P.S. Johnson and D.G. Cathcart

Source: *Regional Studies*, 1979, 13 (3), 269–280.

This paper analyses the role of entirely new firms formed in manufacturing in the Northern Region in recent years. The paper shows that such businesses have made a relatively small direct contribution to employment in the region, although their indirect effects are harder to identify. Mobile plants new to the region appear to be relatively poor incubators for potential founders. Most founders form businesses in the same industrial sector in which they were previously employed, although there is some movement between sub-sectors and from outside the region and manufacturing. New firms are unlikely to provide the major channel for self-sustaining growth in the Northern Region, but they should remain as one important component of regional policy.

Introduction

If it is assumed that the ultimate aim of regional policy is its own demise, i.e. the achievement of a situation where regional disparities stay within politically acceptable limits without recourse to specifically regional policies, then particular attention should be focussed on those mechanisms through which a region's industry is itself able to diversify into more rapidly growing areas and to generate new products and processes as old ones decline. Market forces, expressed through regional variations in factor prices, may lead existing businesses elsewhere to move location, but the experience of the last 30 years suggests that this mechanism alone is unlikely to achieve fully the desired result. Furthermore, immigrant industry – at least as far as the Northern Region is concerned – is likely to play a less significant role in the future [NORTHERN REGION STRATEGY TEAM (NRST), 1977b, p. 112].

There are two ways in which a region's industrial structure can become self-adapting. First, existing businesses may *diversify*, and second, entirely new businesses may be formed. Relatively little is known about either in the regional context although the recent work by GUDGIN (1974) on the East Midlands and FIRN and SWALES (1978) on the West Midlands and Central

Clydeside conurbations has gone some way to improving our information on the latter. (The study by Firn and Swales was however limited to firms of five employees or over.) In this paper we concentrate principally on the new firm mechanism although this does not imply that we necessarily regard it as actually or potentially the more important of the two. Indeed our own view is that it is likely that in quantitative terms most diversification of the region's industry is likely to come through existing firms. At the same time however it should be noted that there is plenty of case-study evidence to suggest that new businesses have often been an important source of innovation (see, for example JOHNSON, 1975, pp. 64–66). It is also worth noting that while the small firms' share of post-war innovations in the UK is lower than their employment share, they appear nevertheless to be more *productive*, per unit of R and D expenditure, than their larger counterparts (FREEMAN, 1971).

This paper divides into four sections. The first discusses the problem of defining new firms, and briefly outlines the sources of data used in the authors' study of such firms in the Northern Region. The second section discusses the relevance of new firm formation to regional policy. It also looks specifically at the employment implications of such formations, since it is against this criterion that regional policies are usually judged. The final section discusses inter-industry differences in formation and fertility rates. All the empirical material used in the last three sections relates to the Northern Region; the majority of this comes directly from the authors' study referred to above.

1. New firms: definitions and sources of data

In this paper, G. C. Allen's definition of the new firm – "one which has no obvious parent in any existing business organisation" (1961, p. 28) – has been used as a starting point. However, the links between an established business and a new operation can be complex and varied. Our own work has shown that the independence implied by Allen's definition can be interpreted in a variety of ways (see JOHNSON, 1978) and that not all of them point in the same direction. For example, a business may be legally independent in the sense of the companies legislation but totally dependent in factor and/or product markets. Two examples from the study may help to illustrate this point. One business was formed to mix detergent concentrate. All the inputs are brought in by a large company which also collects all the output. The large company does not hold any equity in the new business but the latter would be unlikely to survive without the former's business. In another case, the normal supplier of a component required by a large company decided to stop production of this line. The customer company then approached the foreman of the supplier and undertook that if he set up his own (legally independent) business to produce the component, they would buy from him. Virtually all the new firm's output goes to the large company. The degree of legal independence may also vary. Indeed, it may be more helpful to talk in terms of a *spectrum* of legal independence, ranging from the case where an existing business simply expands to the case of the entirely new business of the kind described in this paper. There is of course no 'correct' concept of independence but in any research the definition used should at least be explicit. In the empirical study discussed in the following sections we have chosen to interpret independence in the legal sense and in a fairly strict way. Hence we have examined only those businesses, none of whose principal founders was at the time of formation, a director, shareholder, sole proprietor or partner in any business. (A principal founder is one without whom the business would not have been formed.) Businesses in which other enterprises had major interest were also excluded. The focus of our research therefore is very much on the entirely new spin-off.

The present study is concerned with those manufacturing businesses which met the above requirements and which were incorporated in 1971, 1972 and 1973. The study was limited to new businesses located in the Northern Region.[2]

[The study utilises data from the same 74 businesses and 115 principal founders that form the basis of the study in Chapter 2. A description of how these businesses and founders were identified is given on p. 22.]

These *[companies]* represented the total number of new manufacturing businesses which were 'live' and whose managers or owners were willing to be interviewed. It was not possible to calculate the response rate accurately[3] but it was probably about 75–80 per cent of all 'live' new manufacturing businesses in the region incorporated during the relevant three years.

It had been intended originally also to include businesses which had 'failed' since formation, but although considerable effort was made to trace the former management and shareholders of those companies that had been liquidated or struck off, nearly all seemed to have disappeared without trace. (It may of course be argued that these cases of infant mortality are in many ways of more interest from a policy viewpoint than those that survived.) Some idea of the extent of company dissolution in the Northern Region can be gauged from the fact that of all incorporations in the Region in 1970, about 22 per cent had disappeared in one way or another by 1976.

The sources of data used in this study were far from ideal but they were the best available. It is perhaps worth noting that although a number of government or quasi-government bodies have information that would assist in the identification of new formations, most interpreted the Statistics of Trade Act as prohibiting the disclosure of such information. Factory Inspectorate data which is not covered by the Act and which has in the past been used to good effect by other researchers (e.g. BEESLEY, 1955; GUDGIN, 1974), is not now available for research from which the Health and Safety Executive, its controlling body, is unlikely to receive direct benefit.

The formation and incorporation years of the new businesses covered in the study are given in Table 5.1. The formation year is not self-evident, as is

Table 5.1 Year of formation and incorporation of new businesses in the Northern Region

Year of incorporation	Year of formation										Total
	pre-65	66	67	68	69	70	71	72	73	74	
1971	2	1	1	2	3	4	10	3			26
1972	4			1	3	5	3	9	1		26
1973	1			1	3	1	2	3	8	3	22
										Total	74

implied by some researchers (for example, BOSWELL, 1971). The establishment of a new business is often a long and drawn out process. A business may start initially as a spare-time occupation (in one case it began while the founders were still at school) with relatives becoming involved as the activities expand. A founder may often decide to employ someone else before joining the business himself, thereby reducing his own personal risk. In this study, the formation year was (arbitrarily) defined as the year in which the first full-time employee was taken on, since this usually represents the first major resource decision. Formation in this paper is a firm and not a location based concept. If a business closes down in one location and re-opens in another, the latter is not regarded [as it is in WHITELEGG (1976)] as a birth. Over 70 per cent of companies were 'formed' in a year other than the incorporation year.

In 1975, the total employment of the 61 out of the 74 companies for which we have data was 1323. Total manufacturing employment in the Region in that year was 454,000.

2. New firms and regional policies

We do not propose to examine all aspects of this issue here [FIRN and SWALES (1978) have recently offered a more detailed appraisal], but to concentrate on the relationship between policies designed to attract immigrant industry and new formation at the regional level.

Most regional policies to date have concentrated on the attraction of mobile industry into the depressed regions. Academic research on the regions has been similarly focussed on the movement of industry. (This research has also tended to concentrate on the *plant* irrespective of ownership patterns. However there are good grounds for treating the opening of a new branch plant and of a new business as different economic phenomena.)

Regional policies geared to the attraction of mobile industry – at least until recently – have not been selective in nature and have aimed mainly at the creation of additional jobs, without regard to the *type* of job involved. Clearly these policies have substantially increased the employment opportunities available (MOORE and RHODES, 1973; NRST, 1976). However in the context of this paper, it is important to note that the almost exclusive emphasis on the number of jobs created may reduce the possibilities for self-adaptation if the occupations, industries and functions, for example, have low fertility in terms of 'spin-off', i.e. the formation of new businesses by ex-employees. This does not of course necessarily imply that the sole objective of regional policy should be to maximise the Region's fertility but simply that there may be a trade-off between objectives. Furthermore there is no guarantee that even if regional policy did provide a suitable *initial* industrial structure for maximising fertility, the 'second generation' industrial structure, determined in part by the new firms themselves, would necessarily be similarly characterised. Very little is known about the variations in the fertility rates of different occupations, industries, etc, but it may be plausible to suppose, for example, that spin-off is relatively higher in managerial occupations than in unskilled occupations since the former is likely to give greater exposure to external market opportunities and more relevant experience for forming a new business. (None of the founders for which data were available in the present study had been unskilled manual workers in their previous employment.) In the Northern Region at least there is some tentative evidence to suggest that movement into the Region may have reinforced an occupational structure that was already adverse in this sense (NRST, 1975c, p. 31). There is also some (inter-related) evidence for suggesting that immigrant industry in the North may be a relatively poor incubator environment for potential founders. First, there appears to be no significant relationship between the initial pattern of employment provided by immigrant plants, and that of fertility.[4] Second, none of the new firm founders identified in this study came from immigrant plants defined as those plants which had moved into the area within the five years prior to the founder leaving to set up on his own. Third, immigrant plants may be less fertile as incubators because of their size. The average size (in 1971) of plants moving into the region between 1961 and 1971 was about 200 employees (NRST 1976, p. 23). This figure however underestimates the size of immigrant plants when fully operational since the plants moving into the Region immediately prior to 1971 would not be at full strength. We have shown elsewhere (JOHNSON and CATHCART, forthcoming) that plants of this order of size may have lower fertility than their smaller counterparts.

The above discussion is of particular relevance for the Northern Region since there are good grounds for arguing that the formation rate is low relative to other regions, at least in manufacturing (the NRST saw this as an integral part of the North's "regional problem": NRST, 1977b). There is a much lower percentage of smaller units and self-employment in most manufacturing industries in the region (NRST, 1977a). These characteristics do not of themselves provide direct evidence on formations. However, if it is assumed that the age distribution of small enterprises at national and regional level is the same, then the rate of new firm formation in the Northern Region at least in recent years is also likely to have been relatively low. This conclusion is supported by evidence we have collected on incorporations in the Region over the period 1966–1975.[5] In each year these incorporations accounted for less than 2 per cent of the total for Great Britain, yet the Region has accounted for over 5 per cent of the working population throughout this period. Although there are a number of short-comings in such data – not least that the new *firm* and the new *company* are not necessarily synonymous – it does provide a fairly strong indication that the formation rate is relatively lower in the North. Certainly as far as new technology-based firms are concerned, the Region is heavily under-represented. A recent study by LITTLE (1977) identified 99 such firms in Britain as a whole. None of these firms for whom addresses could be obtained was located in the Region. Although the data sources have limitations there is no reason to think that they are biased against firms located in the Northern Region.

Although we have argued above that immigrant industry has probably not encouraged new firm formation, there are good grounds for supposing that the relatively poor record of the Region in this respect is a long standing one and goes back long before regional policy became active in the mid-1960s (LOEBL, 1978, p. 26).

The employment effects of new businesses

Information on the employment effects of new manufacturing businesses in the Region is very sparse. Department of Industry data on "Enterprises New to Manufacturing" – which are derived from its regional monitoring of new openings – suggests that over the period 1966–71 such firms accounted for about 1500 jobs in 1971, compared with the 23,000 jobs in that year provided by plants entering the region over the same period (NRST, 1976, Table 2.3) However the Department's data are limited to firms of over 11 employees. They also include diversification into manufacturing by enterprises previously engaged in non-manufacturing only. The data are also known to be deficient even within the given criteria (NRST, 1976, p. 9): in the present study it was found that of seven businesses that should have been caught by the Department's monitoring system, five had not been identified. These limitations however are unlikely to affect the validity of the conclusion that the direct employment opportunities provided by recently formed manufacturing businesses are few, relative to other employment. (The authors' own data would suggest a figure of nearly 2000.[6]) We do not however know what the *net* effects of the formations are on the Region's employment. On the one hand, new businesses may *divert* employment from elsewhere in the Region – possibly from the source firm. On the other hand, they may *create* new employment opportunities, for example by exploiting new markets or processes without affecting the markets currently served by existing firms. Usually these effects will be intertwined. For example, the new firm may reduce the markets available to existing firms, thereby diverting employment, but because it is more efficient itself, or because its entry induces existing firms to become more efficient or to seek out new markets to compensate for any losses they may have suffered, its entry may eventually create better long-run employment prospects for the Region. Again, a new firm may take over the markets of the incubator business,[7] i.e. it may appear to divert employment, but if the incubator was going to close anyway, it may be acting to maintain employment above what it would have otherwise been. Even here, however, we cannot be sure that existing firms would not have taken up the slack created by closures. New businesses based on an innovation which does not threaten existing firms may appear at first sight to be creating employment. However, such firms may simply add to the pressures on already scarce skills without increasing the demand for those skills which are readily available among the unemployed. To disentangle these different effects on employment of new business formation would at the very least require a considerable number of detailed micro-studies.

We have so far ignored the multiplier effects of the activities of new businesses on the Region's employment. We have no direct evidence on this score, although we do have some crude estimates of the linkages of such businesses with the Region's industry. The new firms were asked what percentage of their purchases in the last completed financial year were obtained from suppliers in the Northern Region. The results are given in the first column in Table 5.2 below. The second column gives a comparable breakdown of Northern Region plants surveyed by MORLEY (1976). Although Morley does not give the precise nature of his sample, it is known that nearly all the plants belonged to well established firms and that many were immigrants. It is clear that the new firms had more local linkages than Morley's sample of plants taken as a whole.[8] However, there was no significant difference between the distributions when plants of over 50 employees were excluded. (The mean employment in the fifth year after formation of all the new firms for which we have data was nineteen.) These findings must be interpreted very carefully since it may be that the smaller firms use more locally based agents than their larger counterparts. However, this fact alone is unlikely to explain all the differences between the two samples.

Table 5.2 Material purchases in the Northern Region by new firms and plants in the 'Morley' sample

Northern Region purchases as % of total purchases	Number of new firms	Number of plants in 'Morley' sample
0–5	15	37
6–25	11	27
26–75	9	11
76–100	20	8
Total number of firms/plants	55	83

3. New firms as a diversifying force in the Northern Region

The formation of the new firm, as defined in Section 1, usually implies a transfer by the founder *from* a position of paid employment or, more rarely, unemployment, to self-employment.[9] In analysing the role of such firms as a diversifying force therefore we have looked not only at the destination industries, i.e. those in which the formations occur, but also at the source industries, i.e. those from which the founders come. Most previous empirical work in this area has concentrated on the former (MANSFIELD, 1962; FIRN and SWALES, 1978) or has implicitly assumed that the source and destination industries are identical (BEESLEY, 1955) which, as we shall see, is not always the case. The theoretical literature is similarly deficient. The literature on entry (following from the work of BAIN, 1956) and the nature of the firm (COASE, 1937; ALCHIAN and DEMSETZ, 1972) concentrates exclusively on opportunities for profitable operation in the *destination* industry. It ignores the opportunities available to potential founders in paid employment in the same industry. Both factors must surely be relevant in any attempt to explain new firm formation (JOHNSON and DARNELL, 1976). In the cross tabulation in the Appendix, both source and destination industries for new manufacturing firms are given. Industry is defined at the Order Level, although data based on the Minimum List Heading classification are given later.

The following points describe the principal characteristics of the Table. First, 10 per cent of all founders of manufacturing firms – 11 per cent of new business equivalents (NBEs)[10] – came from outside the Region. Thus it is not correct to view the new firm formation process as an entirely indigenous one. Founders, as well as branch plants, can be immigrants. These immigrant founders accounted for five out of the nine new businesses which were based principally on an important innovation. This finding is of particular interest in the context of Loebl's recent study (1978) of new businesses formed in the Region by refugees – immigrants in the truest sense – over the period 1937–1961. He argues (p. 344) that they acted as an important stimulus for diversification in the Region. Second, a further 23 per cent of founders (22 per cent of NBE's) were "indigenous" but came from outside manufacturing, were unemployed, or came from unknown sources. Third, of the remainder (67 per cent of the total of both founders and NBEs), just over 77 per cent of founders (74 per cent of NBEs) represented moves within the *same* order. If electrical engineering, instruments and mechanical engineering are amalgamated, then the percentage becomes very much higher. Thus although there is a substantial movement into the Region's manufacturing from outside manufacturing and outside the Region, nearly all the movement in manufacturing is within individual orders or very closely related orders.

Classification by order is of course at a very high level of aggregation. The same exercise was therefore repeated at MLH level,[11] although it must be remembered that the problem of classifying firms at this level are very much greater; firms, especially young ones, often change MLHs and even when the balance of a firm's activities is relatively stable, there is often a considerable element of arbitrariness about classification. In the interviews, an attempt was made to determine the main balance of the firm's activities since formation. On the basis of this information the firm was allocated to an MLH. Leaving these qualifications aside however, it is clear that there is considerably less stability. The percentage of founders remaining in the same industry, defined at MLH level, is now only 50 per cent (54 per cent of NBEs). Thus although new founders from manufacturing tend to stay in the same broad area of business as that in which they were previously employed, there are nevertheless noticeable shifts within these areas.

We then examined the extent to which the transfer between MLHs represented movement by the founders from a slower to a faster growing environment and/or to industries that were growing less rapidly than Northern Region manufacturing as a whole. Employment growth data for 1967–73 – the only available consistent data – were used. The main drawback of these growth figures is that in some MLHs they are sensitive to small absolute changes occurring, for example as a result of a single new plant setting up production in the region for of the Department of Employment changing the classification of a plant. The 1967 figures were made consistent with those for 1973 using NRST conversion factors (NRST, 1975b). 1967–73 covers the period in which most of the formations in the study occurred. Table 5.3 summarises the results. Clearly the type of transfer involved in new formation is very varied. However the following points are of interest. First, the majority of founders (and NBEs) formed their firms in industries growing faster than the average for all Northern Region manufacturing. Second, the majority of founders

Table 5.3 Movement by founders between MLHs

Type of move		Manufacturing incubator	Non-manu-facturing incubator	Total	of which, total formed in MLHs growing faster than Northern Region manufacturing average
To same MLH	1	39	–	39	21
	2	27.0	–	27.0	15
To faster growing MLH	1	26	9	35	26
	2	13.66	6.5	20.18	14.18
To slower growing MLH	1	12	9	21	12
	2	9.0	5	14.0	8.0
Total	1	77	18	95	59
	2	49.66	11.5	61.18	37.18

Notes
1: Number of founders.
2: NBEs.
A few founders (and NBEs) are excluded because of the absence of suitable growth data, or because they were either unemployed or came from unknown source MLHs.

from manufacturing incubators who moved MLHs, moved to a faster grow-ing environment. The founders from non-manufacturing MLHs were split fairly evenly between faster and slower growing destination industries. (One reason for this may be that the service sector as a whole – in which most non-manufacturing incubators are found is in any case growing very much faster than manufacturing.) Perhaps the most striking feature of the Table is that just over 77 per cent of founders either stayed within the same MLH (i.e. the destination industry growth rate was identical to that of the source industry) or moved to a faster growing MLH.[12]

Data on the industrial environment in which future founders and their new businesses are found does not – even at MLH level – provide information on the particular kinds of markets entered by the latter. A detailed description of the markets served by new businesses is beyond the scope of this paper. However, the following two points are worth noting. First, as already indi-cated above, nine of the 74 businesses could be regarded as being based on a technical innovation. In 1975, these businesses accounted for just under 9 per cent of the total employment provided by the sample firms. Two of these innovation-based businesses had however ceased to market their innovations within three years of formation and a third firm had been taken over because of financial difficulties. Taking employment in the fifth year after formation as a yardstick, three of the remaining businesses were well below, and three were well above, the median (and mean) values for those non-innovating firms for which we have data. Of the firms in the second category, all of which, perhaps significantly, were formed by immigrant founders, one was employing over three hundred by the fifth year and was clearly the success story of the whole study. The above indicates the extremely variable experi-ence of companies attempting to innovate. Overall the picture is certainly not one of the formation of a mass of high potential new businesses based on important innovations.

Second, what evidence we have suggests that many of the new businesses are geared to local markets. Table 5.4 below gives the percentages of total sales in the Northern Region for both the sample firms in this study and for the Morley sample referred to earlier. Half of our new businesses sold three-quarters or more of their sales in the Region. Taken as a whole, new busi-nesses have significantly stronger links with the Region than do the plants in Morley's sample.[13] There are some grounds therefore for arguing that new businesses are not strongly 'export based' and that they are therefore depend-ent for their condition on the general economic state of the Region. It is worth noting in this context that well over 60 per cent of the businesses in this study had *other* manufacturers as their biggest customers

4. Inter-industry differences in formation and fertility rates

GUDGIN (1974) has attempted to explain, via multiple regression analysis, inter-industry differences in formation rates in two counties of the East

Table 5.4 Sales in the Northern Region by new firms and plants in the 'Morley' sample

Sales in Northern Region as % of total sales	Number of new firms	Number of plants in 'Morley' sample
0–5	7	44
6–25	8	19
26–75	15	10
76–100	30	10
Total number of firms/plants	60	83

Midlands in the post-war period. These rates are defined as the number of new firms per thousand employees in the base year (i.e. the year in which the first formation occurred). His independent variables were (i) the percentage of small plants in the industry; and (ii) its employment growth over the period studied.[14] These variables were used principally to reflect, respectively, the extent to which barriers to entry exist in any given industry and the attractiveness of that industry to potential entrants. MANSFIELD (1962) employs similar reasoning although the actual variables that he employs are rather different (he also uses a multiplicative specification). The expected signs on both coefficients are positive. Gudgin found that (i) was significant, but that (ii) was not. This finding is in line with that by WEDERVANG (1965).

We also used similar reasoning in attempting to explain inter-industry differences in formation rates in the Northern Region. In the absence of strong *a priori* arguments in favour of a precise functional form, a linear relationship between the independent and dependent variables was assumed. The following model was specified.

$$NF_i = b_0 + b_1 E_i + b_2 G_i + b_3 S_i + u_i$$

where

NF_i = New formations in industry i[15]
E_i = Employment in industry i in 1972;
G_i = Employment growth in industry i over the period 1965–75;[16]
S_i = Percentage of plants in industry i employing under 100 employees in 1972,[17]

and u_i is the random error term.

In order to eliminate any bias in the formation figures, the new firms which were identified by the only industrial training board which supplied us with some information on its industry, were excluded. We also excluded those industries – orders – which had zero values for NF_i.

The following estimate was obtained:

$$NF_i = -37.3 + 0.36E_i + 0.06G_i + 0.45S_i$$
$$\quad\quad (2.8)\quad (3.9)\quad (1.11)\quad (2.8)$$

$$R^2 = 0.69$$

The F statistic is significant at the 5 per cent level and there is little problem of multi-collinearity. The figures in brackets are the t values. All the coefficients are significant at the 5 per cent level except growth. The findings are therefore in line with the other studies.

However, it must be said that the basic approach adopted in this and previous work is open to question and that this approach may itself be responsible for the insignificant effect of growth. If we start from the basic premise that many founders are myopic and will not even contemplate setting up in business outside the boundaries of the industry in which they are engaged as employees – an assumption given some support by the present study – then any analysis of inter-industry differences in formation rates must take into account not only the relative attractiveness of different industries as a destination for new formations, but also the relative suitability of such industries as generators of spin-off. Thus given the concentration on the diagonal in the cross tabulation (reproduced in the Appendix) which may in part derive from the myopia discussed above, the regression results may be picking up not only the attractiveness of a given industry as a destination industry, but also its 'pushfulness' as a source industry. In both cases the expected sign on the size variable as measured would be positive[18] but there is no way, given the model as it stands, that the two effects can be disentangled. When it comes to growth however the source and destination effects would be expected to generate *different* signs. When viewing an industry as a source industry, relatively low growth (or decline) would be expected to generate *more* spin-offs, i.e. the sign would be negative since founders would be pushed into formations by low prospects in paid employment (a number of writers, SCHUMPETER, 1939, p. 94fn; OXENFELDT, 1943, have suggested that unemployment may stimulate an increase in new enterprises). The same industry as a destination industry is however relatively less attractive to founders. These conflicting forces may go some way towards explaining the insignificant coefficient on the growth variable.[19]

Summary and conclusions

The formation of entirely new firms is one channel through which a region can adapt its industrial structure to the changing pattern of demand. There may however be a conflict between blanket regional policies designed to alleviate unemployment through the attraction of immigrant plants without regard to the type of employment provided and the ability of a region to generate new enterprises. What evidence we have suggests that mobile plants are relatively poor incubators for founders of new businesses. This is significant given that the Northern Region has a low level of new enterprise formation relative to other regions. The total employment accounted for by new enterprises is very small, less than 10 per cent of that created by immigrant industry. The *net* effect of formations on the Region's employment is however difficult to gauge, although it does appear that new enterprises have significantly greater local linkages in their materials purchasing than larger well-established or immigrant plants.

About a third of founders and NBEs in the study moved into manufacturing from either outside manufacturing or outside the region. Most founders from Northern Region manufacturing moved within the same order, but about half of these moved MLH. Where a movement of MLH within Northern Region manufacturing was involved, a substantial majority of the moves were to industries growing at a faster rate. Very few new businesses however were geared to the production of an innovation and the early experience of these businesses was, as might be expected, highly variable. There is also evidence that new businesses are not strongly export based.

Attempts so far to explain inter-industry differences in formation rates cannot be regarded as fully reliable given that many new firms are formed in the same industries as those in which the founders were previously employed.

It is evident from the material presented above that the formation of new firms is unlikely to make a major impact on the difficulties faced by the Northern Region at least in the short run. However, we have also seen that the new firm often has characteristics which should guarantee its place as one element in regional policy (especially as the cost per job is likely to be very much lower than for branch plants). To this extent the recent emphasis on new firms, and moves towards aiding them via the provision of nursery factories, advice and training is to be welcomed. However it should be remembered that many of these moves have been undertaken without any clear view of the nature of the problems they are designed to meet (JOHNSON, 1978). It is therefore essential that, at the very least, some monitoring of their effects should be carried out.

The process of new firm formation cannot be examined in isolation from the industrial structure of the Region as a whole since it is the latter that will determine (a) whether the incubator environment (e.g. in terms of plant sizes and occupational structure) is conducive to spin-off; and (b) whether the types of market suitable for new firms (e.g. sub-contracting and those that do not require heavy capital investment) are available. In this context, it may be worth exploring the possibility of using selective measures to attract immigrant plants with the right characteristics in terms of their potential fertility and/or their likely demand for the products and services of small firms. Selective measures to attract entirely new firms might also be considered; this paper has shown that some new firms – including the business with by far the most rapid growth in the sample – are formed by immigrant founders.

Notes

1 The study on which this paper is based was supported by generous help from the Nuffield Foundation and the Social Science Research Council. We are also grateful for the help and advice received from colleagues in the Department of Economics, Durham University, and from participants in the SSRC Industrial Economics Study Group and the Seminar Programme of the Centre for Urban and Regional Development Studies, Newcastle University.

2 Defined here as Cleveland, Cumbria, Durham, Northumberland and Tyne and Wear.

3 It could not always be established firmly whether a company came within the relevant criteria without an interview. (During the course of the study, several interviews were held with representatives of companies which, on the basis of information obtained in the interview, turned out not to be eligible for inclusion.) Hence it cannot be known with certainty whether a company refusing an interview would in fact have conformed to our requirements.

4 Information on employment provided by immigrant plants by industry was obtained from NRST (1976) Table 2.3. This gives the 1971 employment of plants moving into the Region between 1966 and 1971 and remaining open. Fertility in each industry was measured by the following ratio:

$$\frac{\text{Employees leaving to become a principal founder of a new business}}{\text{Total employment}}$$

The correlation coefficient was less than 0.1.

5 The same data source discussed on p. 22 above was used here.

6 This figure was derived as follows. The number of incorporations in each of the years following 1973 was assumed to be the mean of the number incorporations in 1971, 1972 and 1973, as given in Table 5.1. These incorporations were then assigned a 'formation' year on the basis of the pattern of formations for the incorporations of the three years given in the Table. It was then assumed that each of these formations had the same growth in employment since birth as that given by the mean for our own sample. The 1971 figures were then calculated and added to the 1971 employment of the business in the sample. It should be added that the Department of Industry's formation date is rather vaguely defined.

7 35 per cent of the Northern Region founders for which we have data in our study came from plants which closed either at, or subsequent to, the formation of the new business. In several cases new businesses were formed explicitly to take over the plant in which the founders were working. In some of these the incubator company actively encouraged the formation of the new business to alleviate the adverse effects of their own rationalisation programmes.

8 The chi-squared statistic was significant at the 1 per cent level.

9 Self-employment is not interpreted here in is narrow national insurance sense but refers to any type of employment which is on an 'own account' basis.

10 The new business equivalent of any given founder is the reciprocal of the number of principal founders involved in establishing the relevant business.

11 Because of the size of the cross-tabulation it is not reproduced here. Details can however be obtained from the authors.

12 Unfortunately it was not possible to compare these results with the expected results that would arise from a random process as we did not have data on these founders who *left* manufacturing to form their businesses in non-manufacturing. It should be pointed out that even a random choice of a destination industry by a founder would depend on the source industry in which the latter was employed.

Thus if he was employed in the slowest growing industry in the Northern Region, a random selection of a destination industry would inevitably take him into an industry growing a the same, or a faster pace.

13 The chi-squared statistic is significant at the 1 per cent level. As with material purchases referred to earlier in the text, the difference appears to be related to size, rather than to newness per se.

14 Industry appears to be defined at the order level.

15 The number of principal founders, rather than the number of new businesses, was also used as the dependent variable but the change did not substantially affect the reported results.

16 Several variants of this variable were tried, without any major effect on the results.

17 Several variants of this variable were tried, without any major effect on the results.

18 For a discussion of the reasons why an industry with a higher proportion of small plants might be expected to generate a relatively greater number of spin-offs, see JOHNSON and CATHCART (forthcoming).

19 Further regressions were run using fertility data i.e. the column totals in the cross tabulation. Again although size structure and employment were significant, as was the F test at the 5 per cent level, and the fit was good, $R^2 = 0.69$, growth remained insignificant.

References

ALCHIAN A. and DEMSETZ H. (1972) Production, information costs and economic organisation *Am. Econ. Rev.* **62**, p. 777–795.

ALLEN G. C. (1961) *The Structure of Industry in Britain*. Longman, London.

BAIN J. S. (1956) *Barriers to New Competition*. Harvard University Press, Cambridge, Massachusetts.

BEESLEY, M. E. (1955) The birth and death of industrial establishments: experience in the W. Midlands conurbations *J. Ind. Econ.* **4**, 45–61.

COASE, R. H. (1937) The nature of the firm, *Economica*, **4**, 386–405.

FIRN, J. R. and SWALES, J. K. (1978) The formation of new manufacturing establishments in the central Clydeside and West Midlands conurbations 1963–1972: A comparative analysis, *Reg. Studies*, **12**, 199–213.

FREEMAN, C. *The Role of Small Firms in Innovation in the United Kingdom since 1945*, Committee of Inquiry on Small Firms, Research Report, No. 6, H.M.S.O. London.

GUDGIN, G. (1974) *The East Midlands in the Postwar Period*, Ph.D., Leicester University.

JOHSON, P. S. (1975) *The Economics of Invention and Innovation*, Martin Robertson, London.

JOHNSON, P. S. and DARNELL, A. (1976) *New Firm Formation in Great Britain*, Department of Economics, Durham University, Discussion Paper No. 5.

JOHNSON, P. S. and CATHCART, D. G. (forthcoming) The founders of new manufacturing firms: A note on the size of their 'incubator' plants, *Journal of Industrial Economics*.

JOHNSON, P. S. (1978) *New Firms and Regional Development: Some Issues and Evidence*. Centre for Urban and Regional Development Newcastle University, Discussion Paper No. 11.

LITTLE, A. D. (1977) *New Technology Based Firms in the UK and the Federal Republic of Germany*, Wilton House, London.

LOEBL, H. (1978) *Government Financed Factories and the Establishment of Industries by Refugees in the Special Areas of the North of England* 1937–1961. M.Phil, Durham University.

MANSFIELD, E. (1962) Entry, Gibrat's law, innovation and the growth of firms, *Am. Econ, Rev.* **52**, 1023–51.

MOORE, B. and RHODES, J. (1972) Evaluating the effects of British regional policy, *Econ, J.* **83**, 87–110.

MORLEY, R. (1976) *Employment, Investment and Regional Policy in the Northern Region*, North of England Development Council, Newcastle.

NORTHERN REGION STRATEGY TEAM (1975a) *Change and Efficiency in Manufacturing Industry in the Northern Region*, Technical Report No. 3, NRST, Newcastle.

NORTHERN REGION STRATEGY TEAM (1975b) *Development of Comparable Statistics for Employment and Output*, Working Paper No. 17, NRST, Newcastle.

NORTHERN REGION STRATEGY TEAM (1975c) *First Interim Report* NRST, Newcastle.

NORTHERN REGION STRATEGY TEAM (1976) *Movement of Manufacturing Industry in the Northern Region*, 1961–1973, Technical Report No. 10, NRST, Newcastle.

NORTHERN REGION STRATEGY TEAM (1977a) *Small Business in the Northern Region*, Working Paper No. 12, NRST, Newcastle.

NORTHERN REGION STRATEGY TEAM (1977b) *Strategic Plan for the Northern Region*, Vol. 2: *Economic Development Policies*, H.M.S.O., London.

OXENFELDT, A. R. (1943) *New Firms and Free Enterprise*. American Council on Public Affairs; Washington.

SCHUMPETER, J. (1939) *Business Cycles*, Vol. 1, McGraw-Hill, New York.

WEDERVANG, F. (1965) *Development of a Population of Industrial Firms*. Scandinavian University Books, Oslo.

WHITELEGG, J. (1976) Births and deaths of firms in the inner city, *Urban Studies* **13**, 333–338.

Appendix

The source and destination industries of founders and new businesses

See table opposite.

6 Spatial variations in the determinants and effects of firm births and deaths

Peter Johnson and Simon Parker

NORTHERN REGION INCUBATORS

SOURCE INDUSTRY \\ DESTINATION INDUSTRY	FOOD, DRINK, TOBACCO	COAL, PETROLM.	CHEM. & ALLIED	METALS	MECH. ENG.	INSTRUMENTS	EL. ENG	S/BUILDING	VEHICLES	METAL GOODS	TEXTILES	LEATHER	CLOTHING	BRICKS, GLASS ETC	TIMBER	PAPER, PUBLISHING	OTHER MANUFACTURING	AGRICULTURE AND MINING	CONSTRUCTION	ALL OTHER INDUSTRIES	UNEMPLOYED	DON'T KNOW	MANUFACTURING	NON MANUFACTURING	DON'T KNOW	TOTAL
FOOD, DRINK, TOBACCO			3 / 3.00																	5 / 3.00						5 / 3.00
COAL, PETROLM.																										
CHEM. & ALLIED		1 / 1.00	1 / 0.50															1 / 0.33	2 / 1.50				1 / 1.00	1 / 1.00		4 / 4.00
METALS																										
MECH. ENG.				1 / 0.50	27 / 14.83	5 / 3.50	1 / 1.00			3 / 1.83										4 / 2.00			6 / 4.00			55 / 33.00
INSTRUMENTS					4	4 / 2.00																1 / 1.50				4 / 2.00
EL. ENG.					1 / 0.50	1 / 0.50	3 / 2.00																1 / 0.50	1 / 0.50		6 / 4.00
S/BUILDING					2 / 1.00		1 / 1.00		3 / 2.00											1 / 1.00						6 / 4.00
VEHICLES																										
METAL GOODS					2 / 2.00					2 / 2.00										2 / 1.00						3 / 3.00
TEXTILES					1 / 1.00																					3 / 3.00
LEATHER																										
CLOTHING													1 / 1.00													
BRICKS, GLASS ETC														3 / 2.00							2 / 1.00					6 / 4.00
TIMBER															1 / 1.00					1						
PAPER, PUBLISHING																3 / 3.00				3 / 2.00		2 / 1.00				8
OTHER																	9 / 4.00	1 / 0.33		2 / 1.50				1 / 1.00	2 / 1.50	13 / 7.00
TOTAL	1 / 1.00	1 / 1.00	4 / 3.50	1 / 0.50	31 / 17.83	10 / 6.00	5 / 4.00		3 / 2.00	5 / 3.83			1 / 1.00	3 / 2.00	1 / 1.00	3 / 3.00	9 / 4.00	1 / 0.33	2 / 1.50	16 / 1.50	2 / 1.00	3 / 1.50	7 / 4.50	3 / 2.50	2 / 1.50	115 / 74.00

Note: The top figure in each cell refers to the number of founders; the bottom one to the number of business equivalents.

6 Spatial variations in the determinants and effects of firm births and deaths [1]

Peter Johnson and Simon Parker

Source: *Regional Studies*, 1996, 30 (7), 679–688.

This paper models the interdependence between firm births, firm deaths and economic variables, using county level data for the UK. It examines the determinants of births and deaths, as well as outlining a modelling process which incorporates two other features that have not been considered to any great extent elsewhere: first, a systematic approach to birth / death interdependence; and second, treatment of the economic variables as endogenous, i.e. subject to influence by births and deaths. Since the data relate to the UK counties, the paper is clearly relevant to the analysis of regional development and to the role of flows into and out of the business sector in that development.

Introduction

In recent years there has been a rapid expansion in the literature on the determinants of firm births and deaths. Empirical work has looked at variations in either or both of these rates over time (e.g. ROBSON, 1993), and across industrial sectors (e.g. CREEDY and JOHNSON, 1983; STOREY and JONES, 1987); geographical areas within the same country (e.g. LOVE, 1993; KEEBLE and WALKER, 1994; GUESNIER, 1994; HART and GUDGIN, 1994); and countries (e.g. REYNOLDS *et al.*, 1994). More attention has been paid to births than to deaths.

In all this research, the general approach has been to model the effects of key economic variables, such as unemployment or output, on birth and death rates. Some investigators have argued that births and/or deaths in some previous time period(s) may have a lagged effect on current births and/or deaths, although few studies have explored this relationship in any systematic way. One such study is JOHNSON and PARKER's 1994, investigation into UK retailing, which sought to provide a comprehensive framework for considering birth/death interdependence (see below) and stressed the autoregressive influence of past births and deaths on current births and deaths. It did not, however, examine the wider economic determinants and effects of these phenomena. A further point to note is that, with a few exceptions, the empirical work has assumed that the economic influences on births and deaths are exogenous.

The purpose of this paper is to build on this literature by modelling more fully the interdependence between births, deaths and economic variables, using county level data for the UK. The paper not only examines the determinants of births and deaths, but it also outlines a modelling process which incorporates two other features which have not been considered to any great extent elsewhere: first, a systematic approach to birth/death interdependence; and second, treatment of the economic variables as endogenous, i.e. subject to influence by births and deaths. Since the data relate to the UK counties, the paper is also clearly relevant to the analysis of regional development and the role of flows into and out of the business sector in that development.

The paper is structured as follows. In the next section, previous studies of direct relevance to the current one are briefly reviewed. This review looks first at some of the underlying determinants of births and deaths. It then considers the interrelationships between births and deaths and the impact of births and deaths on economic activity. In the third section the variables and data sources used in the study are briefly discussed. In the fourth section panel data vector auto regression (VAR) econometric techniques, which are designed to best capture the interdependencies central to the paper, are described and the results presented. A final section draws together some concluding comments.

Previous work

Some underlying determinants of births and deaths

Investigators examining spatial variations in birth and death rates have identified a wide range of potential influences: in the review by KEEBLE *et al.*, 1993, pp. 31–33, for example, over 30 such influences were identified. At the risk of some simplification, relevant factors may be grouped under three broad headings.[2]

First, there are those influences which are thought likely to affect the market prospects for those contemplating self employment,[3] sometimes labelled 'demand side' variables. Since new businesses tend to serve local markets, spatial variations in local demand conditions, measured for example in terms of levels or rates of change of GDP and/or population, are likely to be important. *Ceteris paribus*, higher local demand will lead to higher formation activity, and lower deaths. The recent study by KEEBLE and WALKER, 1994, identifies population change as having a significant and important positive effect of births.[4] Variations in population *density* may also have a positive effect on births since the more concentrated the population the greater the local market opportunities are likely to be.

Another demand side influence that may be important is the spatial variation in industry mix. The reasoning here is that since most self employment is in some form of services,[5] a relatively larger emphasis on services will, *ceteris paribus*, provide more opportunities for formation activity and reduce the likelihood of death.

A more direct measure of market prospects for self employment is expected profitability. Data on such profitability are not easily available on a spatial basis, although CREEDY and JOHNSON, 1983, have used a proxy for this measure, to explain cross *industry* variations in formation rates.

The second category of influences represents those which may affect the supply of founders, and the resources required to set-up/remain in business. Unemployment is frequently used to capture variations in the availability of alternative paid employment opportunities for would-be founders and hence the intensity of the 'push' effect on births (e.g. PARKER, 1996).[6] This push effect is also sometimes proxied by an earnings measure (CREEDY and JOHNSON, 1983) or by the ratio of unemployment to vacancies (ROBSON, 1991).

The role of unemployment as a push effect is much debated. One of the difficulties of using the unemployment measure in empirical work is that it may also pick up demand side effects. Thus while a rise in unemployment may provide a greater incentive for people to set up in business because of reduced paid employment opportunities, it may also indicate a fall in market prospects. Empirical work will, of course, only pick up the net effect of these influences, and it is therefore hardly surprising to find a lack of consistency in the results of empirical studies on the effects of unemployment.[7] The ambiguity on the impact of unemployment has been much debated in the literature: see for example, STOREY, 1991.

An area's occupational structure may also influence the supply of founders, since there is evidence to suggest that a large proportion of founders come from skilled technical and managerial grades (BARKHAM, 1992).[8] STOREY, 1994, p. 69, has pointed out that a more professional workforce may indicate the presence of greater employment opportunities, particularly in large firms.

Earlier in this section the industry mix was proposed as a demand side influence. However, it may also be argued that this mix will also capture the extent to which local industry acts as a 'seedbed' for would-be founders who are likely to come, disproportionately, from the service sector. In this way, industry mix may also act on the supply side.

Demographic characteristics may be relevant influences on the supply side. These characteristics include age (the probability of becoming self employed varies with age: see for example EVANS and LEIGHTON, 1989b); sex (females have a lower propensity to go into business: EVANS and LEIGHTON, 1989a); and ethnic origin (some minorities are more likely to set up than others: BORJAS, 1986). Educational qualifications – clearly related to occupational structure – have also been explored although there is some ambiguity in the results of empirical work in this area (see, for example, STOREY, 1982, pp. 106f).

Another supply side influence is the size structure of local industry. A number of studies have shown that the spin-off rate of new firm founders tends to be higher in smaller plants/firms (e.g. JOHNSON and CATHCART, 1979; GUDGIN and FOTHERGILL, 1984).[9] Areas with a relatively greater amount of small scale activity will therefore tend *ceteris paribus* to have higher birth rates. One reason for this is that employees in small businesses are more likely to come into contact with market opportunities that are relevant for small firms, and to be more familiar with small business operations.

Finally, following the time series work by BLACK *et al.*, 1996, it has been suggested that variations in the amount of net housing wealth (the value of the owner occupied stock less outstanding mortgages) may lead to variations in self employment activity, because such wealth, which provides collateral, is likely to have a positive effect on the availability of bank lending. While KEEBLE and WALKER, 1994, find a positive effect of local house values on births,[10] it should be noted that they use average house prices as their measure, apparently with no deduction for outstanding debt. ROBSON, 1994, has however failed to find a positive relationship between net housing wealth and regional rates of firm formation. Indeed, if anything, his results suggest a negative relationship. At the same time, he argued that the availability of external collateral, enhanced by housing equity, may enhance the *survivability* of businesses, at least in the short term. One reason for doubt over the effect of net housing wealth is that it may also pick up demand side effects. Another problem is that, despite popular folklore, founders of small new businesses may typically be reluctant to borrow anything,[11] and that when they do, they do not obtain collateralized finance (CRESSY, 1993, quoted in ROBSON, 1994).

The third set of influences on births and deaths may be categorized under 'the policy environment'. There may, for example, be spatial variations in the supportiveness of local authorities in relation to small business activity. Some investigators have tried to capture this influence by the political orientation of the controlling local political party. The results of this work are mixed (see KEEBLE *et al.*, 1993). Other policy influences – in respect, for example, of taxation or interest rates – are not likely to be very relevant in a spatial context, although they are relevant in time series work at a national level.

The above three-fold categorization is a useful initial classification. However it is clear that the effect of the difference influences may be complex and interrelated, and it is not always clear what the signing of the relevant coefficient should be.

Interrelationships between births and deaths

There is a small but growing literature on the interdependence between births and deaths, including studies by SHAPIRO and KHEMANI, 1987; SLEUWAGEN and DEHANDSCHUTTER, 1991; ROSENBAUM and LAMORT, 1992; LOVE, 1993; CARREE and THURIK, 1993; and JOHNSON and PARKER, 1994. In a detailed study of the likely interdependencies present, Johnson and Parker argued that the effects of births and deaths on subsequent births and deaths may be ambiguous in sign in all cases. For example more births may cause more deaths due to enhanced competition (a 'competition effect'), or lead to fewer deaths, because of a 'multiplier effect', by which the demand for all businesses' products is increased. Births may also have a negative (competition) effect on future births – more formations leave less demand for future new businesses – or a positive (multiplier) effect, with formation activity in one time period encouraging others, via a demonstration effect, subsequently to set up in business. Similarly, deaths may have both competition and multiplier effects on subsequent deaths and births, making it difficult to make any clear predictions about signs. In addition to these effects, births will necessarily be followed after a lag, by their own deaths. Even where firms survive for many years, they will eventually die from 'natural causes'. This effect may be termed the 'Marshall effect', following Alfred Marshall's 'trees of the forest' analogy (MARSHALL, 1920, p. 263).[12] Denoting births and deaths by B and D respectively, Table 6.1 categorizes the different effects.

Although the positive and negative effects of births and deaths on subsequent births and deaths have been separately identified in Table 6.1, the results of empirical work necessarily relate only to the net effects, i.e. they tell us whether it is the negative or positive effects which dominate, but it is not possible to identify the part played by each effect separately. Although this inevitably places some restrictions on interpretation (particularly in respect of the last row in Table 6.1, where any positive net effect of births on deaths could be due to the competition and/or Marshall effects), the net effects will still obviously be of considerable interest to researchers.

It is very important to note that lags go to the very heart of this approach. Births and deaths are not expected to have an impact on other births and deaths instantaneously, but may exert influences that drag on for several years. For example, a past string of business failures may encourage a potential founder to postpone a decision to enter a market. Recognition of long and complex lag structures motivated the use by JOHNSON and PARKER, 1994, of panel-data vector auto regression (VAR) techniques using county level data for retailing from 1990. They found evidence that both multiplier and competition effects were present. Interestingly, they also found evidence of

Table 6.1 The multiplier, competition and Marshall effects: a summary

	Expected sign of each effect		
	Multiplier	*Competition*	*Marshall*
$\partial B_t / \partial B_{t-1}$	+	–	n.a.
$\partial D_t / \partial D_{t-1}$	+	–	n.a.
$\partial B_t / \partial D_{t-1}$	–	+	n.a.
$\partial D_t / \partial B_{t-1}$	–	+	+

Note: n.a. = not applicable.

long and complex lag structures tying births and deaths together, which suggests that interdependence is not a straightforward contemporaneous phenomenon in practice. However no account was taken of any underlying explanatory variables of the kind outlined above in the previous sub-section.

With one exception, the other studies mentioned above take into account other variables but crucially omit considerations of lag lengths. For example, SHAPIRO and KHEMANI, 1987, set up a recursive birth – death model with entry barriers and use contemporaneous entry and exit variables; estimation by FIML on Canadian cross section data provides evidence of a large and significant effect of entry on exit.[13] In contrast, ROSENBAUM and LAMORT, 1992, estimated a simultaneous system, again with contemporaneous variables; applying iterative 3SLS to US Census of Manufacturing data, they found no evidence of endogeneity. From this they concluded there was no causality between births and deaths. However, causality is really the wrong word to use in their context, since it implies the presence of an effect after a lag, whereas they used contemporaneous variables; and of course, in view of the importance of lags in the birth – death process, the omission of lags means that both studies are subject to bias.

The study by LOVE, 1993, is also subject to this drawback. Love estimated a cross section regression using UK county level data from 1984, and explained births and deaths by all four types of variables outlined in the previous sub-section.[14] Love estimated a recursive system and a simultaneous system, but as stated above, omitted considerations of lag structure and reverse causality (see below). Some mixed results were obtained, with a recursive system, in which births can affect deaths (but not vice-versa), providing better econometric performance than a simultaneous system with both effects present.

CARREE and THURIK, 1993, used a pooled time-series/cross-section data-set on retailing in the Netherlands, comprising 23 shop-types, between the years 1981–88. They considered the effect of the level and change in unemployment on births and deaths, as well as consumer expenditure and three types of entry barrier. Unusually, they also considered one-period lagged births and deaths, as well as current-period births and deaths, in their regressions. Simultaneous estimation produced satisfactory results with, for example, profitability and demand growth causing entry and reducing exit (results to which we will return in the next section). However as with the other studies, excepting Johnson and Parker, no account is taken of a richer lag structure of interdependence running from births and deaths to the explanatory variables.

Reverse causality: the impact of births and deaths on economic activity

Although, as indicated at the beginning of this section, a number of studies have examined the effects of underlying economic forces on births and deaths, virtually no attention has been paid to the formal econometric modelling of the latter on the former.[15] It is not difficult to suggest ways in which reverse causation may be generated. For example, a straightforward application of supply and demand analysis would predict that, given certain assumptions about firm size, earnings and house values would be bid up in counties where there were greater births than deaths. Such a scenario would also raise the stock of businesses and the workforce, while lowering unemployment. We attempt in the following to provide a comprehensive framework in which reverse causality is studied alongside the effects of economic variables on births and deaths.

Variables and data

It is the purpose of the empirical work reported later in this paper to estimate county level variations in births and deaths, and in the underlying economic factors which both affect, and are affected by, births and deaths. Due to data limitations the only year for which these variations could be examined was 1990. One of the principal constraints on the data was the need to include lagged values of the variables over a number of years. To have selected one or more years earlier than 1990 would have unduly restricted the data set. Data after 1990 could not be used because of a significant change in the data source for births and deaths (see below).

It should be noted, however, that while the results below therefore apply to county-wide variations in 1990 alone, there are good reasons for regarding 1990 as a favourable year to be analysed, on econometric grounds. This is because of considerable spatial variation in this year, the onset of the early 1990s recession.[16] As is well known, greater variability in the data-set increases the precision of parameter estimates, and so confers greater reliability on statistical inference.

Measure of births (denoted B) and deaths (denoted D) were obtained from data on VAT registrations and deregistrations respectively. These data have a number of limitations when used for these purposes: DALY, 1990; STOREY, 1994, pp. 51, 84–5. *[See also chapter 4.]* Despite these difficulties, the VAT data probably are the best available. In this paper, therefore, a registration is treated as a birth, and a deregistration as a death. The stock of businesses (S) was also available from this source.

Up to 1990 the annual change in VAT threshold moved broadly in line with inflation, keeping the threshold's real value constant. In 1991 there was a major rise in the real value of the threshold, thus affecting the numbers of births and deaths. No data after 1990 were therefore used.

An important issue that needs to be addressed is that of the scaling of births and deaths. Some previous authors (STOREY and JONES, 1987; AUDRETSCH and FRITSCH, 1992; and JOHNSON and PARKER 1994) have used the stock of businesses as a scale measure. ASHCROFT *et al.*, 1991 and LOVE, 1993, on the other hand suggest scaling by workforce. In this paper, it is not necessary to take a position on this issue. The specification of the model, with both stock and workforce (*W*) on the right hand side of the equations, makes a choice unnecessary (see below). However it does mean that the signs of the scaling variables will not be predictable in advance.[17]

The stringent data requirement that all the measures of the economic variables should be (or could be constructed) *for several years on a consistent annual basis at county level* led to the exclusion of three counties and the amalgamation of the Scottish Highlands and Islands.[18] It also meant that not all the factors identified in the previous section could be incorporated. However, it has been possible to utilize some key measures on both the demand and supply sides.

Two demand variables are used: a measure of output (*Q*) and the industrial mix (*M*), measured here as the relative importance of services in employment terms. In addition it should be noted that population effects on the demand side are captured by the inclusion of the workforce variable.[19] On the supply side, unemployment (*U*) is included to capture the attractiveness or otherwise of non self employment activities, as is an earnings measure (*E*). The size structure of a county's industry is proxied by the average size of VAT registered businesses (*W/S*). Because of recent debate about its importance, a measure of real net average housing wealth (*V*) is also included.

Measures for *Q*, *U* and *E* at county level are all taken from various issues of *Regional Trends*. The definitions of these variables are: *Q* = the real per capita GDP at factor cost;[20] *U* = the number unemployed; and *E* = average gross weekly earnings of males on adult rates (data on female earnings at county level are deficient). *M* = the proportion of a county's workforce in employment which is in services, and is calculated from Census of Employment data held in the on-line NOMIS service.[21] County level data for the size of the workforce were also taken from NOMIS. Real net housing wealth per owner occupied house is calculated from data in *Housing and Construction Statistics* using the formula found in ROBSON, 1994. The same real net housing wealth was used for all counties within a given region, which is clearly unsatisfactory; but 'true' county data are unavailable on a consistent basis over the sample. As an independent variable, this measure of net housing wealth will induce some imprecision into the coefficients of a regression but will nevertheless give a good average value of its real effect.

The model and some results

An implication of the section above detailing previous work is the wide range of interdependencies which are relevant to any analysis of births and deaths. As stated earlier, most studies have only recognised limited interdependence between present and past births, deaths and other economic variables. An implicit assumption in such studies is that some variables are exogenous to the analysis, and so can be effectively ignored. In the light of our discussion in the previous section, this is unlikely to be the case in practice. Moreover, in the light of modern econometric practice, assuming exogeneity without testing it, and imposing an *a priori* endogenous – exogenous division between variables is not a state of affairs which many researchers would find satisfactory. This is the essence of SIMS's, 1980, critique of 'conventional' (as it then was) simultaneous equation modelling, which neither allowed full interdependence between variables in the system, nor gave proper consideration to the issue of lag structure.

Sim's solution was to suggest vector auto regression (VAR) techniques, which were originally introduced within a time-series framework. However, work since then by HOLTZ-EAKIN *et al.*, 1988, has extended the VAR methodology to a panel data setting, which is appropriate for our purposes here.

This methodology involves regressing each of the economic variables discussed in the previous two sections on the lagged values of *every* variable in this system. To fix ideas, consider for now just the first variable in the system: births. Denote the number of births in county i at time t by B_{it} ($i = 1, \ldots, 60$). Denote by $\Omega^1 = W$ and $\Omega^2 = S$, so $\Omega^k = \Omega^1$ with Ω^2 depending on whether $k = 1$ or $k = 2$. Then the following equation shows how all lagged variables may affect births, with f_{iB} denoting unobserved county-specified fixed effects, and $v_{it,B}$ denoting a white noise disturbance:

$$
\begin{aligned}
\ln\left(\frac{B_{it}}{\Omega^k_{i,t-1}}\right) = \sum_{j=1}^{p}\Bigg\{ & \alpha_{Bj} \ln\left(\frac{B_{t-j}}{\Omega^k_{t-j-1}}\right)_i \\
& + \beta_{Bj} \ln\left(\frac{D_{t-j}}{\Omega^k_{t-j-1}}\right)_i + \gamma_{Bj} \ln E_{i,t-j} \\
& + \delta_{Bj} \ln\left(\frac{U_{t-j}}{\Omega^1_{t-j-1}}\right)_i \\
& + \varepsilon_{Bj} \ln\left(\frac{Q_{t-j}}{\Omega^k_{t-j-1}}\right)_i \\
& + \zeta_{Bj} \ln V_{i,t-j} + \eta_{Bj} \ln M_{i,t-j} \\
& + \theta_{Bj} \ln\left(\frac{\Omega^1}{\Omega^2}\right)_{i,t-j} \Bigg\} \\
& + \lambda_B f_{iB} + v_{it,B}.
\end{aligned}
\tag{1}
$$

In the above equation, $\alpha_{Bj}, \beta_{Bj} \ldots, \lambda_B$ are coefficients to be estimated. The scale variable Ω^k may be either Ω^1 or Ω^2 and does not need to be specified at this stage. The maximum lag in the model is denoted p, which is to be determined econometrically (qv below); note also that the firm size effect is

$(S/W) = (\Omega^1/\Omega^2)$; this variable, mix and average earnings are already scaled and so are not in need of further re-scaling (see the previous section).[22]

HOLTZ-EAKIN *et al.*, 1988, p. 1,376, demonstrate that, for estimation purposes, equation (1) must be transformed by differencing both sides. This transformation, which removes any county-specific fixed effects, results in the new estimating equation:

$$
\begin{aligned}
\Delta \ln B_{it} = \sum_{j=1}^{p} & \left\{ a_{Bj} \Delta \ln B_{i,t-j} + \beta_{Bj} \Delta \ln D_{i,t-j} \right. \\
& + \gamma_{Bj} \Delta \ln E_{i,t-j} + \delta_{Bj} \Delta \ln U_{i,t-j} \\
& + \varepsilon_{Bj} \Delta \ln Q_{i,t-j} + \xi_{Bj} \Delta \ln V_{i,t-j} \\
& \left. + \eta_{Bj} \Delta \ln M_{i,t-j} - \theta_{Bj} \Delta \ln \Omega_{i,t-j}^2 \right\} \\
& + \Delta \ln \Omega_{i,t-1}^k + \theta_{Bj} \Delta \ln \Omega_{i,t-1}^1 \\
& + \sum_{j=2}^{p+1} \left\{ (\theta_{Bj} - \delta_{Bj}) \Delta \ln \Omega_{i,t-j}^1 \right. \\
& \left. - (a_{Bj} + \beta_{Bj} + \varepsilon_{Bj}) \ \Delta \ln \Omega_{i,t-j}^k \right\} + \phi_{it,B}
\end{aligned}
\tag{2}
$$

where $\phi_{it,B}$ = the new disturbance term.

Two important points need to be made about this equation. First, inspection of it reveals that whereas theoretical priors about the signs of the coefficients on the differences in logs of B D E U Q V and M may be tested, *this is unfortunately not possible for the workforce and stock of business variables, Ω^1 and Ω^2, whatever the choice of k, i.e. whether data are scaled by W or S.* Whatever the choice of scaling, the coefficients on these variables are composites of several parameters, and so cannot be signed. Second, the appropriate econometric format for investigating county-wide variability in the variables of interest is in differences. The use of levels is inappropriate because estimates will be biased by omitting the unobservable fixed effects f_{iB} (these, of course, drop out of the differenced regressions). It should be remembered that the differences of a logarithm of a variable represents a growth rate, so the dependent variable in equation (2) above (and in all the other equations in the system) should be interpreted in terms of growth rates. This does not alter any of the theoretical predictions made above concerning the predicted signs of the coefficients.

The rest of the system of equations is obtained in the same way as for births, leading to equations in $\Delta \ln D_{it}$, $\Delta \ln E_{it}$, etc, analogous to equation (2). The broad structure of these equations will be identical to equation (2) The only differences are: (1) different coefficients (e.g. $a_{Dj}, \ldots, \theta_{Dj}$ in the $\Delta \ln D_{it}$ equation, etc); and (2) different disturbance terms (e.g. $\phi_{it,D}$ in the $\Delta \ln D_{it}$

equation, etc.). There is a three-fold rationale for this 'mandated symmetry' of structure: first, the theoretical framework of the paper suggests total interdependence of all the variables; second, most of the salient influences on each variable are included here; and third, the appropriate econometric structure for panel data of this type is known to be the symmetric Holtz-Eakin *et al.* VAR (see HOLTZ-EAKIN *et al.*, 1988). All the equations of the system can be collected together into the VAR:

$$\Delta \ln Z_{i,90} = \sum_{j=1}^{p+1} A_j \Delta \ln Z_{i,90-j} + \Phi_{i,90} \tag{3}$$

where:

Z = the vector of variables in the system
$\Phi_{i,90}$ = the vector of disturbances for county i at time $t = 1990$
A_j = matrices of coefficients, as described above.

Holtz-Eakin *et al*, show that the identifying assumptions of this VAR are simply standard orthogonality conditions which rule out correlations between the disturbances and the variables in the model, and that the system (3) can be estimated equation by equation. The first task is to determine the VAR lag length empirically, using F tests. On this basis, it transpired that two lags were optimal (F-statistics in this case and for the data-acceptable restrictions described below can be obtained from the authors on request).

OLS estimation of the VAR equation-by-equation is efficient only if each equation includes the same variables on the right-hand side: hence all nine variables lagged up to three periods were present in each equation, as well as an intercept, which was included to capture time-varying effects common to all counties[23]. Data-acceptable restrictions of deflating nominal variables, suppressing the intercept, and dropping four insignificant variables in all equations of the system ($\Delta \ln E_{i,89}$, $\Delta \ln E_{i,88}$, $\Delta \ln D_{i,88}$ and $\Delta \ln U_{i,89}$) were then imposed. It was found, in particular, that the earnings equation was redundant, and so was dropped from the system. The remaining equations of interest are reported in Table 6.2. Goodness-of-fit measures and diagnostic tests for each equation are summarized in Table 6.3.

The interpretation of these results in the following will focus on the significant variables within the VAR. Significance levels of 10 per cent, as well as 5 per cent and 1 per cent, will be considered, because of some possible collinearity inflating the standard errors. Starting with births, we observe that this equation is significant and well specified. Unemployment only enters after a two-year lag, and then with a negative sign, suggesting that any positive recession push influences are dominated by negative demand pull effects. Also, real net housing wealth, lagged two years, has a negative sign, a result which is more in line with ROBSON's 1994, findings than with those of BLACK *et al.*, 1996. It is not possible, for reasons given earlier, to interpret the

Table 6.2 Estimates of the VAR

	$\Delta \ln B_{i,90}$	$\Delta \ln D_{i,90}$	$\Delta \ln U_{i,90}$	$\Delta \ln Q_{i,90}$	$\Delta \ln V_{i,90}$	$\Delta \ln M_{i,90}$	$\Delta \ln S_{i,90}$
$\Delta \ln B_{i,89}$	−0.82	−0.57	−3.54***	3.41**	1.41	−0.33	0.01
$\Delta \ln B_{i,88}$	−0.13	−0.59***	−1.08***	−0.94***	0.67***	0.06	0.06***
$\Delta \ln D_{i,89}$	0.80	0.19	1.79***	−3.21**	−0.15	0.24	0.04
$\Delta \ln U_{i,88}$	−0.23*	0.05	−0.56	−0.24	0.18	0.00	−0.05
$\Delta \ln Q_{i,89}$	0.00	0.00	0.04***	−0.99***	−0.02	0.00	0.00***
$\Delta \ln Q_{i,88}$	−0.03	−0.01	−0.15**	−0.63***	0.04	0.00	0.00
$\Delta \ln V_{i,89}$	−0.14	0.16*	−0.06	−0.07	0.53***	−0.01	−0.03***
$\Delta \ln V_{i,88}$	−0.32***	0.00	−0.19*	0.12	−0.88***	−0.01	−0.04***
$\Delta \ln W_{i,89}$	0.39	0.30	−1.52**	1.42	0.13	0.02	0.06
$\Delta \ln W_{i,88}$	0.34	0.83	1.68**	−1.77	−0.91	−0.04	−0.04
$\Delta \ln S_{i,89}$	5.43	2.57	17.00*	−24.11**	−2.84	2.46**	0.92
$\Delta \ln S_{i,88}$	−5.87*	0.07	−12.53**	24.87**	−0.05	−2.19	−0.46
$\Delta \ln M_{i,89}$	−8.75	17.49	88.81**	181.02**	−56.27	2.95	−1.73
$\Delta \ln M_{i,88}$	7.96	−17.24	−86.47**	−178.91**	54.44	−2.94	1.66

Note: * = significant at 10%; ** = significant at 5%; *** = significant at 1%.

significant negative coefficient on *S* lagged two years because it is picking up a variety of influences. Interestingly, lagged births and deaths do not seem to influence current births.

The deaths equation is also significant and well-specified. The negative effect of births on deaths after a two-year lag suggests that a dominant multiplier effect is at work (see Table 6.1), a finding which confirms the earlier results in JOHNSON and PARKER, 1994. The two-year lag confirms the need to treat lag structure fully in studies of birth and death interdependence. The only other significant effect is the positive one from real net housing wealth (lagged one year), whose sign is consistent with the finding on the birth equation, but not with Robson's proposition that the presence of such wealth may aid survival in the short run.

The unemployment regression is characterized by an excellent fit; the diagnostic tests are also comfortably passed. The equation reveals a considerable number of significant variables. As expected, births have a strongly negative impact: the birth variable lagged one and two years is significant with a Type 1 error of 1 per cent. Increases in business activity, via new firms, reduces unemployment. This result is further reinforced by the significant and positive sign on deaths, lagged one year. The significant and negative sign on output lagged two years is as expected (the positive effect of output lagged one year is, however, puzzling although the effect is small in absolute magnitude; it is possible that it is picking up sluggishness in the responsiveness of unemployment to output change). Real net housing wealth has a small effect, with only the two-year lag being marginally significant (at the 10 per cent level). Both the workforce and stock variables are significant, but as before these are picking up multiple influences as scaling factors so cannot be

Table 6.3 Fit and diagnostic statistics

	$\Delta vB_{i,90}$	$\Delta \ln D_{i,90}$	$\Delta \ln U_{i,90}$	$\Delta \ln Q_{i,90}$	$\Delta \ln V_{i,90}$	$\Delta \ln M_{i,90}$	$\Delta \ln S_{i,90}$
R^2	0.51	0.60	0.81	0.98	0.91	0.21	0.79
$F(13,46)$	3.73***	5.38***	15.45***	149.18***	37.92***	0.94	12.94***
SE	4.38%	4.13%	5.04%	9.87%	5.94%	1.02%	0.56%
RESET: $F(1,45)$	0.21	1.88	0.17	0.78	8.47	5.91	0.02
JB: $\chi^2(2)$	0.72	1.66	1.56	4.87	1.15	0.77	0.37
HETERO: $F(1,58)$	0.54	0.59	3.04	0.37	1.13	0.12	0.19

Note: $F(13,46)$ test significance of the regression; SE is the standard error of the regression; RESET is Ramsey's RESET test, whose test statistic is distributed as $F(1,45)$ in this case (5% critical value: 4.05); JB is Jarque-Bera's normality test, whose statistic is asymptotically distributed as a $\chi^2(2)$ variate (5% critical value: 5.99); and HETERO is White's test for heteroscedasticity (5% critical value: 4.01).

signed. Finally, industrial mix seems to play an important role in determining county-level unemployment. It proves possible in this regression to combine $\Delta\ln M_{t-1}$ and $\Delta\ln M_{t-2}$ by imposing a restriction on the coefficients; this forms the composite variable $\Delta\Delta\ln M_{t-1}$, which can be interpreted as the acceleration of the move towards the service sector in the local economy. The fact that it is positive in the regression indicates that an acceleration towards services (away from manufacturing) causes unemployment overall. One explanation for this is the labour mismatching that may arise from a changing industrial structure.

The output equation also possess excellent goodness-of-fit and passes all of the diagnostic tests. Births lagged one year have a strongly positive effect on output, but a two-year lag has a smaller negative (but still significant) effect; this again reflects an 'acceleration' effect, i.e. an increase in the growth of the growth rate of births serves to raise output. In line with the positive sign on births lagged one year, deaths with the same lag have a negative sign. The significant negative effects of lagged output reflect the general economic downturn that occurred in 1990. As in the unemployment regression, an accelerating move towards the service sector is present. The coefficient on this term indicates that it increases output as the economy redistributes its resources towards more rapidly growing sectors. As before, stock and workforce coefficients cannot be interpreted.

This concludes our discussion of the salient empirical results of the model. Although it would be possible to consider also the housing wealth and industrial mix equations, there are doubts about the validity of inference which may be made in these equations engendered by failure of the Ramsey RESET tests for correct functional form. Finally, we note that the equation describing growth in the stock of businesses is well-specified and gives a good fit. Not surprisingly the equation picks up a significant positive effect of births on stock. The significant negative sign on net housing wealth is consistent with the births equation.

Conclusions

In this paper a preliminary attempt has been made to set up and estimate a small model of county-level economic behaviour. The role of births and deaths has been stressed, but the importance of modelling full interdependence between all the variables in the model has also been emphasized. Overall the model performed quite well, with mostly well specified and tight fitting equations. Although the data used here have important limitations which should be borne in mind in the interpretation of the results, they are nevertheless the best currently available at county level.

The following results may be highlighted. First, relatively little direct birth – death interdependence was detected, a result perhaps of allowing for wide-ranging influences from a relatively large number of economic variables on business activity. The interdependence that we *did* identify – the negative effect of lagged births on deaths – is at odds with the findings of a number of other studies (e.g. KEEBLE and WALKER, 1994) and is not at first sight easily reconcilable with the well established fact that the mortality rate among newly born firms is very high (STOREY, 1994, p. 93). However, it should be remembered that our study is picking up the *combined* impact of the competition, multiplier and Marshall effects of births on deaths of all types of firms, and not just of new ones.

Second, we found that the widely held view that net housing wealth acts as a proxy for collateral and so is associated positively with births needs to be reassessed; we found a negative association, which may suggest that increasing housing equity may to some extent reflect improving economic conditions which, in turn, expands opportunities for paid employment. Third, confirmation was found of the need to take account of lags greater than one year when modelling births and deaths. Fourthly, there is robust evidence that the growth in births and reductions in deaths *significantly* lowers unemployment.

We would be the first to recognize the tentative nature of the results contained in this paper. However, it is hoped that the paper will act as a stimulus for further work in a number of directions. First, the results suggest that considerable progress could be made in this area by models which more fully recognize interdependence between variables through time, not only between births and deaths, but between births and deaths and other economic variables. Second, and more specifically, it would be helpful to examine in greater detail the effects of real net housing wealth on business activity. At the moment there is conflicting evidence. (It is possible, of course, that our results are specific to 1990, a year in which there were very considerable spatial variations in house price behaviour.) Finally, it may be interesting for future researchers to repeat the analysis conducted here in order to perform some robustness tests on our specifications. Data limitations currently prevent us from doing this here.

Indeed, how far further progress is possible will depend on the availability of good time series data at county-level. Although the VAT data, despite its limitations, is a relatively good source of births and deaths, its quality is not generally matched by the other measures available. This is particularly true of net housing wealth.

Notes

1 This is a version of a paper given to the ESRC Industrial Economics Study Group held at the University of Edinburgh in February 1995. The authors are grateful to colleagues in the Department of Economics, University of Durham, and to participants in a staff seminar in the Department of Business Studies, University of Edinburgh, for helpful comments on their work. The comments of two anonymous referees were also very helpful. All errors and omissions however remain the responsibility of the authors.

2 This categorization broadly follows that contained in KEEBLE *et al.*, 1993, pp. 28f.

3 The term self employment is used here to embrace all forms of own account activity.

4 Keeble and Walker also find that population change has a significant and important positive effect on *deaths*. Their explanation for this is that new firms are 'inherently vulnerable, high risk and prone to failure. New firm death rates are thus much higher than those for established firms'.

5 At the beginning of 1991, nearly two-thirds of the stock of VAT registered businesses were in services.

6 The possibility, implied by this approach, that a reduction in paid employment prospects may stimulate births, by lowering expected returns in the alternatives to self employment, has long been recognized in the literature: see for example SCHUMPETER, 1939, p. 94, and OXENFELDT, 1943, pp. 120–23.

7 Compare for example ROBSON, 1993, and PARKER, 1996, with BLACK *et al.*, 1996. Although these studies use time series data, the underlying issues are the same as those relevant for spatial analyses.

8 Barkham's study related to high growth new firms only. However the point is likely to be more generally valid (see, for example, JOHNSON and RODGER, 1983).

9 The evidence is not wholly unanimous on this point. For example, KEEBLE *et al.*, 1992, suggest that in information intensive business services, large firms may be relatively more important incubators. However, the weight of evidence supports the proposition in the text.

10 They also find a positive effect on deaths. Reasoning similar to that found in note 4 may be used to justify this finding.

11 In an as yet unpublished study of new VAT registrations being undertaken by one of the authors (Johnson) two-thirds of the business surveyed had not raised significant funds from financial institutions (see also BASU, 1995).

12 Some firms may of course be taken over. However, such take overs are likely to affect only a small minority of old businesses.

13 These authors cite CAVES and PORTER, 1976, as the first study to put entry into an exit equation.

14 Specifically: gross domestic product per capita; the level and change in the unemployment rate; the average annual wage; the percentage of dwellings that are owner occupied (proxying house collateral); population density; and proxies for small firm background and management skills.

15 An exception is the recent paper by ASHCROFT and LOVE, 1994, which looked at the impact of births on employment. There is of course a substantial 'job accounting' literature that purports to look at the impact of births and deaths on employment, but none of this literature is based on any formal modelling.

16 We are grateful to an anonymous referee for making this point.

17 This is because some of the other variables which appear in the births and deaths regressions are also scaled by these variables. Working in logarithms, the sum of the coefficients of the variables will determine the overall coefficient on the scaling variables.

18 The excluded counties were the Isle of Wight, Powys and the Borders.

19 While this is, of course, a different measure from total population, the two measures are very highly correlated. Inclusion of both measures in the regressions would be highly undesirable, since this procedure would not only use up valuable degrees of freedom, but would also undoubtedly induce damaging multicollinearity into the estimates.

20 Unfortunately GDP figures by county are not available for all the years covered in this study. However annual data by county for manufacturing value added *are* published. An annual series for GDP by county was obtained by applying the ratio (which can be derived from annually published data) of manufacturing GDP to total GDP for the region in which the county is found. The resulting series was

converted into real terms by the GDP deflator. A county's population is proxied here by its workforce.

21 Data for any missing years were obtained by interpolation.

22 It will be noted that the equation enters all variables in logarithmic form. This is advantageous because any constant measurement error in the data will be separated out by the log rule: $\ln(ab) = \ln(a) + \ln(b)$. If b is the 'true' value of the variable, and a is a constant multiplicative error factor, then differencing will remove this factor from the regression.

23 For example, with the price level changing from year to year, an effect for each year will be present. If these are common to all counties, the sum of these effects will simply be a constant in these regressions.

References

ASHCROFT B., LOVE J. and MALLOY E. (1991) New firm formation in the UK counties with special reference to Scotland, *Reg. Studies* **25**, 395–410.

ASHCROFT B. and LOVE J. (1994) Employment change and new firm formation in GB counties: 1981–90, paper presented at the ESRC Urban and Regional Economics Seminar Group, Craigie College, Ayr, January.

AUDRETSCH D. and FRITSCH M. (1992) Market dynamics and regional development in the Federal Republic of Germany, Discussion Paper FS IV 92–6, Wissenschaftszentrum Berlin.

BARKHAM R. (1992) Regional variations in entrepreneurship: some evidence from the United Kingdom, *Entrepreneurship & Reg. Develop.* **4**, 225–44.

BASU A. (1995) Asian small businesses in Britain: an exploration of entrepreneurial activity, Discussion Paper No. 303, University of Reading.

BLACK J., DE MEZA D. and JEFFREYS D. (1996) House prices, the supply of collateral and the enterprise economy, *Econ. J.* **106**, 60–75.

BORJAS G. (1986) The self employment of immigrants, *J. Human Res.* **21**, 485–506.

CARREE M. and THURIK R. (1993) Entry and exit in retailing: incentives, barriers, displacement and replacement, Centre for Advanced Small Business Economics, Erasmus University, Rotterdam, and the Department of Fundamental Research, Research Institute for Small and Medium Sized Business (mimeo).

CAVES R. E. and PORTER M. E. (1976) Barriers to exit, in MASSON R. T. and QUALLS P. D. (Eds) *Essays on Industrial Organization in Honour of Joe S. Bain*, pp. 39–69. Cambridge University Press, Cambridge.

CREEDY J. and JOHNSON P. S. (1983) Firm formation in manufacturing industry, *Appl. Econ.* **15**, 177–85.

CRESSY R. (1993) Loan commitments and business starts: an empirical investigation on UK data, Working Paper 12, Centre for Small and Medium Sized Enterprises, University of Warwick.

DALY M. (1990) The 1980s: a decade of growth in enterprise, *Emp. Gazette* **98**, 553–65.

EVANS D. S. and LEIGHTON L. S. (1989a) Some empirical aspects of entrepreneurship, *Am. Econ. Rev.* **79**, 519–35.

EVANS D. S. and LEIGHTON L. S (1989b) The determinants of changes in US self-employment, 1968–1987, *Small Bus. Econ.* **1**, 11–19.

GUDGIN G. and FOTHERGILL S. (1984) Geographical variation in the rate of formation of new manufacturing firms, *Reg. Studies* **18**, 203–06.

GUESNIER B. (1994) Regional variations in new firm formation in France, *Reg. Studies* **28**, 347–58.

HART M. and GUDGIN G. (1994) Spatial variations in new firm formation in the Republic of Ireland, 1980–1990, *Reg. Studies* **28**, 367–80.

HOLTZ-EAKIN D., NEWEY D. and ROSEN D. (1988) Estimating vector autoregressions with panel data, *Econometrica* **56**, 1,371–95.

JOHNSON P. S. and CATHCART G. (1979) The founders of new manufacturing firms: a note on the size of their incubator plants, *J. Ind. Econ.* **28**, 19–24.

JOHNSON P. S. and PARKER S. C. (1994) The interrelationships between births and deaths, *Small Bus. Econ.* **6**, 283–90.

JOHNSON P. S. and RODGER J. (1983) *Self Employment Among Redundant Employees.* Manpower Services Commission, Sheffield.

KEEBLE D. and WALKER S. (1994) New firms, small firms and dead firms: spatial patterns and determinants in the United Kingdom, *Reg. Studies* **28**, 411–27.

KEEBLE D., BRYSON J. R. and WOOD P. (1992) Entrepreneurship and flexibility in business services: the rise of small management consultancy and market research firms in the United Kingdom, in CALEY K., CHITTENDEN F., CHELL E. and MASON C. (Eds) *Small Enterprise Development: Policy and Practice in Action*, pp. 43–58. Paul Chapman, London.

KEEBLE D., WALKER S. and ROBSON M. (1993) *New Firm Formation and Small Business Growth in the United Kingdom: Spatial and Temporal Variations and Determinants*, Department of Employment Research Series No 15. Department of Employment, London.

LOVE J. (1993) Spatial entry and exit: recursive and simultaneous estimations, Strathclyde Papers in Economics 93/7, University of Strathclyde.

MARSHALL A. (1920) *Principles of Economics*, 8th edition (reset 1949). Macmillan, London.

OXENFELDT A. R. (1943) *New Firms and Free Enterprise*. American Council on Public Affairs, Washington, DC.

PARKER S. C. (1996) A time series model of self-employment under uncertainty, *Economica* (forthcoming).

REYNOLDS R., STOREY D. J. and WESTHEAD P. (1994) Cross national comparisons of the variation in new firm formation rates, *Reg. Studies* **28**, 443–56.

ROBSON M. (1991) Self-employment and new firm formation, *Scot. J. Pol. Econ.* **38**, 352–68.

ROBSON M. (1993) Macroeconomic factors in the birth and death of UK firms: evidence from quarterly VAT registrations, Department of Economics, University of Newcastle upon Tyne.

ROBSON M. (1994) Housing wealth, business creation and dissolution in the UK regions, Department of Economics, University of Newcastle upon Tyne (mimeo).

ROSENBAUM D. I. and LAMORT F. (1992) Entry, barriers to exit and sunk costs: an analysis, *Appl. Econ*, **24**, 297–304.

SCHUMPETER J. A. (1939) *Business Cycles*, vol. 1. McGraw Hill, New York.

SHAPIRO D. and KHEMANI R. S. (1987) The determinants of entry and exit reconsidered, *Int. J. Ind. Org.* **5**, 15–26.

SIMS C. A. (1980) Macroeconomics and reality. *Econometrica* **48**, 1–48.

SLEUWAGEN L. and DEHANDSCHUTTER W. (1991) Entry and exit in Belgian manufacturing, in GEROSKI P. A. and SCHWALBACH J. (Eds) *Entry and Market Contestability: An International Comparison*. Oxford University Press, Oxford.

STOREY D. (1982) *Entrepreneurship and the New Firm*, Croom Helm, London.

STOREY D. (1991) The birth of new firms – does unemployment matter? A review of the literature, *Small Bus. Econ.* **3**, 167–78.

STOREY D. (1994) *Understanding the Small Business Sector*. Routledge, London.

STOREY D. and JONES A. M. (1987) New firm formation – a labour market approach to industrial entry, *Scot. J. Pol. Econ.* **34**, 37–51.

7 Differences in regional firm formation rates

A decomposition analysis

Peter Johnson

Source: *Entrepreneurship Theory and Practice*, 2004, 28, (5), 431–445.

This article examines regional differences in recent business formation activity in the United Kingdom over the period 1994–2001. It considers the extent to which regional differences can be accounted for by (i) variations in industrial structure, with some regions having a greater or lesser share of sectors where the formation rate tends to be high; and (ii) variations across regions in the formation rate in the *same* sector. The article shows wide variations across regions and over time in the relative importance of these two factors. The article explores some policy implications of this decomposition.

Introduction

There are wide spatial variations in business formation rates. Variations across countries are highlighted by the Global Entrepreneurship Monitor (GEM) studies. The 2002 GEM study which covered thirty-seven countries, shows that the Total Entrepreneurial Activity (TEA) prevalence index – defined as the percentage of the labour force involved in setting up or running a new business – varied from 18.7 in Thailand to only 1.8 in Japan (Reynolds et al., 2002, p. 4). The same study shows (p. 10) wide variations across regions of the world, with the highest rates occurring in Latin America and the developing Asian economies. *Within* countries, there is also considerable spatial variation. Reynolds et al. (1994), using annual firm births per 10,000 persons as their measure of regional birth rates, show that the ratio of the highest to the lowest rate was at least 2.2 in each of the six countries they looked at and was as high as 4.1 in the United States.

These spatial variations in formation rates generate important opportunities and challenges for policy makers. Business births are an important expression of entrepreneurial activity, an activity that is, in turn, a key element in economic development and growth (Organisation for Economic Co-operation and Development, 1998). Not surprisingly, there is now a considerable body of empirical evidence to suggest that new firms have a significant role to play in employment generation (e.g. Ashcroft and

Love, 1996; Gallagher et al., 1996; Hart and Oulton, 2001), innovation (e.g. Audretsch, 1999, esp. pp. 8–10), economic growth (e.g. Schmitz, 1989) and the reduction in unemployment (e.g. Thurik, 1999). Thus where policy-makers are charged with improving the ranking of a region or country, in terms of its economic performance – a task with which they have been charged in the United Kingdom (UK) (HM Treasury, 2003; Office of the Deputy Prime Minister, 2004) – they may need to examine, inter alia, whether there any effective ways in which the formation rate can be encouraged in relative terms.[1]

It is against this background of the policy interest in formation activity and the need to understand more fully why spatial variations in such activity exists, that this article examines regional[2] differences in business formation activity in the UK over the period 1994–2001. It considers the extent to which regional differences can be accounted for by (i) variations in industrial structure, with some regions having a greater or lesser share of sectors where the formation rate tends to be high; and (ii) variations across regions in the formation rate in the *same* sector. This decomposition has potentially important implications for policy. For example, where the policy objective is to increase formation activity, the analysis provides some clues about the most appropriate ways of doing so. The statistical evidence in this article suggests that in some UK regions a key challenge arises from an industrial structure that is biased against industries in which the formation rate tends to be high. A central question for policy makers here is how far intervention might be able to adjust that structure. In other regions, the results suggests that a dominant policy concern should be the inability of some industries to match the formation rates experienced *in the same industries* in other regions.

It should be noted that although the decomposition technique is applied only to UK data in this article, the same approach can be utilised in the analysis of spatial variations in formation activity anywhere in the world.

The structure of the article is as follows. The next section describes the data sources and sets out the methodology of the study. The third section briefly reviews the results of earlier studies. In the fourth section some results are presented. The final section concludes the study.

Data sources and methodology

The data

Throughout this article VAT registrations are used as proxies for the number of births and the number of "live" registrations is treated as a proxy for the business stock. These VAT statistics have some well-known limitations (Daly, 1990; Storey, 1994, pp. 50–51). *[See also chapter 4 in this volume]*. In particular it is known that registration data do not pick up all births. In 1999, the Small Business Service (2000b, p. 5) estimated that there were 3.7m businesses in the UK, compared with only 1.7m VAT registrations (Small Business Service 2000a, p. 6). Given their very small average size, new firms are likely to be even more under-represented, with registration often occurring (if it happens at all) some time after the business starts trading (Johnson and Conway, 1997). Changes in the real value of the VAT turnover threshold – below which businesses do not have to be registered – mean that time series analyses need to be approached with caution. Notwithstanding these limitations, however, the VAT figures still represent the best available data set for measuring births (Keeble and Walker 1994), and it is not surprising to find them widely used by both the English Regional Development Agencies (RDAs) and the U.K. central government: see for example, East Midlands Development Agency (1999, p. 60); Northwest Development Agency (1999, p. 63); One NorthEast (1999, p. 103); and Department of Trade and Industry (1999, p. 48). They have also been used in evaluations of regional competitiveness (e.g. Gudgin, 1996; Brooksbank and Pickernell, 1999; Department of Trade and Industry, 2000).

Methodology

Formation rates may be measured in different ways. Consider sector i in region r. The formation rate for this sector (ignoring time subscripts) may be defined as follows:

$$f_{i,r} = \frac{VR_{i,r}}{VS_{i,r}}$$

where $VR_{i,r}$ = the annual number of VAT registrations in sector i in region r and $VS_{i,r}$ = the stock of registered VAT businesses at the beginning of the year in sector i in region r.

Aggregating over all sectors, the formation rate for region r, f_r, is

$$f_r = \frac{\sum_{i=1}^{n} VR_{i,r}}{\sum_{i=1}^{n} VS_{i,r}}$$

where n = the number of sectors.

The formation rate in sector i *in the country as a whole* (here the UK), $f_{i,UK}$, may then be defined as

$$f_{i,UK} = \frac{\sum_{r=1}^{m} VR_{i,r}}{\sum_{r=1}^{m} VS_{i,r}}$$

where m = the number of regions.

The UK formation rate, aggregating over all regions and sectors, f_{UK}, is

$$f_{UK} = \frac{\sum_{i=1}^{n}\sum_{r=1}^{m} VR_{i,r}}{\sum_{i=1}^{n}\sum_{r=1}^{m} VS_{i,r}}$$

All the above formation rates ($f_{i,r}, f_r, f_{i,UK}, f_{UK}$) use the stock of VAT registered businesses, defined appropriately, as the denominator. The use of the
registration stock figures is particularly helpful for analysing the extent to
which the business sector is being rejuvenated since the resultant formation
rate measures what proportion of the stock is "new blood". This way of
measuring the birth rate is sometimes referred to as the "ecological"
approach: Armington and Acs (2002). An alternative measure – designated
the "labor market" approach by Armington and Acs – utilises population (or
work force) as the denominator and is more relevant for examining how
"entrepreneurial" a region's people are i.e., what proportion of the population is setting up new business. Thus, for example, the alternative specification
for the formation rate for region r, aggregating across all sectors, denoted
here as f_r^*, may be defined as $\dfrac{\sum_{i=1}^{n} VR_{i,r}}{P_r}$ where P_r is some measure of the
population (or work force) in region r[3]. The two formation rates for each of
the UK regions/countries are set out in Table 7.1. The two measures generate some differences in regional rankings. They are however highly correlated
($r = 0.79$) – a finding consistent with U.S. data (Armington and Acs, 2002) –
even though their focus is different.

The two measures may also generate different policy implications. For
example, in the North East of England, the Regional Development Agency,
One North East, set itself (in 1999) the target of raising the region's annual
birth rate, defined as f_r, to that of the rest of the UK by 2010 (One NorthEast,
1999). Using 1999 data as a base, that would have required 315 new registrations;[4] on the alternative measure, f_r^*, the number required would have been

Table 7.1 Formation rates in the UK regions: alternative specifications, 1994–2001, all sectors

Region/country	f_r (see Note 1)	f_r^* (see Note 2)
North East	0.099	2.032
North West	0.109	3.191
Yorks and Humberside	0.098	2.885
East Midlands	0.103	3.376
West Midlands	0.103	3.309
East of England	0.107	3.935
London	0.139	6.080
South East	0.115	4.365
South West	0.098	3.632
Wales	0.081	2.600
Scotland	0.097	2.804
Northern Ireland	0.067	2.806
United Kingdom	0.108	3.687

Notes
1 Number of registrations as a proportion of the registered stock of businesses at the beginning of the year: weighted average.
2 Average annual number of registrations per 1000 in the adult population.

Source: Based on data from the UK's Small Business Service (http://www.sbs.gov.uk).

3787 (Johnson, forthcoming). This substantial variation in the numbers of new firms required is likely to be mirrored in the scale of policy inputs required to achieve the target. Clearly, the choice of measure is critical for policy formulation and execution.

In the rest of the article we utilise the stock of registered businesses at the beginning of the year as the denominator in the annual birth rate. The starting point for the analysis is the very considerable variation across sectors in the formation rate at national level. Table 7.2 provides some data on $f_{i,UK}$ for eleven sectors. The highest formation rates are found in "Hotels and restaurants" and in "Real estate, renting, and business activities". The lowest rates are in "Agriculture, forestry and fishing" and in "Manufacturing". We should note in passing that the correlation between sectoral birth rates and death rates is high and positive ($r = 0.77$), confirming findings from elsewhere: see Geroski (1995). Geroski argues that "... entry and exit seem to be part of a process of change in which large numbers of new firms displace large numbers of older firms without changing the total number of firms in operation at any given time by very much." (p. 424)

The following analysis starts with a comparison of the actual number of births in region r, denoted here as A_r, and the "National Standard" number of births in region r, denoted here as NS_r. The latter may be defined as the number of births region r would have had if (i) the stock of registered businesses in the region had displayed the same industrial distribution as that in

Table 7.2 Formation rates by sector: 1994–2001

Sector	$f_{i,UK}$
Agriculture, forestry and fishing	0.025
Mining and quarrying; electricity, gas, and water supply	0.101
Manufacturing	0.080
Construction	0.098
Wholesale, retail, and repairs	0.092
Hotels and restaurants	0.159
Transport, storage, and communications	0.123
Financial intermediation	0.111
Real estate, renting, and business activities	0.155
Public administration; other community, social, and personal services	0.123
Education; health and social work	0.100
All sectors	0.108

Source: Based on data from Small Business Service's website (http://www.sbs.gov.uk).

the UK as whole; and (ii) if the birth rate in each sector had also been the same as that in the UK. More formally,

$$NS_r = \sum_{i=1}^{n} \left(\frac{VS_r VS_{i,UK} f_{i,UK}}{VS_{UK}} \right)$$

where the notation is as before, and
   VS_r = total stock of businesses in region r
   $VS_{i,UK}$ = UK stock of businesses in sector i
   VS_{UK} = total UK stock of businesses (in all sectors).
   We may define A_r minus NS_r as the regional 'deficit' where it is negative and the regional 'surplus' where it is positive.
   Now the *difference* between A_r and NS_r may be broken down into a Structural Component, S_r, and a Formation Component, F_r, as follows

$$S_r = \sum_{i=1}^{n} \left(VS_{i,r} - VS_r \frac{VS_{i,UK}}{VS_{UK}} \right) f_{i,UK}$$

$$F_r = \sum_{i=1}^{N} VS_{i,r}(f_{i,r} - f_{i,UK})$$

   Thus the Structural Component shows how many new registrations would be generated by applying the national formation rate in each sector to the *difference* between the actual stock of registered businesses in each sector and what that stock would have been if the region had had the same industrial structure of registered businesses as the UK as a whole. The Formation

Component on the other hand shows the number of registrations that would be generated by applying the difference between the regional and national formation rates in each sector to the regional stock of businesses in that sector.

Earlier work

There is now a wealth of empirical research on spatial differences in business formation activity: see for example the special issue of *Regional Studies* (1994), which contained articles covering experience in several countries and, more recently, Armington and Acs (2002). The determinants of regional variations are clearly complex: for example, Keeble and Walker (1994) identified over 30 potential influences. These covered factors affecting the market prospects of those setting up in business; those affecting the supply of founders and of the resources necessary to set up in business; and those arising from the policy environment within which formation takes place. A summary review of these influences is contained in Johnson and Parker (1996). This literature on regional differences in formation activity should be set in the context of the wider analysis of the economics of self-employment. For an excellent survey in this area, see Le (1999).

In this article, we effectively collapse the sources of regional differences in formation activity into two. The first is differences in industrial structure. As Table 7.2 demonstrates, industries vary significantly in their formation rates; ceteris paribus therefore, variations in industrial structure across regions are likely to generate differences in regional formation rates.[5] Second, there may be differences across regions that are not attributable to industrial structure. In this case, even in the same industry, there may be regional variations in the formation rate. Factors behind such variation might include regional differences in culture, the opportunities for self-employment, the supply of founders, agglomeration economies and local economic policy.

This decomposition has been the basis of earlier work on formation activity. In Johnson (1983), the author applied the technique to UK manufacturing. The analysis was applied to those formations between 1966 and 1977 which reached 11 employees and survived to 1977. Thus it excluded new firms that either died before reaching 11 employees or that survived the period but did not reach such a number. The birth rate for each of the 17 sectors was defined as the number of formations over the average *employment* in the sector, the implicit assumption being that most formations in an industrial sector are undertaken by people employed in that sector. There is some empirical support for this assumption: see for example, Johnson and Cathcart (1979). The analysis demonstrated the overwhelming importance of the Formation Component in "explaining" regional differences in births. In only one region, the East Midlands, did the Structural Component dominate.

Storey and Johnson (1987) subsequently repeated the exercise utilising VAT registration data for the period 1980–83. Unlike Johnson (1983), they used, as here, the stock of registrations as the denominator in their measure of the formation rate. Their analysis was not limited to manufacturing but was applied to data for (i) all sectors, not just manufacturing; and (ii) all sectors, *less* Agriculture. The all sectors results showed that the Structural Component exceeded the Formation Component in most regions. In only three regions (Yorkshire and Humberside, West Midlands and Scotland) was the Formation Component dominant. However when agriculture was excluded, the Formation Component once again dominated in all regions, a result which closely reflected that in the Johnson (1983) study.

The conclusion from these two studies was that when manufacturing was considered in isolation or in conjunction with services, the Formation Component was dominant; when Agriculture was added, structural factors became paramount. The sectoral coverage of any analysis clearly has an important part to play in determining the results. The advantage of the current study over its predecessors is that it provides yearly data. It is of course also more up to date.

Results

Table 7.3 provides data on the A_r/NS_r ratio for the UK regions/countries for the period 1994–2001. The Storey and Johnson (1987) results for 1980–83 are added for comparative purposes although it should be noted that some of their regions do not have the same geographical boundaries as those used here. The bold figures are for all sectors. The unbold, italicised figures exclude Agriculture from the calculations.

The results for all sectors show that only London and the South East have had ratios that have been consistently greater than one. In London, the "excess" has been very substantial in all years. In two further regions, the ratio is one or above in specified years: in the North West between 1996 and 2001 and in the East of England in 1995, 1997, 2000, and 2001.

Not surprisingly, the exclusion of Agriculture has the effect of significantly lowering the ratio for London and the South East – in the case of the latter, taking it marginally below one in 1999 and 2000 – and raising it for the South West, Wales, Scotland and Northern Ireland. These changes reflect the fact that the UK formation rate is very low in Agriculture – as Table 7.2 shows, it averaged 0.025 over the period 1994–2001 in this sector compared with 0.108 for all sectors – and that in London and the South East, Agriculture is very underrepresented in terms of its share of the stock of registered businesses, whereas in the areas where the A_r/NS_r ratio rises with the exclusion of the sector, it accounts for a substantially higher share. In the UK as a whole, Agriculture accounted for just under 9 per cent of the stock of registered businesses in 2001; in Northern Ireland it was over one-third. The exclusion of Agriculture does not however fundamentally alter the picture as far as the A_r/NS_r ratio is concerned. London continues to have higher than expected formation activity; and this is also true for the South East except in 1999 and 2001.

Table 7.3 Ratio of actual to National Standard formations for UK regions, all industries

Region	Current study: 1994–2001								Average 1994/2001	Storey and Johnson study: 1980–83
	1994	1995	1996	1997	1998	1999	2000	2001		
North East	**0.98**	**0.92**	**0.92**	**0.87**	**0.88**	**0.93**	**0.92**	**0.91**	**0.92**	**0.92***
Ex Agriculture	*0.97*	*0.92*	*0.92*	*0.87*	*0.88*	*0.93*	*0.92*	*0.92*	*0.92*	*0.95*￼
North West	**0.98**	**0.98**	**1.00**	**1.02**	**1.03**	**1.05**	**1.04**	**1.03**	**1.01**	**1.02****
Ex Agriculture	*0.96*	*0.96*	*0.98*	*1.00*	*1.01*	*1.03*	*1.02*	*1.01*	*1.00*	*0.97***
Yorks and Humberside	**0.92**	**0.90**	**0.91**	**0.88**	**0.88**	**0.91**	**0.93**	**0.95**	**0.91**	**0.95**
Ex Agriculture	*0.92*	*0.91*	*0.91*	*0.89*	*0.88*	*0.92*	*0.93*	*0.96*	*0.91*	*0.95*
East Midlands	**0.94**	**0.95**	**0.94**	**0.94**	**0.94**	**0.94**	**0.98**	**0.99**	**0.95**	**0.95**
Ex Agriculture	*0.95*	*0.96*	*0.95*	*0.95*	*0.95*	*0.94*	*0.99*	*0.99*	*0.96*	*0.98*
West Midlands	**0.96**	**0.95**	**0.94**	**0.89**	**0.97**	**0.98**	**0.96**	**0.98**	**0.95**	**1.00**
Ex Agriculture	*0.96*	*0.95*	*0.93*	*0.88*	*0.97*	*0.97*	*0.96*	*0.98*	*0.95*	*1.00*
East of England	**0.98**	**1.00**	**0.98**	**1.02**	**0.98**	**0.97**	**1.02**	**1.00**	**0.99**	**0.89*****
Ex Agriculture	*0.97*	*0.99*	*0.97*	*1.01*	*0.96*	*0.96*	*1.01*	*0.99*	*0.98*	*0.98*****
London	**1.30**	**1.33**	**1.32**	**1.31**	**1.34**	**1.28**	**1.25**	**1.20**	**1.29**	**n/a**
Ex Agriculture	*1.20*	*1.23*	*1.23*	*1.21*	*1.24*	*1.19*	*1.16*	*1.11*	*1.20*	*n/a*
South East	**1.09**	**1.08**	**1.07**	**1.09**	**1.06**	**1.04**	**1.03**	**1.05**	**1.06**	**1.15******
Ex Agriculture	*1.05*	*1.03*	*1.03*	*1.04*	*1.01*	*0.99*	*0.99*	*1.00*	*1.02*	*1.08*******
South West	**0.90**	**0.85**	**0.89**	**0.91**	**0.91**	**0.94**	**0.93**	**0.92**	**0.91**	**0.88**
Ex Agriculture	*0.94*	*0.89*	*0.94*	*0.96*	*0.96*	*0.98*	*0.98*	*0.97*	*0.95*	*0.94*
Wales	**0.76**	**0.76**	**0.76**	**0.73**	**0.71**	**0.74**	**0.75**	**0.77**	**0.75**	**0.81**
Ex Agriculture	*0.86*	*0.85*	*0.86*	*0.81*	*0.80*	*0.83*	*0.86*	*0.87*	*0.85*	*0.91*
Scotland	**0.92**	**0.93**	**0.91**	**0.92**	**0.87**	**0.89**	**0.87**	**0.92**	**0.90**	**0.81**
Ex Agriculture	*0.97*	*0.97*	*0.96*	*0.97*	*0.92*	*0.94*	*0.92*	*0.98*	*0.95*	*0.86*
Northern Ireland	**0.63**	**0.68**	**0.67**	**0.63**	**0.60**	**0.60**	**0.57**	**0.63**	**0.63**	**0.64**
Ex Agriculture	*0.72*	*0.79*	*0.78*	*0.74*	*0.73*	*0.76*	*0.73*	*0.80*	*0.76*	*0.74*

Notes: * North (including Cumbria); **excluding Cumbria); ***East Anglia; ****including London.

Source: Based on analyses of VAT Registrations available from the UK's Small Business Service (see http://www.sbs.gov.uk/).

The table shows that the results are broadly consistent with those obtained for the early 1980s by Storey and Johnson ($r = 0.89$ for all industry; $r = 0.83$ excluding Agriculture). Comparison of the two sets of results shows that of the regions which are (broadly) defined the same geographically, Yorks and Humberside, West Midlands and Wales showed some noticeable deterioration in the A_r/NS_r ratio, while Scotland's ratio improved.

Table 7.4 presents data for 1994–2001 on the Formation and Structural Components when all sectors are included in the calculations. The shaded figures relate to those where the A_r/NS_r is equal to or greater than one. The overall picture varies considerably from region to region. In two of the deficit regions, the North East, and Yorks and Humberside, the Formation Component dominates. In four further deficit regions, East Midlands, Wales, Scotland and Northern Ireland, it is the Structural Component that consistently accounts for the majority of the difference between A_r and NS_r. (In Wales however there are a number of years where the two components are of a similar magnitude.) In the West Midlands and South West, the Structural Component also dominates in all but one or two years.

In those regions where A_r/NS_r is greater than one in some or all of the years the picture is also varied. In the South East, the Structural Component considerably outweighs the Formation counterpart in all years whereas in London, the latter is more important in all but two of the years. No clear pattern emerges in the East of England. In the North West, the Formation Component dominates in all years. These results do not sit well with the all sector results of Storey and Johnson, but they are more in line with Johnson's work on manufacturing.

Table 7.5 recalculates the figures excluding agriculture. The Formation Component still dominates in the North East and Yorks and Humberside (except in 1994 in the former region and in 2001 in the latter region). In three further deficit regions, Wales, Scotland and Northern Ireland, it is now the Formation Component rather than its structural counterpart that accounts for the majority of the difference between A_r and NS_r. In the East Midlands, the Structural Component continues to dominate. In the South West, the exclusion of Agriculture causes the dominant element to switch from the Structural Component to the Formation Component in all years. In the West Midlands too, the Structural Component is now quantitatively more significant except in two years.

In those regions where A_r/NS_r is greater than one in some or all of the years, the picture remains varied. In the South East, the Formation Component now outweighs its Structural counterpart in most years where A_r/NS_r is one or greater (except 1994). In London, the Formation Component is the dominant factor in all years. This is also true for all except one year in the East of England. In the North West the picture is a little mixed, although in all the years where the region is in "surplus", the Formation Component dominates.

Table 7.4 Formation (F) and Structural (S) Components (numbers of registrations): 1994–2001, all sectors

Region	1994		1995		1996		1997		1998		1999		2000		2001	
	F	S	F	S	F	S	F	S	F	S	F	S	F	S	F	S
North East	-65	-40	-296	-43	-321	-57	-524	-94	-475	-114	-259	-49	-292	-64	-331	-46
North West	-305	-50	-333	-41	-49	-26	376	-85	493	1	617	175	588	156	388	124
Yorks and Humberside	-611	-404	-798	-381	-712	-418	-1,044	-530	-1,086	-561	-726	-357	-574	-392	-194	-382
East Midlands	-195	-488	-143	-441	-249	-460	-163	-562	-148	-595	-327	-434	220	-462	241	-407
West Midlands	-167	-437	-257	-379	-523	-389	-1,213	-506	125	-554	97	-417	-155	-449	142	-398
East of England	-501	98	-223	187	-524	173	50	287	-751	292	-702	201	167	201	-168	233
London	3,748	3,777	4,654	3,394	4,707	3,594	4,737	3,982	5,718	4,239	4,712	3,455	3,857	3,706	2,475	3,234
South East	679	1,552	307	1,604	56	1,725	321	2,096	-534	2,178	-677	1,663	-785	1,726	-315	1,627
South West	-798	-836	-1,486	-848	-772	-894	-483	-952	-461	-996	-191	-844	-262	-861	-532	-742
Wales	-879	-1,051	-857	-1,022	-794	-1,091	-1,138	-1,211	-1,245	-1,275	-1,065	-1,069	-924	-1,122	-823	-1,007
Scotland	-276	-752	-169	-710	-348	-753	-256	-847	-836	-924	-668	-797	-882	-829	-270	-713
Northern Ireland	-639	-1,364	-414	-1,317	-447	-1,401	-668	-1,575	-801	-1,688	-813	-1,523	-966	-1,606	-620	-1,520

Source: Based on analyses of VAT Registrations available from the UK's Small Business Service (see http://www.sbs.gov.uk/).

Table 7.5 Formation (F) and Structural (S) Components (numbers of registrations): 1994–2001, excluding agriculture

Region	1994		1995		1996		1997		1998		1999		2000		2001	
	F	S	F	S	F	S	F	S	F	S	F	S	F	S	F	S
North East	-63	-66	-272	-66	-281	-76	-485	-115	-458	-131	-248	-61	-292	-73	-316	-50
North West	-237	-408	-269	-375	26	-357	443	-437	533	-362	637	-165	582	-190	400	-205
Yorks and Humberside	-570	-412	-721	-379	-645	-409	-984	-516	-1,025	-534	-681	-322	-565	-353	-174	-338
East Midlands	-178	-401	-125	-359	-212	-382	-125	-479	-160	-510	-325	-351	-207	-377	254	-329
West Midlands	-100	-527	-188	-461	-484	-472	-1,147	-597	150	-638	106	-489	-137	-521	177	-463
East of England	-439	-64	-164	27	461	-4	60	81	-768	57	-695	-27	180	-45	-166	-8
London	3,662	1,820	4,602	1,489	4,689	1,591	4,719	1,763	5,699	1,851	4,705	1,146	3,852	1,341	2,464	994
South East	651	555	214	625	-37	709	247	983	-584	991	-714	519	-863	551	-398	510
South West	-790	-69	-1,433	-103	-765	-125	-486	-114	-491	-121	-212	-22	-285	-35	-533	24
Wales	-760	-174	-795	-172	-736	-206	-1,092	-235	-1,164	-236	-1,047	-77	-828	-101	-779	-44
Scotland	-389	10	-324	21	-496	5	-364	-14	-901	-41	-732	52	-944	41	-319	122
Northern Ireland	-796	-264	-537	-247	-579	-273	-789	-320	-835	-324	-795	-203	-914	-237	-618	-211

Source: Based on analyses of VAT Registrations available from the UK's Small Business Service (see http://www.sbs.gov.uk/).

Some concluding reflections

The ratios in Table 7.3 provide a useful shorthand way of evaluating a region's relative performance in terms of birth rates. The relevance of these ratios has been given added emphasis in the UK in recent years by the implicit or explicit commitment of a number of Regional Development Agencies to matching their regions' formation rate to that of the country as a whole. It is clear from the data in Table 7.3 that a policy aimed at raising a region's formation activity in relative terms faces a significant challenge: no region was able to sustain a continuous year on year rise in its A_r/NS_r ratio over the period covered. The two regions that started the period with the lowest ratio (Wales and Northern Ireland) saw no significant improvement in their relative position over the period. The high correlation between Storey and Johnson's data for the early 1980s and those presented here further emphasises the long run nature of the challenge for regions seeking to raise relatively low formation rates.

The article has also applied a decomposition analysis to the difference between a region's actual formation rate and what that formation would have been if the region had reflected the national picture in terms of both industrial structure and formation activity in each industry. Before the implications of the results are examined, it is important to be aware of some of the limitations of the decomposition technique. Two may be mentioned. First, the technique is essentially an "accounting" tool that does not seek to identify causal relationships. It may however provide hints on these relationships. Second, it treats the Structural and Formation Components as independent elements when in fact there may be some interdependencies between them. For example, the structural characteristics of a region may influence formation activity in that region. One reason for this is that industries differ in the scope that they offer for both upstream and downstream small firm activity and hence formations. Conversely, formation activity is one of the mechanisms by which the structure of a region is shaped, with growing industries attracting new firms and declining industries shedding firms.

The limitations of the data must also be recognised. Some of these have been outlined above. A further potential limitation arises from the level of industrial aggregation in the data. We simply do not know how sensitive the results are to the level chosen.

Notwithstanding the above deficiencies, the technique provides a number of useful initial insights into regional differences in births and pointers to the direction for future research. First, the results point to a wide variety of experience across regions and in some regions, over time. In some cases the results are very sensitive to whether or not agriculture is excluded. This variation highlights the complexity of the processes involved and suggests that different policy responses are likely to be appropriate in different regions and at different times. The application of a standard policy "package" across regions is likely to be misguided.

Second, the data suggest that the explanation for relatively low birth rates is likely to vary across regions. Two contrasting examples may help to illustrate this point. In the North East, it is clear from both Tables 7.4 and 7.5 that a key reason behind this region's birth rate "deficit" is that, *sector by sector*, the birth rate tends to be lower than elsewhere. This in turn raises the question of how far the North East's relatively low formation rate in a sector is due to region-wide influences, e.g. a culture that is less supportive of business formation generally, and how far to sector specific differences, relating for example to market opportunities, supply constraints and agglomeration economies. The central policy issue here is the question whether these influences are amenable to intervention. Relatively little research has been undertaken into regional variations in the formation rate *in particular sectors*. Such research would best be carried out at a lower level of aggregation than that on which this article is based.

In contrast, the East Midlands deficit is dominated by the Structural Component, even when agriculture is allowed for. In this region, rather more attention might be given to why the structure of industry is as it is and to the question of whether this structure might be adapted by policy measures. Care is needed here: the industrial structure of a region is a reflection of a wide range of influences and it may be inappropriate to seek to alter that structure simply to raise the formation rate. Careful analysis of the reasons for the current structure and of the implications of seeking to alter it is necessary.

Finally, it is important to note the dominance of London. Its A_r/NS_r ratio is very significantly higher than that for any other region in the United Kingdom, even when adjustment is made for agriculture. Furthermore, the capital has a very substantial advantage in both structural and formation terms when it comes to business births. This in turn reflects the financial and other attractions of a capital city as a center for entrepreneurial activity. No other region is likely to be able to match these unique advantages and it would be a mistake to endeavour to emulate the record of what is clearly a special case.

It is evident that there is still much research to be undertaken on regional variations in formation rates. More disaggregated studies would be valuable. But perhaps the most pressing need is to develop a better understanding of regional differences in specific sectors. Such work might also usefully encompass an analysis of regional variations in the *quality* of formations, in terms of their subsequent long run survival and growth.

Notes

1 Barkham (1992) has shown that the characteristics of new firms and not only the formation rate, may also vary across regions. He found that in the UK, new firms in the South East tend to be more successful than their counterparts in other regions. For more recent evidence on this issue – this time for Austria – see Tödtling and Wanzenböck (2003).

2 Simply for economy of words, *regional* and *region* in this article relate to the English Standard Regions and Northern Ireland, Scotland and Wales.
3 We have specified here only the *aggregate* regional formation rate using population or the workforce as denominator. However it should be noted that population is not meaningful when it comes to sectors. It should also be noted that disaggregation by sector carries the implication that it is the workforce *working within the sector* that is the only relevant one. It is difficult to utilise the workforce denominator when VAT registration data are used at the level of the individual sector because the sectoral classification boundaries used for the VAT data are not identical to those used to calculate the workforce.
4 This figure is based on the stock remaining the same. Of course changes in the registration numbers will have implications for the stock. Such an impact will depend on how the survival rate changes as the result of the changes in registrations.
5 This may not follow if the mix of industries varies from region to region, but that mix is such that the *overall* formation rates are similar.

References

Armington, C. and Acs, Z.J. (2002). The determinants of regional variation in new firm formation. *Regional Studies*, 36(1), 33–45.
Audretsch, D.B. (1999). Linking entrepreneurship to economic growth. In G.D. Libecap (Ed.), *The sources of entrepreneurial activity. Advances in the study of entrepreneurship and economic growth*, vol. 11, 1–28. Stamford, Connecticut: JAI Press.
Ashcroft, B. & Love, J.H. (1996). Employment change and new firm formation in UK counties, 1981–9. In M.W. Danson (ed.) *Small firm formation and regional economic development*, 17–35. London: Routledge.
Barkham, R. (1992). Regional variations in entrepreneurship: some evidence from the United Kingdom. *Entrepreneurship and Regional Development*, 4(3), 225–244.
Brooksbank, D.J. & Pickernell, D.G. (1999). Regional competitiveness indicators. A reassessment of method. *Local Economy*, 13(4), 310–326.
Daly, M. (1990). The 1980s – a decade of growth of enterprise. *Employment Gazette*, 98, 553–565.
Department of Trade and Industry (1999). *Our competitive future. UK competitiveness indicators*. London: DTI.
Department of Trade and Industry (2000). *Regional competitiveness indicators*. London: DTI.
East Midlands Development Agency (1999). *Economic development strategy for the East Midlands. Regional delivery plan 2000–2003*. Nottingham: East Midlands Development Agency.
Gallagher, C., Kidd J., & Miller, P. (1996). Empirical research on the role of new firms in Scotland. In M.W. Danson (ed.) *Small firm formation and regional economic development*, 65–80. London: Routledge.
Geroski, P. (1995). What do we know about entry? *International Journal of Industrial Organization*, 13, 421–440.
Gudgin, G. (1996). Prosperity and growth in UK regions. *Local Economy*, 11(1), 7–26.
Hart, P.E. & Oulton, N. (2001). Galtonian regression, company age and job generation, 1986–95. *Scottish Journal of Political Economy*, 48(1), 82–98.
HM Treasury (2003). *A modern regional policy*. London: HM Treasury.
Johnson, P.S. (1983). A note on new manufacturing firms in the UK regions. *Scottish Journal of Political Economy*, 30(1), 75–79.

Johnson, P.S. (forthcoming). Targeting firm births and economic regeneration in a lagging region: the case of the North East of England. *Small Business Economics.*

Johnson, P.S. & Cathcart, G. (1979). New manufacturing firms and regional development: some evidence from the Northern region. *Regional Studies*, 13(3), 269–280.

Johnson, P.S. & Conway C. (1997). How good are the UK VAT registration data at measuring firm births? *Small Business Economics*, 9(5), 403–409.

Johnson, P.S. & Parker, S. (1996). Spatial variations in the determinants and effects of firm births and deaths. *Regional Studies*, 30(7), 679–688.

Keeble, D. & Walker, S. (1994). New firms, small firms and dead firms: spatial patterns and determinants in the United Kingdom. *Regional Studies* 28(4), 411–427.

Le, A.T. (1999). Empirical studies of self-employment. *Journal of Economic Surveys*, 13(4), 381–416.

Northwest Development Agency (1999). *England's North West. A strategy towards 2020.* Warrington: Northwest Development Agency.

Office of the Deputy Prime Minister (2004). *ODPM Public Service Agreement: technical note.* London: ODPM.

One NorthEast (1999). *Regional economic strategy for the North East. Unlocking our potential.* Newcastle: One North East.

Organisation for Economic Co-operation and Development (1998). *Fostering entrepreneurship.* Paris: OECD.

Regional Studies (1994). Special issue: regional variations in new firm formation. Guest editors: P Reynolds, D. Storey and P. Westhead. 28(4), 343–456.

Reynolds P., Storey, D. & Westhead, P. (1994). Cross-national comparisons of the variation in new firm formation rates. *Regional Studies* 28(4), 443–456.

Reynolds, P., Bygrave, W., Erkko, A. and Hay, M. (2002). *Global Entrepreneurship Monitor 2002 Summary Report.* November. Babson Park, MA: Babson College, Ewing Marion Kauffman Foundation and the London Business School.

Schmitz, J.A. (1989). Imitation, entrepreneurship and long-run growth. *Journal of Political Economy*, 97(3), 721–739.

Small Business Service (2000a). *Business start-ups and closures: VAT registrations and de-registrations, 1980–99.* URN00/111. October. Sheffield, U.K. Research and Evaluation Unit, Small Business Service.

Small Business Service (2000b). *Small and medium enterprise (SME) statistics for the United Kingdom.* URN00/92. September. Sheffield, UK Research and Evaluation Unit, Small Business Service.

Storey, D. (1994). *Understanding the small business sector.* London: Routledge.

Storey, D. and Johnson, S. (1987). Regional variations in entrepreneurship in the UK. *Scottish Journal of Political Economy*, 34(2), 161–173.

Tödtling, F. & Wanzenböck, H. (2003). Regional differences in structural characteristics of start-ups. *Entrepreneurship and Regional Development*, 15(4), 351–370.

Thurik, A.R. (1999). 'Entrepreneurship, industrial transformation and growth. In G.D. Libecap (ed.) *The sources of entrepreneurial activity. Advances in the study of entrepreneurship and economic growth*, 11, 29–65. Stamford, Connecticut: JAI Press.

Part III
Employment

8   Unemployment and self-employment

A survey

Peter Johnson

Source: *Industrial Relations Journal* 1981, 12 (5), 5–15.

The currently high level of unemployment emphasises the importance (in policy terms) of the potential contribution of a self-employment alternative. Here the author examines the available UK evidence on the degree of movement from unemployment to self-employment, the factors influencing this movement and the role of labour market information and training.

This paper examines the movement into self-employment of people who are either unemployed or likely to become so as a result of redundancy. 'Self-employment' is used here in a broad non-technical sense, and covers all situations where people have set up in business on their own account. The businesses so formed may take different organisational forms – sole proprietorships, companies or partnerships – and cover very different types of activity, from window cleaning to manufacturing. Our justification for providing a survey of the work that has been undertaken in this field is two-fold. First, we have so far been unable to trace any study that has focused specifically on this issue although, as we shall see, a number of studies have made passing reference to it. On the theoretical level the establishment of a new business by an unemployed person or indeed someone still in paid employment has not (as far as we can see) received explicit recognition as a possible option in the job search literature. Perhaps this fact in itself is not of any technical significance: self-employment may be incorporated into the models as simply another job option. However, the absence of explicit mention does serve to emphasise the lack of interest in the transfer phenomenon that is the topic of this paper.

Second, the currently high levels of unemployment emphasis the importance of the issue from a policy viewpoint: if opportunities in *paid* employment are limited, to what extent can redundant and unemployed people create their *own* work by setting up in business? The present government is currently sponsoring training courses aimed specifically at assisting people to make this transition (see Section III) and it clearly sees the formation of entirely new enterprises by redundant workers as one means of alleviating unemployment. (The March 1981 Budget contained measures designed specifically to encourage this activity.) We shall examine the likely impact on employment of such transfers later. More generally, the government is devoting considerable effort to the encouragement of the small firm sector as a whole, in the belief that it is in this sector that the main hope for additional employment lies [1].

This paper is divided into three parts. In Section I we look briefly at the factors affecting the transfer from unemployment to self-employment. Section II examines the available empirical evidence in the UK on the transfer from unemployment (or threatened unemployment) to self-employment. The final section examines the role of labour market information and training in this area.

I Factors affecting the transfer from unemployment to self-employment

In principle, the unemployed person faces several possible options in the future allocation of his time. These options may be grouped into three main categories. First, he may remain unemployed. Second, he may become an employee, i.e. enter *paid* employment. Third, he may enter *self*-employment. He may of course try to combine these categories, e.g. he may run a business 'on the side' while still remaining an employee of another company.[1] Within the paid and self-employment categories there may be several options open to him (e.g. he may work as an employee for x, y *or* z; he may found a business in industries a, b *or* c).

At a theoretical level, it is helpful to view the unemployed worker as comparing the anticipated returns, discounted, in each of the options open to him. These returns include non-financial elements. For example, a number of studies (e.g. Boswell, 1973, chap. 3; Cooper, 1973; Goldby and Johns, 1971; Roberts and Wainer, 1971; Scott, 1978)[2] have pointed to the importance of such factors as the degree of independence, job satisfaction, social status, control over others and challenge in the returns that founders obtain from their businesses. The non-financial *costs* of running a business (e.g. disruption of family life, anxiety, the possibility of bankruptcy) have to be set against these returns. Similarly, the net returns from unemployment and paid employment will also be determined in part by non-monetary factors. Some options may not of course be open to the unemployed worker: he may be unable to obtain *any* kind of paid employment even if he wanted to. Other options may not even be considered: for example, probably most unemployed manual workers do not give any thought to setting up on their own account. For our purposes, we can represent these possibilities as yielding zero or negative returns in respect of the options involved.

We are of course concerned here with the subjective assessment of future returns in the different options. Such assessment might be based on wildly inaccurate estimates of what the present values of those benefits are likely to be. Several writers have argued (although not usually on the basis of firm empirical evidence) that the high failure rate of small businesses (see the survey by Gudgin, 1974, and Brough, 1970) may in part be due to the tendency of people to go into well established markets which are already saturated by existing producers (for example, see Davis and Kelly, 1972, p.60, and Beesley, 1955) [4]. Such entrants may have grossly miscalculated their prospects. It is also likely that many potential founders will bias their calculations in the opposite direction, i.e. they will *underestimate* the possible returns to self-employment.[3]

These returns will be subject to a constant process of adjustment. For example, the unemployed person's circumstances, his position in the labour market, his perceptions of market opportunities, social attitudes towards the different options and government policies are unlikely to remain static and all are likely to play some part in the determination of anticipated returns. The individual may also directly alter his perceptions of the returns by engaging in search activity in order to improve his knowledge about the possible options (e.g. the person considering self-employment may undertake some market research in order to identify commercially viable activities).

The unemployed person will move into self-employment when he perceives that the discounted value of future returns from that activity exceed those from either unemployment or paid employment.[4] This may occur not only because anticipated returns from self-employment have *risen*, but because returns from the alternatives have *fallen*. Thus a perceived decline in employment prospects of a fall in unemployment pay will, other things being equal, generate movement into self-employment. It is not therefore surprising to see that a number of authors have argued that unemployment may stimulate new business formation [5].

II Previous studies on unemployment and self-employment

As we have already mentioned, we have been unable to trace any UK study that was specifically geared to examining the role of self-employment among people who had either been made redundant or who were unemployed [6]. However, there are three areas of empirical research more general in nature that might be expected to deal, in greater or lesser degree, with this particular issue. These areas are: studies of redundant workers and their subsequent experience in obtaining re-employment; studies of the unemployed and their subsequent experience; and studies of new firm formation and the backgrounds of the founders. We examine the findings of each of these in turn (we delay the main *interpretation* of the findings until the end of the section). Before we do this, however, we should note that all the studies mentioned were undertaken *before* the recent policy emphasis on small business: the results, therefore, provide a useful yardstick against which the effects of the new policy initiatives might be assessed.

(i) Redundancy studies

These are principally of two kinds.

(a) Case studies

There is now a very considerable number of studies of particular redundancies and of the subsequent job histories of the people involved. Among industries covered in the studies undertaken in the post-war period in the UK are the following: aircraft and missiles (Thomas, 1969; Wedderburn, 1964): engineering (Daniel, 1972); mining (HMSO, 1970; Bulmer, 1971); motor vehicles (Kahn, 1964; Pearson and Greenwood, 1977); railways (Wedderburn, 1965); textiles (Martin and Fryer, 1973) and shipbuilding (Sams and Simpson, 1968; Herron, 1975; Hart, 1979).[5]

It is difficult to summarise the findings of such a diverse collection of studies. However, it is striking that all either do not mention self-employment among redundant workers or, where they do, such employment is clearly very unimportant in quantitative terms as a source of re-employment. However, it should be noted that some of the studies were not set up in a way that would elicit a clear indication of whether someone had gone into business on his own account. Many of the classifications adopted for deciding the subsequent employment of the redundant workers could have applied equally to paid employment or self-employment. Furthermore, even where an explicit question on self-employment was included in a study, it is not always clear whether or not such employment refers only to those who *in National Insurance terms* are self-employed, or whether it also includes those who are 'self-employed' in the broad, non-technical sense of 'working for themselves' but who for National Insurance purposes, because they have set up a *company* of which they are technically 'employees', are not self-employed.[6] However, even allowing for these problems, it is quite clear that self-employment was not an important avenue for re-employment. The following table gives some indication of its importance in those case studies that give firm data. The very small percentage of people going into business on their own account may in part be a reflection of the nature of the samples, in particular their emphasis on manual occupations. (This emphasis is also apparent in most of the redundancy studies which make no mention at all of self-employment.) Data on differences in the rate at which redundant people go into self-employment across occupations are very sparse in these case studies, but there is tentative evidence in the studies by Martin and Fryer (1973) and more recently by Hart (1979), to suggest that *non*-manual workers are more likely to set up on their own.[7] In an unpublished study of male 'staff' personnel who had taken voluntary severance from a large chemical company, the author found that the percentage going into business by themselves was about 7 per cent, very much higher than any of the percentages reported in the first four studies in Table 8.1. (The 'Casterton Mills' study did not indicate how many had *actually* set up in business, it is not, therefore, directly comparable with the others). We

Table 8.1 Redundancy and self-employment: some case studies

Industry	Company/Companies involved	Number in sample	Nature of sample	% of sample going into self-employment	Source
Engineering	Mainly GEC	529	Males who received lump sum payment at redundancy. 67% of total sample were unskilled, semi-skilled or skilled manual workers.	3	Daniel (1972) p.97
Motor vehicles	Mainly BMC	215	Males who did not go back to original employer. Total sample of 447 males made redundant. 86% of total sample either semi-skilled or manual workers.	2	Kahn (1964) p.177
Shipbuilding	Upper Clyde Shipbuilders	264	Males who had obtained re-employment out of 300 active job seekers. Total sample of 328 useable interviews out of 400 approached. 91% of the 400 were unskilled, semi-skilled or skilled manual workers.		Herron (1975) p.85
Shipbuilding (Oil rig construction)	RDL	795	Total (mostly males) entering employment after redundancy. Total sample of 1030 made redundant. 85% of 795 were skilled or unskilled manual workers.	1	Hart (1979) table 55
Textiles	"Casterton Mills"	107	Males who received redundancy pay, out of a total sample of 328 male leavers. 55% of 107 were manual workers.	7 mentioned starting up own business as one use to which redundancy money would be put (respondents could state two uses)	Martin and Fryer (1973) p.126

shall return to this point later. It may also be true that the more entrepreneurially inclined of the work force in the closing plant may have left prior to the
closure to set up on their own. In most cases such people would not be
covered by these studies.

(b) More general studies

These include the studies by MacKay and by Parker *et al* [7], the latter being
aimed at evaluating the effects of the Redundancy Payments Act. MacKay's
study makes no explicit mention of self-employment, although the possibility that some of his respondents set up in business on their own account
cannot be ruled out. Parker *et al* [8] found in their study of a random sample
of just over 2000 redundant workers that at the time interviews took place
about 1 per cent were self-employed.[8] The percentage was the same both for
workers who received no statutory payment, and for those who did receive
such a payment. This suggests that redundancy payments may not be an
important stimulus for people to set up by themselves. Indeed, it might be
argued that redundancy payments may in part act to make unemployment
relatively more attractive. In view of the comment earlier about differences
across occupations, it is worth reproducing in full here their findings on different classes of redundant employees, about 80 per cent of whom were
males, who had received a statutory payment and who had subsequently gone
into self-employment (see Table 8.2).

It is very striking that the percentages are substantially greater in the professional and management categories. While there may be other factors which
explain part of these differences, straight occupational differences are still
likely to account for a substantial residual. The finding that manual and
clerical workers are relatively less important sources of self-employment is
confirmed in another 'general' study undertaken by Daniel (1972).

Table 8.2 Findings of Parker, *et al*

Last job prior to redundancy	% in self-employment (first job after redundancy)	Base figure* on which % is calculated
Senior managers	8	78
Junior managers	11	55
Professional and technical		
Higher	14	42
Lower	–	50
Clerical	2	157
Skilled	4	458
Semi-skilled	3	245
Unskilled	3	470

Source: Parker, *et al* (1971), Table 3.38, p.100.

Note: *Relates to those who *found* a post-redundancy job.

(ii) Studies of the unemployed

The fairly large scale studies conducted by Daniel (1974) and Daniel and Stilgoe (1977) make no mention, in their analyses of the jobs to which the unemployed go, of self-employment, although, as with the redundancy studies, the research was not designed to elicit specific responses in this area. The large scale study by the Department of Employment (1977) on the characteristics of the unemployed conducted in 1976–1977 showed that 1 per cent of males in the sample had become self-employed six months after their initial interview. (This represents nearly 2 per cent of all those who had left the unemployment register.) Grossed up to 1976 totals this would have represented a flow of 9100 people from unemployment into self-employment. (It is not clear whether self-employment is defined in National Insurance or broader terms here.) These figures are not broken down by duration of unemployment or occupation.

Disney (1976) has shown in his study of movements between classes for a cohort of 1630 males, all of whom were born in 1933, that about 5 per cent of all those who had experienced any period of sickness or unemployment in 1972 paid at least one month of Class 2 stamps in 1973 (although only 1 per cent paid Class 2 stamps for the *whole* of 1973, suggesting that a significant number may have tried self-employment for a short experimental period). Again, we do not have any further breakdown of these data.

(iii) Studies of new firms

The published work on new firm formation and on the background of founders in the UK in the post-war period is relatively sparse. The studies by Boswell (1972), Gudgin (1978), Firn and Swales (1978), Little (1977), Johnson and Cathcart (1979 a and b), Gudgin *et al* (1979) and Storey and Robinson (1979)[9] probably constitute the bulk of the material [9].

None of these studies was set up to look specifically at new firms formed by redundant employees or unemployed people. However, our own study provided some background data on the previous experience and working environment of the founders. This study covered 74 entirely new *manufacturing* businesses (115 founders) founded in the Northern Region in recent years. Details of the sample can be found in Johnson and Cathcart (1979a) [10]; it is sufficient to say here that it was not, as far as we are aware, systematically biased in any way.

The finding which is of particular relevance in the context of this survey is that a substantial minority (about one-third) of founders came from incubator plants that either were actually closing at the time of the formation of the new business or were about to close. Table 8.3 provides the relevant data. New Business Equivalents (NBEs)[10] give the number of founders weighted by their contribution to business formations.

The occupational breakdown of the founders who came from plants closing at or subsequent to formation of the new business is given in Table 8.4.

Table 8.3 Status of incubator plants of a sample of Northern Region founders

	NBEs		Founders	
Status of incubator plant	*Number*	*%*	*Number*	*%*
Closed at time of formation of new business	19.0	25.7	29.0	23.5
Closed subsequent to formation of new business	7.5	10.1	11.0	9.6
Taken over by another (existing) business at time of formation	4.0	5.4	8.0	7.0
Remaining open	34.0	45.9	56.0	48.7
Founders unemployed	1.0	1.4	2.0	1.7
Don't know	8.5	11.5	11.0	9.6
Total	74.0	100.0	115.0	100.0

Table 8.4 Occupational breakdown of a sample of Northern Region founders

	Founders	*%*
Semi-skilled manual	2	5.0
Skilled manual	4	10.0
Clerical	1	2.5
Sales representatives	5	12.5
Commercial	4	10.0
Technical	3	7.5
Supervisory (foreman or equivalent)	6	15.0
Managerial (above foreman level)	15	37.5
Total	40	100.0

There were *no* unskilled manual workers in the group. Eighty-five per cent were white collar workers: and the biggest single group in this second category was management (above foreman level). The data do not of course provide information on formation *rates* across occupations since we do not know how many in total in each occupation were made redundant over the relevant period; however, it should be clear that managerial and supervisory occupations have a much higher propensity to set up in manufacturing business than manual workers, and that within the latter category, unskilled workers are less likely to set up than skilled workers. These findings are in line with the findings from the redundancy and unemployment studies (the latter are not of course limited to self-employment in *manufacturing*).

We also found from our study that 'fertility' in terms of manufacturing spin-off declines with incubator plant size, even when industry effects are accounted for. This finding is based on an analysis of the incubator size of *all* founders, whether or not they were affected by closure. However, none of the 28 founders who came from a manufacturing incubator which closed at (or subsequent to) the formation of the new firm and for whom we have data came from incubator plants or more than 500 employees. Unfortunately, data on the number of employees involved in the closure of plants of different sizes are not available. Consequently, we do not know whether the absence of spin-off from the 500 plus plants represents a relatively lower fertility *rate*, although on the basis of the other evidence, we suspect that it does.

None of the research in the three categories mentioned above provided very detailed information on the transfer from redundancy/unemployment to self-employment. However, the following conclusions seem reasonably clear. First, the total size of the transfer is probably very small. Consequently, even if substantial policy initiatives were taken in this area the outcome, in terms of the reduction in unemployment, would be of a low magnitude. (Such initiatives may, nevertheless, be justified in cost benefit terms but their absolute impact on the unemployment problem would be limited.) It may of course be argued that a new business created by a person affected by unemployment may also provide employment for others and thereby *indirectly* reduce unemployment. However, the majority of new businesses are formed in the service sectors and they will often employ – even at their largest – only a few employees.[11] Of 43 businesses formed by ex-staff employees of the large chemical company referred to earlier, only one was employing more than five, three years after formation. (Storey, 1980, has shown that not one of the new *manufacturing* firms formed between 1965 and 1976 in Cleveland employed more than 100 people in 1976; he also shows that this finding is not unique to Cleveland.) Such firms may remain small not only because the market is limited but because the owner does not want to relinquish either internal or external control. Some businesses may of course have very high growth potential in employment terms and it is likely that the founders of such businesses will be drawn from managerial ranks rather than from manual grades.

The estimation of the *actual* numbers of people employed in the new businesses is unlikely of course to be a good guide to the overall impact of formations on unemployment since the 'new' jobs may displace workers in other businesses. Such displacement effects are difficult to estimate, although information on the nature of the employment in the new businesses may provide some guide.

Second, manual workers (and especially unskilled manual workers) seem less likely to make the transfer than managerial grades. The latter are likely to have higher anticipated earnings in self-employment than the former. Not only is their expertise more complete in terms of running a business, but they are also more aware of possible market opportunities. Skilled manual workers are likely to have more expertise to sell on a self-employment basis than their unskilled counterparts.

Third, there are reasonable grounds for supposing that ex-employees from small plants are more likely to set up in business than those from larger plants. Employees in the smaller plants will have greater contact with individuals who have themselves set up in business. They will gain greater familiarity with the types of market that could be served by a new business which in the early years at least is almost inevitably going to be small. They are also likely to gain greater all-round experience in the running of a business. At the same time, it must be said that the evidence we have is consistent with some pre-selection by potential founders: they may deliberately seek employment in small plants before setting up in order to gain relevant experience. Nevertheless, even if this is the case, the lower fertility of large plants implies that the depressed regions of the UK are likely to be at a relative disadvantage as far as new formations are concerned.

III The role of labour market policies

Our discussion in Section II suggested two basic objectives which labour market policies might have in this area. Before we examine these below, it is worth stressing the general point that such policies cannot be considered in isolation from those relating to *paid* employment and unemployment. If, for example, labour market policies make paid employment more attractive, then (ceteris paribus) the flow into self-employment will diminish. Lowering unemployment benefit will have an opposite effect.

(i) Improvement in the *accuracy* with which potential founders perceive their likely prospects in self-employment. (For one way in which these prospects can be affected, see Jackson, 1979, p.3.) Such activity may involve broadening or narrowing the potential founder's horizons. It may even generate an interest in self-employment that did not previously exist. In some cases it may lead to the abandonment of proposals for a new business, by making potential founders more realistic about (for example) their own abilities, market prospects, the availability of finance, premises, labour etc.[12] This improvement in accuracy of perceptions may occur *directly*, through the provision of information and advice, and/or *indirectly*, through the provision of certain types of experience which are likely to raise perceived prospects in self-employment. There can be little doubt that the overwhelming emphasis in the provision of information in redundancy situations (and, indeed, in the labour market generally) is on paid employment opportunities. As far as we can see most companies and official agencies adopt a *responsive* attitude towards self-employment, i.e. they may provide a 'sign-posting' and/or advisory service to those who express an interest, but they do not actively promote self-employment as an option. This bias stems in part from the fact that labour market information in the self-employment area must of necessity be more nebulous in character. No 'vacancy' lists exist as such. Indeed, it is in the interests of the currently self-employed to conceal as far as they can the 'vacancies' in their particular line of business. This raises the question of whether it would be possible to formulate a positive approach to information provision on self-employment opportunities which might attract people whose 'natural' perceptions of such opportunities are very limited or non-existent (for example because of their previous work experience) but for whom the probability of success in self-employment is high.

The provision of information is, in general, likely to have a cumulative impact, and our own research suggests that founders have often considered the idea of founding a business for several years before actually launching out (Johnson and Cathcart, 1979a). The impact (in terms of new formations) of information provided only immediately prior to redundancy is therefore likely to be much less than where there has been a build-up over several years. In this connection we should note the absence of such positive promotion of self-employment as a career option in the UK. A cursory examination of the official careers publications for example shows a marked absence of discussion on the opportunities for setting up (perhaps at a later date) on an 'own account' basis. It is likely that schools could take a much more active part in sowing the seeds that might bear fruit at a later stage. *Indirect* methods of altering perceptions might be achieved through (for example) employment experience in a small firm.

So far we have considered only the perceived prospects of potential *founders*. However, large *companies* making personnel redundant might also be encouraged to question whether activities that they are shutting down or rationalising might not be viable on a smaller scale, if run by some of their ex-employees as independent businesses. Such businesses often have lower unit costs than sections of a similar size which are part of a large company (often because of lower overhead costs). 'Buy-outs' of this kind appear to have become much more frequent as the result of the present recession, partly because the unit cost difference between small and large company operations becomes more marked as output falls (the overhead element becomes more significant). Companies engaged in rationalisation might also be able to assist start-ups by ex-employees by making available equipment and premises which have a low real cost in terms of alternative uses. They might also provide ex-employees with some initial orders where those employees are providing goods or services which were previously 'in house' activities of the large company. Such a policy might provide the new start-up with the breathing space in which to establish other customer contacts. The costs of such a buying policy might be small in relation to the gains in industrial terms resulting from a smoother rationalisation process.

(ii) The alteration of actual prospects through (a) changes in the economic and social environment in which formation and subsequent growth can occur; and/or (b) changes in potential founders' own capabilities via training both on and off the job. Under (a) there can be no doubt that the general political environment has become much sympathetic towards small firms in recent years. One effect of this has been a growth in 'local initiatives' (see Foundation for Alternatives, 1979) and of bodies which provide various forms of assistance to new business.[13] Tax and other reliefs for small firms have also been introduced; how substantially these moves have shifted the balance of advantage towards self-employment remains, however, an open question. (It must be remembered that the impact on formations of any measures which also improve the returns from paid employment – a lowering of income tax rates is one example – will be greatly reduced; it may even be zero or negative.)

In the longer term it may be possible to change social attitudes towards setting up in business on an own account basis through (for example) special schools programmes. Social attitudes towards business failure may also affect the formation rate. It is, for example, a commonly held view that bankruptcy has a social stigma attached to it in this country which is much less than that in the United States. (We have no definite evidence on this score.) The removal of such a stigma might thus raise perceived prospects in self-employment.

Many of the above measures cannot of course be regarded as *labour* market policies. However, it may be misconceived to focus exclusive attention on such policies since there may be far greater returns in terms of formation and growth rates of new businesses from changes in *general* economic and social policies.

Under (b), there may be scope for providing some form of formal training for self-employment. The MSC has recently introduced training schemes for unemployed personnel wishing to set up in business. It is difficult, and probably too early, to assess the overall impact of these schemes. (The measurement of 'output' from the training presents formidable problems for any evaluation.) However, it should be remembered that the underlying aim of these courses is not to train an entrepreneur from scratch, but to improve the performance of someone already committed to the formation of a business. The demand for such courses is therefore dependent to a large extent on the factors mentioned under (a).

It is doubtful whether there is much scope for explicit on-the-job training of would-be entrepreneurs, especially if the firm providing the training knows that the trainee will set up as a competitor. However, as we have seen, the provision of small firm experience in a more general context may lead to a greater awareness of options in self-employment on the part of people so employed.

We have discussed various ways in which policies might influence the extent and nature of transfer between unemployment and self-employment. Whether any or all of these policies would represent an efficient use of resources remains of course an open question.

IV Conclusions

This article has considered the movement from unemployment or redundancy to self-employment, broadly interpreted. We have suggested that an increase in unemployment or actual (or threatened) redundancy may increase the rate of new firm formation although we know very little about the elasticity of this response. Redundant workers or workers threatened by redundancy are an important source of founders for new manufacturing firms, at least in the Northern Region. Notwithstanding this finding, the formation of a new business does not appear to be an important avenue for re-employment among redundant workers. The studies of redundancy and the unemployed so far undertaken suggest that no more than about 5 per cent of people affected by redundancies attempt to set up on their own, although the studies are biased towards manual workers and therefore towards a group that is likely to be less 'fertile' in terms of the setting up of businesses. Managerial grades have higher fertility. Nevertheless, our findings should generate caution in arguing that new business formations by unemployed / redundant workers can make a big impact on the unemployment figures. This need for caution is further emphasised when the nature of the businesses formed and the size of their subsequent labour force are analysed. This is *not* to say, however, that policies in this area would not be cost effective. In the depressed regions of the UK, where unemployment is by definition higher, the problem is exacerbated by the relatively high concentrations of larger plants, since fertility appears to be inversely related to plant size.

The enhancement of labour market information by training policies for self-employment (which cannot be seen in isolation from those for *paid* employment or unemployment) may be viewed as having two main aims: improvement in the *accuracy* of workers' perceptions of self-employment possibilities; and the alteration of actual self-employment prospects via changes in the economic and social environment and training. The improvement in the accuracy of perceptions may lead *inter alia* to some people who would otherwise have gone into business and then failed, deciding against self-employment. It is important to see the training / information inputs in the context of the *whole* range of economic and social variables that influence formation rates.

To date nearly all self-employment information has been provided on a responsive basis. An active approach to such information provision, though difficult to formulate, might attract successful founders who might not otherwise set up. We have also argued that the provision of information on self-employment needs to be viewed in a longer term context in shaping attitudes; there may, therefore, be a role for stimulating interest in this area at school level.

Notes

1 The formation of a co-operative represents another form of activity in which the categories mentioned in the text may be combined. The worker becomes *both* an employee – often at a wage less than the going rate – and an owner of the business, from which he receives his share of any profits. In this sense he can be regarded as being in both self-employment and paid employment. For a review of the development of co-operatives, see Wilson and Coyne [2].

2 The studies by Cooper and Roberts and Wainer [3], are limited to founders of new technologically orientated companies.

3 Some preliminary work with ex-employees of a large (private) UK company has indicated that a substantial percentage of founders may be too pessimistic about their prospects when setting up. Of a sample of 28 ex-employees who had left at

various times in the past to set up in business on their own, 12 thought in retrospect that they had been *more* successful than they had anticipated when launching out originally. These answers may of course reflect some ex-post rationalisation and in any case the sample size is too small to warrant firm conclusions. However, despite these difficulties the figures serve as a useful counterbalance to the views expressed in the text.

4 Movement into any of the three states is not an irreversible decision. Indeed, *at any point in time* an individual may envisage a future career pattern that involves all three at different stages. This complication need not worry us here.

5 At the time of writing, a number of other redundancy studies are being undertaken or are at the report stage. These include investigations into particular redundancies in the shipbuilding, jute and cash register industries.

6 Even if the studies exclude those who start their own *companies* it is unlikely that the data on self-employment would significantly understate the number of new businesses since most firms that do become incorporated start off life in a way which would make their employees self-employed in the normal National Insurance sense.

7 This statement draws on the data Martin and Fryer provide on the use made of redundancy payments. It may be of course that non-manual workers, for various reasons, received *higher* redundancy payments and were, therefore, in a better position to set up on their own.

8 2 per cent of those who received statutory redundancy payments claimed that the 'major use' to which they put them was to set up in business. This suggests that by the time of the interview some had already moved away from running their own business.

9 Individual business histories do of course abound. However, it would be a major task to synthesise the findings of these studies. Without such a synthesis any comments would be of an anecdotal kind and would not, therefore, be particularly helpful in the present context.

10 The NBE of any given founder is the reciprocal of the number of founders involved in the formation of the relevant business.

11 Even if the businesses involved employed large numbers, we would still not know what would have happened to employment in the absence of such firms.

12 Thus a *reduction* in the rate of formations by such potential founders may be an indicator of success of policies in this area, if the people who would otherwise fail are deterred from setting up.

13 The London Enterprise Agency, the Hackney Project and the St Helen's Trust, are examples of this kind of activity.

References

[1] This view of the employment potential of the small firm sector received a considerable boost from Birch, D. L., *The Job Generation Process*, MIT Program on Neighborhood and Regional Change, Cambridge, Mass., 1979. Birch estimated that, over the period 1969–1976, 52 per cent of *net* employment creation came from independent businesses which had less than 20 employees in 1969. (Employment in new businesses formed *during* the period are included in this figure.) There are, however, a number of problems with Birch's data and his findings have been widely misinterpreted: see Storey, D. J., *Job Generation and Small Firms Policy in Britain*, Policy Series 11, Centre for Environmental Studies, March, 1980. For recent estimates for employment creation by *new* firms in various regions of the UK, see Firn, J. and Swales, J. K., 'The Formation of New Manufacturing Establishments in the Central Clydeside and West Midlands Conurbations 1963–1972',

Regional Studies, 1978, 12, pp. 119–213, Gudgin, G., Brunskill, I. and Fothergill, S., *New Manufacturing Firms in Regional Employment Growth*, paper given to the Conference on New Firm Formation, Centre for Environmental Studies, October, 1979, Johnson, P. S. and Cathcart, D. G., 'New Manufacturing Firms and Regional Development: Some Evidence from the Northern Region', *Regional Studies*, 1979a, 13, pp. 269–280, Storey, D. J. and Robinson, J. F. F., *Entrepreneurship and New Firm Formation. The Case of Cleveland County*, paper given to the Conference on New Firm Formation, Centre for Environmental Studies, London, October, 1979. For a comparison between the US and Britain, see Fothergill, S. and Gudgin, G., *The Job Generation Process in Britain*, Centre for Environmental Studies, Research Series 32, London, 1979. None of these studies, however, answers the question of what would have happened to employment in the absence of these formations.

[2] Wilson, N. and Coyne, J., 'Co-operatives and the Promotion of Co-operative Development in Great Britain', *Industrial Relations Journal*, Vol. 12 No. 2, 1981.
[3] Cooper, A. C., 'Technical Entrepreneurship. What do we know?', *R & D Management 3(2)*, 1973, pp. 59–64, Roberts, E. B. and Wainer, H. A., 'Some Characteristics of Technical Entrepreneurs', *IEEE Transactions on Engineeering Management*, EM-18(3), 1971, pp. 100–109.
[4] See Gudgin, G., *The East Midlands in the Post-war Period*, PhD, Leicester University, 1974, Brough, R., 'Business Failures in England and Wales', *Business Ratios* (Summer) 1970, pp. 8–11, Davis, J. R. and Kelly, M., *Small Firms in the Manufacturing Sector*, Committee of Inquiry on Small Firms, Research Report No. 3, HMSO, London, 1972, p. 60, and Beesley, M. E., 'The Birth and Death of Industrial Establishments. Experience in the West Midlands conurbation', *Journal of Industrial Economics*, 4(1), 1955, pp. 45–61.
[5] See, for example, the findings and the studies quoted on Johnson, P. S. and Darnell, A. C., *New Firm Formation in Britain*, Department of Economics, Durham University, Working Paper No. 5, 1976.
[6] Some limited follow-up studies of unemployed personnel who have participated in self-employment courses have been undertaken see Watkins, D., 'Practical Support for the Establishment of New Businesses', paper given to the Smaller Business Research Conference, Durham University, November, 1978. However, by their very nature these studies cover samples which have very specific characteristics.
[7] McKay, D. I., 'After the Shake Out', *Oxford Economic Papers*, 24, 1972, pp. 89–110, Parker, S. R., Thomas, C. G., Ellis, N. D. and McCarthy, W. E. G., *Effects of the Redundancy Payments Act*, HMSO, London, 1971.
[8] Ibid., p. 97.
[9] Boswell, J., *The Rise and Decline of Small Firms*, Allen & Unwin, London, 1973; Gudgin, G., *Industrial Location Processes and Regional Employment*, Saxon House, 1978; Firn, J. and Swales, J. K., 1978, op. cit.; Little, A. D., *New Technology Based Firms in the UK and Germany*, Anglo-German Foundation for the Study of Industrial Society, London, 1977; Johnson, P. S. and Cathcart, D. G., 1979a, op. cit.; Johnson, P. S. and Cathcart, D. G., 'The Founders of New Manufacturing Firms A Note on the Size of their 'Incubator' Plants', *Journal of Industrial Economics*, XXVIII, 2, 1979b, pp. 219–224; Gudgin et al., 1979, op. cit.; Storey, D. J. and Robinson, J. F. F., 1979, op. cit.
[10] Johnson and Cathcart, 1979a, op. cit.

Bibliography

Boswell, J., *The Rise and Decline of Small Firms*, Allen & Unwin, London, 1973.
Brown, G., 'Characteristics of New Enterprises', *New England Business Review*, 1957.

Bulmer, M. I. A., 'Mining Redundancy A Case Study of the working of the Redundancy Payments Act in the Durham Coalfield', *Industrial Relations Journal*, Vol. 2 No. 4, 1971, pp. 3–21.

Cooper, A. D., 'Technical Entrepreneurship. What do we know?', *R & D Management*, 3(2), 1973, pp. 59–64.

Daniel, W. W., *Whatever Happened to the Workers at Woolwich?*, PEP Broadsheet No. 537, 1972.

Daniel, W. W., *A National Survey of the Unemployed*. PEP Broadsheet 546, PEP, London, 1974.

Daniel, W. W. and Stilgoe, E., *Where are they now? A follow-up study of the unemployed*, PEP Broadsheet No. 572, PEP, London, 1977.

Department of Employment, 'Characteristics of the Unemployed Sample Survey, June 1976'. *Department of Employment Gazette*, 1977, June.

Disney, R., *The Distribution of Unemployment and Sickness among the United Kingdom Population*, University of Reading, Department of Economics, Discussion Paper No. 87, 1976.

Foundation for Alternatives, *Local Initiatives in Britain*, mimeo, Adderbury, 1979.

Golby, C. W. and Johns, G., *Attitudes and Motivation*, Committee of Inquiry on Small Firms, Research Report No. 7, HMSO, London, 1971.

Hart, D. M., Internal MSC paper on redundancies at RDL (North Sea) Ltd., at Methil, Scotland, 1979.

Herron, F., *Labour Market in Crisis*, Macmillan, London, 1975.

HMSO, *Ryhope a pit closes a study in redevelopment* (for the Department of Employment and Productivity), HMSO, London, 1970.

Kahn, H. R., *Repercussions of Redundancy, a local survey*, Allen & Unwin, London, 1964.

Martin, R. and Fryer, R. H., *Redundancy and Paternalist Capitalism a Study in the Sociology of Work*, Allen & Unwin, London, 1973.

Pearson, R. and Greenwood, J., *Redundancies and Displacement. A Study of the Maidstone Labour Market*, Institute of Manpower Studies, Sussex University, 1977.

Roberts, E. B. and Wainer, H. A., 'Some Characteristics of Technical Entrepreneurs', *IEEE Transactions on Engineering Management*, 1971, EM-18 (3), pp. 100–109.

Sams, K. I. and Simpson, J. V., 'A Case Study of a Ship-building Redundancy in Northern Ireland', *Scottish Journal of Political Economy*, 1968, pp. 267–282.

Scott, M., 'Independence and the Flight from Large Scale: Sociological Factors in the Founding Process', paper given to the Smaller Business Research Conference, Durham University Business School, November, 1978.

Thomas, R. (ed.), *An Exercise in Redeployment*, Pergamon, Oxford, 1969.

Wedderburn, D. E., *White Collar Redundancy. A Case Study*, University of Cambridge, Department of Applied Economics, Occasional Paper No. 1, Cambridge U. P., 1964.

Wedderburn, D. E., *Redundancy and the Railwaymen*, University of Cambridge, Department of Applied Economics, Occasional Paper No. 4, Cambridge U. P., 1965.

9 New firms and employment creation

P. S. Johnson and R. B. Thomas

Source: *Managerial and Decision Economics*, 1982, 3 (4), 218–224.

This paper uses some simple microeconomic tools to explain the net effect on employment of different types of new firm formation. The first section of the paper examines the way in which actual employment in new firms has been calculated in recent empirical studies. The next section looks at the relationship between the actual and net employment effects of formations and argues that the former may not be a good guide to the latter. The final section examines the policy implications of the analysis.

1. Introduction

With the growth in unemployment in the late 1970s and early 1980s, policy makers have increasingly focused on the formation of entirely new businesses as a mechanism through which increased employment opportunities may be provided. In May 1979, the Queen's Speech referred to the government's intention to 'stimulate the development of small businesses *on which the creation of new jobs so heavily depends*'[1] (our italics; it is quite clear from other government statements that 'development' here includes 'formation'). More recently, the Chancellor of the Exchequer, while discussing possible tax relief for industry, argued that 'if there is any room for help and relief at all, it will be directed . . . at new business because *that is where the jobs will come*[2] (our italics). Similar sentiments were expressed by the Chancellor in his budget speech of March 1981. Indeed, some of the measures announced then were designed to encourage not only the development of new business generally, but also the direct transition from unemployment to self-employment.

This policy emphasis on new firms as employment generators has been translated into a considerable array of measure designed to assist formations. However, little serious attention has been paid to the examination of the underlying issue: the net effect of new firm formation on employment, i.e. the difference between employment with formations and what it could be without them. It can of course be argued that *all* current employment in the private sector is the result of new firm formation at *some* stage in the past. However, the net employment effect of *particular* formations remains an important one for policy. This paper provides an initial exploration of this issue using some simple microeconomic tools. In section 2 we examine recent efforts to measure actual employment. In section 3 we look at the net employment effect of new formations. We shall argue that the former may be only a poor guide to the latter. In section 4 we examine some of the policy implications of our discussion.

Our sole concern in this paper is with *employment*. We do not consider explicitly the issue of whether or not the labour is employed efficiently. However, the current interest in employment generation per se justifies our more limited approach.

The definition of a 'new firm' is not without difficulties.[3] However, in broad terms, we are interested in the business that is set up from 'scratch'. Diversification or expansion by an existing business is excluded from our consideration. This is broadly the definition adopted in the studies referred to in section 2, although differences in the data bases used have inevitably led to some variation.

2. Actual employment in new firms

In recent years a good deal of effort has gone into 'components of change' analysis of employment. The degree of detail in the studies using basically this approach has varied considerably, primarily because of differences in the data bases used, but the underlying methodology has been the same and is briefly described below. (The formation of new firms does of course only represent one factor in employment change; however, we describe the other possible influences on such change in order to place formation in its proper context).

Components of change analysis decomposes employment change in any given period into the categories given in Table 9.1.

Table 9.1 Components of employment change

	A. Gross job expansion		B. Gross job loss
A1.	Employment in end year of new *firms* born between base and end years and surviving in end year.	B1.	Employment in base year of *firms* existing in base year but dying between the base and end years.
A2.	Employment in end year of new *plants* (of existing firms) opened between base and end years and surviving in end year.	B2.	Employment in base year of plants existing in base years but dying between the base and end years.
A3.	End year less base year employment in plants which have expanded over the period.	B3.	Base year less end year employment in plants which have contracted during the period.

Category A2 is sometimes further sub-divided to distinguish between the opening of new plants which are *additional* to the firm's capacity, and the opening of plants in the area/region under consideration which have resulted from the *transfer* of productive capacity from outside. (B2 may be sub-divided on similar lines.)

We cannot here attempt a full appraisal of this methodology. However, two limitations in respect of new firm employment – to which attention has often been drawn – should be noted. First, this method does not catch those firms which opened and closed between the end and base years. Second, total employment in new firms in the end year will be very sensitive to the age distribution of the new firms in that year, which in turn may be related to the particular period chosen. Despite these difficulties, the method provides useful data on actual end year employment in new firms in relation to actual employment change in other types of enterprise. In recent years, studies involving components of change analysis have been undertaken both inside and outside government. Masey[4] has recently provided a breakdown of employment change for particular regions of the UK, using UK data. Although this study has the advantage that data for the different regions are comparable, it suffers from the defect that only plants of above ten employees are included. This problem has, in part, been overcome by a number of 'unofficial' studies[5–10] which have provided components of change for particular areas or regions of the UK and have tried to include the smaller size units in their analyses. Unfortunately, however, the cost of this improvement in coverage is a loss in comparability across studies since they use different data bases, time periods and definitions. In the US, Birch's study[11] has provided data on employment change for both the US as a whole and individual States.

Components of change analysis has been used by the investigators to provide *inter alia* estimates of the contribution of new firms to overall employment change over the chosen period, usually by expressing end year new firm employment as a percentage either of the total gross job expansion (see Table 9.1) or of total base year employment.[12] For example, Fothergill and Gudgin in their components of employment change analysis for manufacturing in the East Midlands between 1968 and 1975 concluded that 'new firms were responsible for about one in six of all job gains and added a little over 4 per cent to manufacturing employment' (see Ref. 7, p. 7). In similar vein, Storey shows that in Cleveland 'about 12 per cent of gross new manufacturing jobs are created by new firms' (see Ref. 10, p. 7). In his US study, Birch concluded that 'about 40 per cent of birth generated jobs are produced by independent, free standing entrepreneurs' (see Ref. 11, p. 6). (Births accounted for about 50 per cent of gross job expansion). See Ref. 8, p. 83 and Ref. 9, p. 12, for findings in other areas.

Now these estimates are based on end year actual employment in new firms. They are of little help, therefore, in the analysis of the *net* employment effects of formation, yet it is surely these net effects that are of crucial policy significance.[13] The reason of course why actual employment may not be a good guide to net employment is that the various components in Table 9.1 are *interdependent*. The formation and subsequent growth of a new firm may lead, as we shall see in section 4 below, to expansion, contraction or the death of *other* firms (or to less expansion/greater contraction than would otherwise be the case). Although some investigators have briefly acknowledged the existence of this interdependence (see Ref. 7, p. 24 and Ref. 15), no attempt has been made to investigate it further. One reason for the absence of meas-urement in this area is that it requires much more detailed knowledge of a new firm's products, operations and market(s) than is usually available in components of change analyses.[16] In the absence of such information, esti-mates of actual end year employment in new firms give little indication of net employment effects unless the heroic assumption is made that the relation-ship between actual and net employment is the same for all three categories of gross job expansion given in Table 9.1 (thereby allowing for a *pro rata* distribution of gross job losses across the categories).

In the next section, we look at some of the interrelationships between actual employment in new firms and the net effect of formations.

3. The net employment effects of new firms

In this section we are concerned with two questions. The first is the extent to which new firms increase employment above what it would be in their absence. The second is the relationship between actual employment in new firms and the net employment effects generally. We have already argued that actual employment is unlikely to give good guidance on this score because of the effect of formations on other businesses' employment.

Some indication of factors likely to affect the answers to these questions can be provided by examination of a number of simple illustrative cases. Consider the formation of a new firm (or firms) which enter some industry i. By definition

$$NE_i \equiv Lp_i - La_i \tag{1}$$

where NE_i is the net employment effect in the ith industry, Lp_i is the post-entry and La_i the pre-entry employment in that industry. $NE \gtreqless 0$ as $Lp \gtreqless La$. Let λ be the ratio of employment in the new entrant(s) to the total post-entry employment. We can thus write,

$$A = \lambda Lp_i \quad 0 < \lambda \leqslant 1 \tag{2}$$

where A is the actual employment in the newly-formed entrant(s). A is always positive.

In the analysis below, the important simplifying assumptions are as follows.

(a) There are constant costs for all firms and no external economies or diseconomies. The labour-output ratio is constant. (We shall also assume that this ratio is equal to one so that employment and output can be drawn on the same axis in the following diagrams).

(b) The supply of labour to each firm is perfectly elastic so there is no labour constraint. Jobs are thus equal to employment.

(c) The products of all established and new firms are homogeneous.

(d) Firms have equal market shares. This means that

$$\lambda_i = B_i / F_i$$

where B_i is the number of newly-formed firms setting up in industry i and F_i is the total number of post-entry firms.

(e) The industry demand is static and negatively sloped.

(f) Net employment effects are limited to the industry entered (so we can drop the i subscripts).

(g) There are no employment multiplier effects and there is immediate adjustment to equilibrium after entry.

We now examine some cases where the cost structure of the entrant[17] is the same as that in existing firms.

Case I: A competitive market structure exists and a new firm enters. This simply leads to a reduction in the average size of firm. $Lp = La$ so $A > NE = 0$.

Case II: A monopoly (involving a single firm or a group of colluding firms) exists and a new firm enters. This is shown in Fig. 9.1. D_m is the market demand curve and MR the relevant marginal revenue curve. Pre-entry (monopoly) price and output are P_m and L_a.

IIa: If the new firm joins the monopoly or collusive agreement then $Lp = La$ and again $A > NE = 0$.

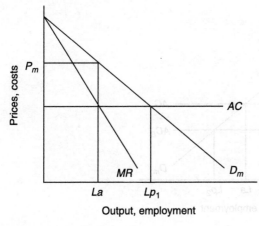

Figure 9.1

IIb: If the new firm does not join the monopoly, output and employment expand to the competitive level so that *Lp* is now to the right of *La*, shown as Lp_1 in Fig. 9.1. Thus, $NE > 0$ and, given equal market shares, $A = NE > 0$.[18]

In cases where the new entrant has a lower average cost curve (AC_B) than existing firms *(AC)* the position is slightly changed.

Case III: A competitive market structure exists initially.

IIIa: The new firm, with its lower costs, becomes a monopolist and sets output and employment where $AC_B = MR$. Price will be set at P_m. Assume $P_m > P_c$, where P_c is the previously prevailing competitive price. In this case if old firms cannot match the lower costs and cannot re-enter then the new employment is Lp_i in Fig. 9.2. Note that $Lp_1 < La$ so $A > 0 > NE$. the new firm has displaced more jobs than it has created.

IIIb: If there were a threat of the old firms re-entering when $P_m > P_c = AC$ then the new monopolist may be forced to price at P_c. *Lp* would then coincide with *La* in Fig. 9.2 so that $A > NE = 0$.

IIIc: Where old firms are able to match the new cost levels, i.e. *AC* drops to AC_B, then employment will expand to Lp_2. Since $Lp_2 > La$ then $NE > 0$ but we cannot say whether this is greater or less than *A*. This case is quite likely to occur since entry itself may lead existing firms to institute a search for lower costs.

It is straightforward matter to extend these examples. One can easily show, for instance, the consequences of the new entrant in Case III pricing such that $P_m \leq P_c$. It would be tedious to describe all these and a summary of some of them, together with the cases already discussed is shown in Table 9.2. The list is by no means exhaustive. It does not, for instance, examine (the relatively straightforward) cases where a newly-formed lower cost firm enters a monopolistic industry. However, the table shows quite clearly that whereas *A* is

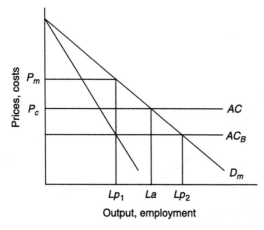

Figure 9.2

Table 9.2

Case No. in text	New firm's costs compared with existing firms' costs	Market structure		Other remarks	Relationship between A and NE
		Pre-entry	Post-entry		
I	Same	Competition	Competition		$A > NE = 0$
IIa	Same	Monopoly	Monopoly		$A > NE = 0$
IIb	Same	Monopoly	Competition		$A = NE > 0$
IIIa	Lower	Competition	Monopoly	$P_m > P_c$, existing firms cannot match new firm's lower costs. No re-entry possible by existing firms	$A > NE < 0$
IIIb	Lower	Competition	Monopoly	$P_m > P_c$, existing firms cannot match new firm's lower costs. Re-entry possible by existing firms	$A > NE = 0$
IIIc	Lower	Competition	Competition	$P_m > P_c$, existing firms match new firm's lower costs.	$A \gtrless NE > 0$
–	Lower	Competition	Competition	$P_m < P_c$, existing firms match new firm's lower costs.	$A \gtrless NE > 0$
–	Lower	Competition	Monopoly	$P_m < P_c$, existing firms cannot match new firm's lower costs.	$A > NE > 0$
–	Lower	Competition	Competition	$P_m = P_c$, existing firms match new firm's lower costs.	$A \gtrless NE > 0$
–	Lower	Competition	Monopoly	$P_m = P_c$, existing firms cannot match new firm's lower costs.	$A > NE = 0$

invariably positive, *NE* is not so. The formation of a new firm is no guarantee of additional jobs being created and in some instances there may be a net fall in employment. The net employment effect will be positive wherever the market structure becomes more competitive. (If the cases in which costs of the new entrant were lower than existing firms had been presented with monopoly

as a stating point, these would have all showed $NE > 0$). Where market structure remains unchanged, some reduction in costs is necessary for NE to be
positive.

We can see from Eqns 1 and 2 that,

$$NE = \frac{A}{\lambda} - L_a$$

so the net employment effect varies inversely with λ. For any given level of A
the Lp will be as shown in Fig. 9.3. The curve will shift upwards or down-
wards as A rises or falls. The vertical gap between Lp and La is NE and where
the La level is sufficiently low not to cut the Lp curve as with La_1, then there
will not be net displacement of jobs. Where La cuts Lp, as with La_2, then for
$\lambda > \lambda_1$ there will be net displacement, i.e. $NE < 0$. The assumptions under
which our discussion so far has been carried out have been very restrictive.
Therefore, we explore below some of the implications of relaxing some
of them.

Growing industry demand

If the industry demand curve is shifting to the right then the formation of a
new firm may simply soak up the increase in demand and may not, therefore,
lead to the loss of any actual jobs in established firms. However, to establish
the size of NE we would have to make a judgement on whether or not the

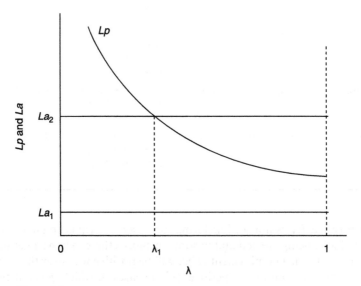

Figure 9.3

established firms would have expanded in any case to meet the increased demand. If they would have done so, the *NE* is zero.

A new firm may of course identify hitherto untapped demand for the industry's product, e.g. in an export market or through import substitution. Insofar as new firms alone meet that demand, *A* will be equal to *NE*. If the identification of this market leads to other established firms coming in, then *NE* will exceed *A*, assuming equal market shares.

New and improved products

A new firm may introduce a new or improved product. We may treat any such departure from our assumption of homogeneity as involving the formation of a new industry (i.e. where $La = 0$). It may have been possible to produce the 'new' product under existing technology. The innovation may, however, make *economically viable* production possible for the first time. The size of *NE* will depend on the extent to which other firms, established in other industries or entirely new, are willing and able to imitate the innovation. Where no imitation is possible, the innovator will price as a monopolist and *NE* will equal *A*. (Since $La = 0$ and $\lambda = 1$ then Eqns 1 and 2 give $NE = Lp = A$). If other firms come in, then output and employment will grow to the competitive level. In this case $\lambda < 1$ and since $NE_1 = Lp_1$ then $A < NE$.

Direct effects in other industries

So far we have assumed that other industries are unaffected by developments in the industry which the new firm enters. Clearly, in many instances, this assumption will be unrealistic for several reasons. First, an increase or a reduction in quantity demanded in one industry may, itself, lead to changes in the demand for the products of *other* industries (and, hence, their employment) as customers switch their purchasing power. This switch may occur as the result either of lower prices for the same good, or of an innovation or improvement. Although these 'ripple' effects may be difficult to detect and measure, they are, nevertheless, an essential element in the accurate calculation of *NE*. Second, an innovation or cost reduction in *one* industry may have widespread effects outside the industry in which it is introduced. An innovation may, for example, lead to the development of other industries by providing 'a missing link' in some technology. A cost reduction may allow profitable production in an industry to commence for the first time. In these cases *NE* may far exceed the employment in the innovating firm. On the other hand, the products of other industries may be *displaced* by the innovation.

Indirect effects through the employment multiplier

If, after all the direct implications of the formation of the new firm have been worked out, there is a positive net effect, then there are also likely to be *additional* effects resulting from the generation of the employment multiplier (provided there is less than full employment).

We have shown above that estimating the net employment effects of new formations may be complex. We have only examined the relaxation of *some* of the assumptions made at the beginning of this section, and then usually one by one, and not in combination. We have not looked at the effects of abandoning the other assumptions (e.g. the constant labour output ratio, constant costs, the absence of external economies and diseconomies, immediate adjustment to equilibrium). All these factors will further complicate the picture presented here.[19] Furthermore, it must be remembered that Table 9.2 is based on exercises in comparative statics. Different *equilibrium* positions were compared and no attempt was made to analyse *how* these positions were attained. It was simply assumed that adjustment was instantaneous. In reality of course, firms do not usually have the level of knowledge of demand and costs that this approach implies. In such a world of uncertainty, new firms may be one mechanism through which the market feels its way towards equilibrium. The formation of a new firm by a founder who thinks (correctly, as it turns out) that he is better informed about market conditions than established firms, may expand employment overall in the industry simply because the latter was in a position of disequilibrium before the formation. The formation may also – by providing additional market information – stimulate other firms to expand. This information providing role of new firms cannot be examined in detail here. However, it should be borne in mind in any analysis based on the comparative statics of the kind described earlier.

4. Some policy implications

We have shown that observed employment in new firms is unlikely to provide any guide to the net employment effects of formations. At one extreme, these effects will be near to zero where the new firm has little new to offer and enters established markets which are already highly competitive. At the other, they could be very substantial given an appropriate mix of new firm and market characteristics. For example, a new firm which introduces an innovation which is quickly taken up by other firms and which leads to the opening up of new markets, may generate a large *NE*, especially if it leads to the introduction of relatively more labour intensive methods. Many formations, will, of course, generate a mixture of both positive and negative effects on *NE*. (For example, few innovations will not adversely affect other markets in *some* way).

While the hard evidence is rather thin, it is probably true to say that the majority of new businesses formed probably do not have a substantial *NE*. Davis and Kelly[20] have argued, following Oxenfeldt,[21] that,

> Most new businesses set up in the manufacturing sector do not have anything new to offer. They do not generally rely on process or product innovations and have little administrative skill, and it is hardly surprising

that the average life expectancy is low. The new small firm tends to enter industries with low capital, technological and managerial requirements and has consequently to contend with fierce competition.

The view of these authors in relation to the non-innovatory nature of most new businesses gains some support from other studies. In a study of 74 new manufacturing firms formed in the Northern Region in recent years in the U.K.,[3] we were only able to identify nine that could be classed as innovative in a technical sense. Two of these ceased to market their innovations within three years of formation. The recent Arthur D. Little study[22] of new technology based firms formed in the UK between 1950 and 1977, found only just over 100 meeting the relevant criteria. Gudgin in his comprehensive study of the East Midlands formed the impression 'that most new firms began life without any innovation.[23] Now these studies relate primarily to manufacturing and to technical innovations. However, there is no reason to think that the position will be substantially different in the non-manufacturing sector or in relation to other types of innovation. It is unlikely that the majority of new firms will serve to break down monopolies. As Davis and Kelly imply, most will enter industries that are already highly competitive and will remain small for virtually the whole of their lives. Those new firms that enter more oligopolistic industries will not usually provide a challenge to the leaders of industry. (Their presence may, however, serve to modify monopolistic tendencies among such leaders).

The above does not, of course, imply that *some* new firms may not provide a substantial *NE*. Indeed, as we pointed out at the beginning of this paper, it could be argued that all current employment represents a *NE* of formation. Some new firms may contribute significantly to employment. For example, one of the innovating firms identified in the Northern Region study was employing over 300 by the first year of employment and it is likely that its *NE* has been substantial. It may also be the case that there may be a positive *NE* in the *region* in which the firm is formed, but not in the country taken as a whole. New firm formation could thus be used to provide a geographical redistribution of employment. Certainly, it has been seen as one means of reviving depressed regions. See Ref. 24, p. 176.

In view of the differences in *NE* across new firms, there may be a case for making any policy of assistance towards new firms as employment generators *selective* in nature. Whether, however, it is possible to devise a policy of selecting 'winners' without, at the same time, supporting a large number of losers, remains an open question. What is clear, however, is that for large numbers of new firms, the net effect on employment is very small indeed and may bear little relation to the actual numbers employed.

The measurement of *NE* in particular formations – whether *ex post* or *ex ante* – is bound to be rather tentative because of the many factors involved. Any assessment will almost certainly have to be limited to the effects of a formation in closely related markets in a particular geographical area. It will also be necessary to limit fairly rigorously the time period over which the effects of the formation on employment are considered. Such limitations are inevitable given the complex nature of the task. However, provided these limitations are explicitly recognised, any quantification of *NE* would represent a significant advance on current knowledge.

References

1. *Hansard*, House of Lords, Vol. 400. Col. 7.
2. Reported in the *Times*, 31st January, 1981. See also the Chancellor's comments in *Employment News*, No. 85 (May 1981).
3. P. S. Johnson and D. G. Cathcart, New manufacturing firms and regional development, *Regional Studies* **13**, 269–280 (1979).
4. R. Massey, 'Components of Regional Employment Change'. Paper given to a Conference on Industry and the Inner City, Sunningdale (December 1980).
5. J. Firn and J. K. Swales, The formation of new manufacturing establishments in the central Clydeside and West Midlands conurbations, 1963–72: A comparative analysis. *Regional Studies* **12**, 199–213 (1978).
6. G. Gudgin, *Industrial Location Processes and Regional Employment Growth*. Saxon House, Farnborough (1978).
7. S. Fothergill and G. Gudgin, *The Job Generation Process in Britain*, Centre for Environmental Studies, Research Series 32, CES, London (1979).
8. M. Cross, *New Firm Formation and Regional Development*. Gower, Farnborough (1980).
9. D. Hamilton, L. Moar and I. Orton, *Job Generation in Scottish Manufacturing Industry*. Fraser of Allander Institute, University of Strathclyde, Glasgow (1981).
10. D. Storey, *Job Generation and Small Firms Policy*, Centre for Environmental Studies Policy Series No. 11, CES, London (1980).
11. D. L. Birch, *The Job Generation Process*, MIT Program on Neighbourhood and Regional Change, MIT, Cambridge, Massachusetts (1979).
12. In one case (see Ref. 11), end year employment in new firms was expressed in terms of the net employment change over the period. Birch has rightly been criticised for this approach (See Ref. 10, p. 4).
13. The difference between the actual employment and net employment effect is not always appreciated. For example, in a recent (well received) research study commissioned by the Department of Industry on the value of publicly financed counselling for small firms, it was argued that the service had 'saved or created' 3,500 jobs. This estimate was based on the views of the service's clients on the likely effects of the counselling *on their own businesses*. No account whatsoever was taken of effects on *other* businesses. (See Ref. 14, p. 25) Of course, as a special case, actual may equal net.
14. Department of Industry, *The Value of the Counselling Activity of the Small Firms Service*. A Report for the Department of Industry by Research Associates Ltd (1981).
15. J. F. F. Robinson and D. J. Storey, Employment change in manufacturing industry in Cleveland, 1965–1976. *Regional Studies* **15**, 161–172 (1981).
16. In some studies (see Ref. 11) the net effect of *gross* job gains and losses for different *size* categories of firm have been estimated. (Size is measured in the base year except for births where end year size is used). However, this does not meet our need as it is not possible to separate out the effects of new firms only; nor is it necessarily true that new firms in a given end year size category will only affect existing firms who were in that size category in the base year.

17. It is assumed hereafter that only one firm enters the industry. However, extension of the analysis to the case where several new firms enter presents no major problems.

18. In this particular instance $\lambda = \frac{1}{2}$ and the linear demand curve implies $Lp = 2La$, so by substituting into Eqns 1 and 2 we have,

$$NE = 2La - La = La$$
$$A = \frac{1}{2}(2La) = La$$

So $NE = A$.

A group of colluding firms acting as a single monopoly is treated as such.

19. For instance, a variable labour output ratio will alter the employment implications of any change in output. For any expansion in industry output the employment will rise more or less than proportionately depending on whether the labour output ratio is falling or rising.

20. J. R. Davis and M. Kelly, *Small Firms in the Manufacturing Sector*. Committee of Inquiry on Small firms, Research Report No. 3, HMSO, London (1970).

21. A. R. Oxenfeldt, *New Firms and Free Enterprise*. American Council on Public Affairs, Washington (1943).

22. A. D. Little, *New Technology Based Firms in the UK and the Federal Republic of Germany*. Wilton House, London (1977).

23. See Ref. 6, p. 102. Gudgin does, however, point out that the more successful firms 'later evolved their own proprietary products which would often have some element of originality'. This illustrates the very considerable difficulty mentioned earlier in the text, of estimating the *NE* effect many years after birth. Such firms are still likely, however, to constitute only a minority of *all* firms.

24. Northern Region Strategy Team (NRST), *Strategic Plan for the Northern Region Vol. 2: Economic Development Policies*. NRST, Newcastle (1977).

10 Employment change in the small establishment sector in UK manufacturing [1]

Peter Johnson

Source: *Applied Economics*, 1989, 21 (2), 251–260.

In 1971, the Bolton Committee of Inquiry on Small Firms (HMSO, 1971) expressed concern over the declining share of small firms in economic activity. Its report showed, *inter alia*, that the employment share of small establishments, defined as those with less than 200 employees, in manufacturing had been declining since the mid-1920s. Since 1971, however, the trend has been reversed, with the small establishment sector (SES) accounting for a growing share of total employment. Now the published *Annual Census of Production* (ACOP)[2] data from which these trends are calculated do not give any indication of the relative importance of flows of employment into or out of the 'small' category, or of employment change among establishments that remain in the category. Yet such information is likely to be important for policy. For example, the implications for industrial policy of a small establishment sector which is growing because large establishments are getting smaller are likely to be different from those where the reason for growth is an expansion of births.

This paper takes a first step towards supplying the relevant information by presenting the results of some special tabulations obtained from the ACOP data for the period 1979–83. These tabulations show that over a period when the share of total employment accounted for by the SES in manufacturing rose by over 20 per cent, small establishments have in general become much less able to generate employment. Furthermore, it is clear that the share of the SES has been boosted by small establishments becoming *less* able *to grow out of* the SES, and by a greater contraction of large establishments *into* the sector. Neither of these phenomena can be said to reflect industrial vigour in the SES.

This paper is divided into four sections. The first looks briefly at trends in the SES since 1975. The second section describes relevant features of the ACOP data base. The third section looks at components of employment change using the specially prepared tabulations. The final section concludes the paper and provides suggestions for further work.

I. Trends in the SES since 1975

Fig. 10.1 sets out employment trends in manufacturing since 1975. It is clear that while the *share* of the SES in total manufacturing employment has steadily increased (from 28.9 per cent to 37.8 per cent) since that year, the sector's absolute level of employment has declined. (There has, however, been some marginal increase in the absolute employment in establishments of under 20 employees.)

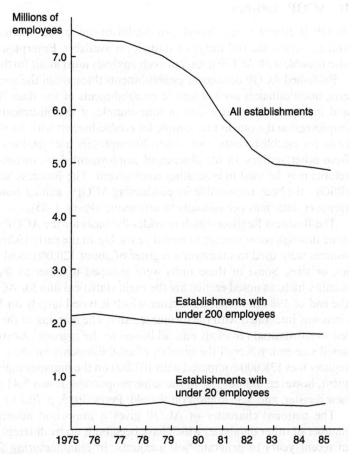

	Millions of employees										
	7.0										
	6.0							All establishments			
	5.0										
	4.0										
	3.0										
	2.0					Establishments with under 200 employees					
	1.0					Establishments with under 20 employees					
	1975	76	77	78	79	80	81	82	83	84	85
% Employment share of establishments with under 200 employees	28.9	29.8	29.6	29.6	29.8	31.9	33.9	34.2	36.2	37.8	37.8
% Employment share of establishments with under 20 employees	6.7	7.0	6.9	7.3	7.6	8.2	10.0	10.0	11.0	11.5	11.6

Figure 10.1 Employment in small establishments in manufacturing.

Source: Annual Census of Production.

Note: 1979 figures use 1968 SIC.

In terms of the *numbers of establishments*, the SES has also increased its share over the period (from 93.9 per cent to 96.7 per cent). The absolute numbers of establishments in the SES has also increased dramatically (by over 40,000) since 1982. Some of this increase may, however, be due to the changes in the register of establishments used as the basis for ACOP (see below).

II. ACOP statistics

ACOP is establishment based. An establishment is the smallest productive unit for which the full range of statistics is available. Enterprise analyses are also feasible with ACOP data, but such analyses must await further resources.[3]

Published ACOP data cover establishments throughout the size range. However, questionnaires are not sent to establishments of less than 20 employees,[4] and in general there is a one in four sample of establishments with 20–49 employees[5] and a one in two sample for establishments with 50–99 employees.[6] Data for establishments with under 20 employees are obtained or estimated from other sources. In the absence of employment data, turnover from VAT returns may be used in estimating employment. The Business Statistics Office (BSO) – the body responsible for conducting ACOP – admits, however, that the turnover data 'may occasionally be erroneous' (Perry, 1985).

The Business Register which provides the basis for the ACOP enquiries has gone through some change in recent years. Up to the early 1980s, a variety of sources were used to maintain a register of about 120,000 local units, factories, or sites. Some of these units were grouped together to form establishments which, as noted earlier, are the main statistical unit for ACOP. Towards the end of 1984 the separate register which is based largely on VAT registrations was integrated with the former register. The merging of the two registers led to substantial removals and additions to the register,[7] mostly at the very small size end. (Overall the number of establishments on the new integrated register was 138,000 compared with 107,000 on the previous register. Employment, however, did not rise in the same proportion: it was 5.41 million in the new register, and 5.33 million on the old: Perry, 1985, p. 70.14.)

The national character of ACOP gives it important advantages over a number of other databases which have been built up by different investigators in recent years to generate 'job accounts' in manufacturing for particular areas of the UK (Fothergill and Gudgin, 1979; Gudgin, 1978; Cross, 1981; Lloyd and Dicken, 1981; Storey, 1982). These databases have often used different data sources, a variation which makes direct comparisons rather hazardous. The Dun and Bradstreet database now being developed by Cohn Gallagher at Newcastle University (Gallagher and Stewart, 1986) *is* national and has the further advantage that it covers all industry. However, it contains less information on each reporting unit than the ACOP file and the representativeness of its coverage, particularly at the smaller size end has been questioned (Storey and Johnson, 1986).

Because of statutory restrictions and disclosure, the raw ACOP data cannot be made available to outsiders. (There are also restrictions on its use within government.) The tabulations on which this paper is based do not, however, infringe the statutory restrictions. They were drawn up to the author's specification, with the necessary computer programming being undertaken internally by the BSO. Such an exercise is costly; hence the tabulations are rather restricted in their scope and detail; however, they do illustrate the potential for using ACOP data for longitudinal purposes. (This potential is not of course restricted to small-scale operations.)

III. Components of employment change

Employment trends in the SES are the net effect of (a) employment lost by units moving out of the small size band; (b) employment gained by units moving into the size band; and (c) employment change in units which remain in the size band. Employment losses in (a) may arise from deaths and/or the movement of units into a larger size band. Gains in (b) may result from births and/or from units previously in a larger size band moving into the small size band as a result of contraction.

To identify the various components of employment change in the SES in manufacturing it is necessary to look at:

(i)   the *end* year status of all establishments classified as small and in manufacturing in the *base* year; and

(ii) the *base* year status of all establishments classified as small and in manufacturing in the *end* year.

'Status' here refers to the following:

(i)   *Whether or not the establishment exists in manufacturing.* If it does not, it is referred to as 'untraceable'. It may, however, still exist in non-manufacturing. It is not possible with the ACOP database to distinguish between 'untraceable and ceased business' and 'untraceable but continuing in business outside manufacturing'.

(ii) *Whether, if it does exist in manufacturing, it is small or large.*

Of course each establishment included in the analysis must have been small and in manufacturing in at least one of the years.

Since an establishment in the ACOP database retains the same establishment number while it remains in existence, it is a relatively straightforward matter to obtain the end (base) year status of establishments classified as small and in manufacturing in the base (end) year.

The period chosen for the study of components of employment change was 1975–83. Because of changes in the standard industrial classification (SIC) in 1980 it is not possible to undertake an analysis for the whole period. The period has therefore been broken down into two subperiods of equal length: 1975–9 and 1979–83 (the 1979 data are available under the two SICs). A division at 1979 is particularly useful because this year marks the beginning of a greatly enhanced policy commitment to the encouragement of small-scale enterprise. Although at the time of the analysis, 1984 data were available it was decided to stop a year earlier because of the problems that might be caused by the changes in the Business Register.

Table 10.Al summarizes the results of the analysis. (These results rely on a small amount of estimation which was necessary to overcome disclosure restrictions on the ACOP data[8].) It may be seen that in the first subperiod 87 per cent of establishments classified to the SES in 1975 were still small in 1979. Their share of 1975 employment was rather lower. The proportion of establishments moving into the large category between 1975 and 1979 was less than 10 per cent although their share of 1975 employment was significantly higher (at 4 per cent). The percentage of (1975) small establishments becoming untraceable over the period was 12 per cent (16 per cent employment). This broad pattern is maintained in the 1979–83 subperiod although the proportion of the total numbers of establishments and of employment accounted for by establishments (i) remaining in the SES; and (ii) moving into the large category, both fell. Establishments which became untraceable accounted for a substantially larger proportion of the base year SES total in the second period. The composition of the two *end* years, 1979 and 1983, is broadly similar with those establishments which have remained small throughout accounting for around 80–85 per cent of all the SES establishments and employment in them. Perhaps the most notable difference between the two end-year compositions is the greatly increased employment accounted for by the contraction of large plants into the SES in the second subperiod.

Table 10.1, which is derived from Table 10.Al, examines the employment implications of the changes that have taken place.

The pace of employment decline (as measured by the percentage change in base year total employment in the SES) was clearly much faster in the second period (bottom row). This faster decline may be largely accounted for by the following factors:

(i)   The establishments that remained small throughout each subperiod registered a substantial employment loss during 1979–83, whereas these establishments increased employment during 1975–9.

(ii) The net loss from establishments becoming untraceable was much larger in the second subperiod. While those establishments which moved *from* 'untraceable' in the base year provided roughly the same employment, those establishments moving *to* the untraceable category accounted for a considerably increased employment loss.

The higher losses in the second subperiod from the above two sources more than offset the increase in the net gain made by the SES as a result of the movement between small and large categories. This higher net gain arose

Table 10.1 Components of employment change in the SES

Description of establishment	1975/9		1979/83	
	Employment change	% of total base year employment in SES	Employment change	% of total base year employment in SES
Small in base and end years	+51,741	+2.4	−140,105	−6.8
Small in base year; large in end year	−86,426	−4.0	−48,633	−2.3
Small in base year, untraceable in end year	−348,123	−16.1	−428,714	−20.6
Small in end year; large in base year	+84,269	+3.9	+157,581	+7.6
Small in end year; untraceable in base year	+212,036	+9.8	+216,496	+10.4
Total employment change in SES	−86,503	−4.0	−243,376	−11.7

Source: See Table 10.Al.

because there was a smaller employment loss from establishments moving from small to large (i.e. lower expansion of small establishments) and a bigger employment gain from establishments moving in the opposite direction (i.e. greater contraction).

As Table 10.Al shows the net movement between small and large and small and untraceable is mirrored in the number of establishments.

Table 10.2 provides data on employment change by size of establishment in the base year. Establishments that were large in the base year (but which became small by the end year) are excluded from the table. The first column provides data on employment growth or decline in those small establishments which were small in the base year and which either remained small or grew out of the SES. It should be noted that establishments in all size bands showed a lower capacity to generate jobs in the second subperiod. However the decline in this capacity between the two subperiods was greater in the larger size bands.

The second column also shows a greater proportionate loss due to establishments becoming untraceable in the second subperiod. The increase in employment shedding is greatest among the very small establishments, i.e. those of ten employees or under. Indeed whereas the loss due to establishments in this size band becoming untraceable was substantially more than offset by the growth of those that remained in existence in the first subperiod, this was not the case in the second subperiod (and employment growth of 8.4 per cent was more than wiped out by a loss of 17.7 per cent).

Table 10.2 Employment change in the SES by size of establishment

| | Change in employment as a % of base year employment: | | | | | | | |
| | 1 In establishments that remained small or became large during the period | | 2 Due to establishments becoming untraceable during the period | | 3 Due to previously untraceable establishments entering the SES | | 4 Balance of 2 and 3 | |
Establishment size	1975/9	1979/83	1975/9	1979/83	1975/9	1979/83	1975/9	1979/83
1–10	+20.0	+8.4	–8.8	–17.7	+19.1	+13.9	+10.3	–3.8
11–19	+4.8	+1.7	–14.0	–18.3	+14.4	+18.0	+0.4	–0.3
20–49	+4.7	–4.4	–19.7	–20.3	+11.1	+13.0	+8.6	–7.3
50–99	+7.0	–9.9	–17.3	–22.4	+7.4	+7.5	–9.9	–14.9
100–199	+4.3	–13.6	–16.4	–21.5	+5.7	+6.4	–10.7	–15.1
Total	+5.8	–4.4	–16.1	–20.6	+9.8	+10.4	–6.3	–10.2

Source: Author's data.

From the third column it is clear that the employment gain from untraceables entering the SES was lower in all size bands but most particularly in the smaller bands.

So far attention has focused almost exclusively on employment. However, it is also instructive to examine what is happening to the numbers of establishments. As Table 10.A1 shows the main movement in and out of the SES relates to those which were untraceable in one of the years. Data on such movement is given by size band in Table 10.3. It is not known how far movement to and movement from 'untraceable' correspond, respectively, to business failure and business birth but the links are likely to be close. The failure rate (first two columns) increased between the two periods – both in total and in all size bands. The increase was most marked in the smallest size band. The birth rate also declined overall, although experience varied by size band: in the smallest size band it fell substantially, whereas in the top three size bands it increased substantially.

IV. Discussion and conclusion

This paper shows that the SES in manufacturing has become less able to generate employment over the period 1975–83, despite its growing *share* of total employment. Employment change (as a proportion of base year employment) in those establishments which were classified as small in the base year and which were still in existence in the end year (as either small or large) changed from positive in the first subperiod to negative in the second subperiod (Table 10.2). In the second subperiod the employment loss from small establishments that became untraceable was also higher. The employment generated from previously untraceable establishments moving into the

Table 10.3 Movement of establishments between the SES and the untraceable category

	% change in the number of establishments as a proportion of the total number of establishments in the size band in the base year			
	Small to untraceable		Untraceable to small	
Establishment	*1975/9*	*1979/83*	*1975/9*	*1979/83*
1–10	8.6	18.1	20.0	8.6
11–19	13.7	15.7	14.5	13.7
20–49	20.0	20.3	11.4	20.0
50–99	17.5	22.4	7.5	17.5
100–199	16.3	21.4	5.8	16.3
Total	12.3	18.9	16.1	12.3

Source: Author's data.

SES was however maintained in the second subperiod in terms of both base year employment and absolute numbers of employees.

In interpreting the growing share of employment accounted for by the SES, it is important to remember that this share has been boosted by small establishments becoming *less* able to grow out of the SES, and by a greater contraction of large establishments into the sector.

The above suggests that any attempt to use the growing share of the SES as evidence of increased vigour and dynamism among small firms should be viewed cautiously. However the maintenance of the employment contribution of small establishments which have moved into the SES from being untraceable at a time when there was a substantial employment decline in the SES as a whole does provide some support for the view that the introduction of policies to stimulate small business activity has had some success.

The data provided in this paper do not of course show the *interrelationships* between the various categories of establishments. The following questions, for example, have not been addressed:

(i) Does the arrival of previously untraceable establishments in the SES lead to *other* establishments being forced out through the competitive process?
(ii) Does the growth of existing establishments cause decline in others?
(iii) Does decline generate entry by providing market 'space'?
(iv) Does growth (decline) in some establishments encourage growth (decline) in other establishments?

The answers to these kinds of question would require a detailed study of the influences on, and effects of employment growth at the level of the individual establishment.

This paper has involved the 'tracking' of individual establishments through

time. Cost constraints have meant that this has been done for two years only –
a 'base' and an 'end' year – in each sub-period but there is no reason in
principle, given the *annual* nature of the Census, why a year by year profile of
the experience of individual establishments and indeed enterprises should not
be constructed. The national character of ACOP and the extent of the data
collected through it would ensure a very rich base for the testing of a wide
range of hypotheses concerned with the determinants of employment
growth. Developments of ACOP in this way would however involve much
broader issues relating to the government's resource commitment to statistics
and its priorities in this area. At the present time the use of ACOP data is
circumscribed by statutory restrictions on disclosure, but it would not be
difficult to maintain the requirements on disclosure while enabling a far more
intensive use of the data-base. The BSO might itself also consider undertaking and publishing longitudinal studies. Annual 'snapshot' pictures of industrial activity are of course helpful; but their value would be greatly enhanced
if they were complemented by studies of what is happening over time to
particular groups of establishments. The returns from a wider usage of
ACOP would more than compensate for the marginal costs involved. Such
usage would also eliminate the need for the development of the kind of 'one
off' databases that have been set up by researchers in recent years.

Appendix

Table 10.A1. Components of employment change in the SES: detailed results

Establishment category	Variable Emp: Employment Est: Establishment	Numbers (% of total employment or total numbers of establishments in SES in year in brackets)			
		1975	1979	1979	1983
Small in base year; small in end year	Emp	1,725,852 (79.9)	1,777,593 (85.7)	1,606,726 (77.1)	1,466,621 (79.7)
	Est	85,149 (87.1)	85,149 (83.9)	83,268 (80.8)	83,268 (85.0)
Small in base year; large in end year	Emp	86,425.5 (4.0)	160,521	48,633 (2.3)	96.851
	Est	595 (6.0)	595	350 (3.4)	350
Small in base year; untraceable in end year	Emp	348,123 (16.1)	n.a.	428,714 (20.6)	n.a
	Est	11,980 (12.3)	n.a	19,439 (18.9)	n.a.
Small in end year; large in base year	Emp	153,089	84,268.5 (4.1)	319,270	157,580.5 (8.6)
	Est	550.5	550.5 (0.5)	1,103	1,103 (1.1)
Small in end year, untraceable in base year	Emp	n.a.	212,036 (10.2)	n.a.	216,496 (11.8)
	Est	n.a.	15,751 (15.5)	n.a.	13,643 (13.9)
SES Total	Emp	2,160,400.5 (100.0)	2,073,897.5 (100.0)	2,084,073 (100.0)	1,840,697.5 (100.0)
	Est	97,724 (100.0)	101,450.5 (100.0)	103,057 (100.0)	98,014 (100.0)

Source: Author's data.

Notes

1 The author's thanks are due to the University of Durham for providing the necessary funds to purchase the cross tabulations from the BSO. He is also grateful to Dr Bernard Mitchell and Mr John Smith of the BSO for their assistance, and to Mr Richard Morley and Dr Lynne Evans for their comments on an earlier draft. All errors and omissions do of course remain the author's alone.

2 Prior to 1970, the *Census of Production* was conducted on a much less frequent basis.

3 Small establishment and small enterprise analyses may not yield such different results as may be seen from the following data. In 1984 there were 131,080 small establishments in the private and public sectors in UK manufacturing. Of these, 122,039 were owned by the 116,576 small enterprises in the private sector. The

difference is made up of small establishments owned by the public sector and by large enterprises. Unfortunately no published data are available on the split between these two, nor has it been possible to exclude the small establishments owned either by large enterprises or by the public sector from the cross tabulations in this note.

On the not unreasonable assumption that no small enterprise in the private sector owned more than two establishments in 1984, the probability that a small establishment selected at random from all (public and private) small establishments in the UK in 1984 would belong to a single establishment small enterprise is 0.85

$$\left(\text{i.e. } \frac{116{,}576 - (122{,}039 - 116{,}576)}{131{,}080}\right).$$

4 In 1978, however, questionnaires were sent to a 1 in 10 sample of establishments in this size band.

5 In 1978 and 1979, census coverage was cut to 1 in 2 for establishments in this size band in 68 industries. Then in 1980 it was reduced to 1 in 4.

6 There are a number of exceptions to the sampling rules, one of which is that the BSO samples more intensely in industries where it believes that there would otherwise be an unacceptable level of estimation. It should also be noted that until 1986 all establishments with an employment of 20 or more which covered sites at more than one address were required to complete a questionnaire, and that, prior to 1980, all establishments in the 50–99 size band were included in the survey. (For the 'benchmark' census in 1984, all establishments with an employment of 50 or more were sent questionnaires and in general 1 in 2 of those with an employment of between 20 and 49.)

7 Some idea of the change in establishments covered by the 1984 figures may be gauged from the following data. In 1979, 12 per cent of the small establishments in existence in that year had disappeared by 1983 (see Table 10.A1). However 72 per cent of the 1979 small establishments had disappeared by 1985. There is less difference between the employment percentages – 16 per cent and 44 per cent respectively – but it is still very substantial. In 1983, 14 per cent of small establishments existing in that year did not exist in 1979, whereas in 1985 the percentage that were untraceable in 1979 was 79 per cent. The corresponding employment figures were 14 per cent and 38 per cent respectively.

8 The possibility of disclosure arose because of the way in which the BSO's data were presented to the author. Each of the establishment categories in Table 10.A1 were analysed in terms of base and end year size *bands*. (Where an establishment was untraceable in one of the years, its employment size was treated as zero). Each cell in the cross tabulations therefore provided (i) the number of establishments (the same in both base and end years); (ii) the total base year employment of establishments in that cell; and (iii) the total end year employment of establishments in that cell. Data for cells with two establishments or less were not however disclosed. In these cases, it was assumed that there were 1.5 establishments in the cell. Base and end year employment were each assumed to be $\dfrac{(1 \times B_L) + (2 \times B_U)}{2}$ where B_L and B_U are the lower and upper bounds of the relevant size bands respectively. $(1 \times B_L)$ and $(2 \times B_U)$ provide, respectively, the minimum and maximum employment possible in the cell. Thus if the base and end year employment of establishments moving from the 50–99 size band in the base year to the 100–99 size band in the end year were not disclosed, it was assumed that base year employment was $\dfrac{(50 \times 1) + (99 \times 2)}{2}$ and that end year employment was $\dfrac{(100 \times 1) + (199 \times 2)}{2}$. Only 18 out of 128 cells required estimation in this way and many of these cells involved

the very small size bands thus making the possible magnitude (in employment terms) of any estimation error very low.

References

Cross, M. (1981) *New Firm Formation and Regional Development*, Gower, Farnborough.

Fothergill, S. and Gudgin, G. (1979) *The Job Generation Process in Britain*, Research Series 32, Centre for Environmental Studies, London.

Gallagher, C. C. and Stewart, M. (1986) Jobs and the business life cycle in the UK, *Applied Economics*, 18, 875–900.

Gudgin, G. (1978) *Industrial Location Processes and Regional Employment Growth*, Saxon House, Farnborough.

HMSO (1971) *Small Firms*. Report of the 'Bolton' Committee of Inquiry on Small Firms, Cmnd 4811, HMSO, London.

Johnson, P. S. (1986) *New Firms: an Economic Perspective*, Allen and Unwin, London.

Lloyd, P. and Dicken, P. (1981) *Industrial Change: Local Manufacturing Firms in Manchester and Merseyside*, Inner Cities Research Programme, Department of the Environment, London.

Perry, J. A. (1985) The development of a new register of businesses, *Statistical News*, 70, 70.13–70.14.

Storey, D. J. (1982) *Entreprenewship and the New Firm*, Croom Helm, London.

Storey, D. J. and Johnson, S. (1986) Job generation in Britain: a review of recent studies, Centre for Urban and Regional Development Studies, Newcastle University, Mimeograph.

Part IV

Growth and development

11 How good are small firms at predicting employment?[1]

John Ashworth, Peter Johnson and Cheryl Conway

Source: *Small Business Economics*, 1998, 10 (4), 379–387.

This paper utilises some data from an interview survey of very small firms in the North of England to examine the relationship between actual and forecast employment in small firms over a twelve month period. The paper first provides some summary statistics on actual and forecast employment for the survey firms over the reference period. It then looks at how successful the firms are in their short term forecasts, and finds that there is systematic over-estimation. The causes of the systematic forecast error are investigated. It is suggested, tentatively, that the firms may in some way be incorrectly interpreting the information embodied in their own employment figures when making their forecasts. The paper concludes with a brief review of the results and possible policy implications. Avenues for future work are also proposed.

I. Introduction

In recent years much has been written about employment in small firms. (For a good overview, see Storey, 1994, ch. 6). Studies have examined a wide variety of issues, such as the relative contribution of such firms to net employment change, using a job accounting approach (e.g. Daly et al., 1991), and the *nature* of their employment, including the remuneration employees receive (e.g. Brown et al., 1990, ch. 4; Curran et al., 1993, ch. 8; Morissette, 1993; Reilly, 1995); the break-down between full and part-time work (Storey and Johnson, 1987, p. 184; Scott et al., 1989, ch. 5; Curran et al., 1993; p. 10f); the extent of fringe wage benefits (e.g. Brown et al., 1990, ch. 5); and the employment profile of small firms since birth (e.g. Johnson, 1986, p. 86). Despite this extensive interest in small firms, little work appears to have been done on the expectations of these firms about future employment, and on how accurate their estimates are.[2]

This paper offers a contribution to the literature by examining the relationship between small firms' short term employment forecasts – over six and twelve months – made in interview surveys, and their subsequent employment record. It thus provides some indication of the extent to which small firms tend to over-estimate or under-estimate their future employment prospects. Such knowledge is likely to be important for public policy, not least in the devising of appropriate training and advisory services aimed at helping firms to evaluate their prospects in a realistic way. It is also likely to be of value in the evaluation, by both private and public sector agencies, of business plans drawn up by small firms – for example, in applications for bank loans – and of the results of more general surveys of small firm prospects, such as those carried out by the Confederation of British Industry, and other similar bodies.

The plan of the paper is as follows. In section II the sample of firms used in the study is described. Section III outlines the way in which information on actual and forecast employment was collected, and presents some summary data on both. Section IV briefly examines some sources of forecast error. In section V, the divergence between actual and forecast employment is further explored. The final section reviews the work and suggests ways in which further research might be developed.

Unless otherwise stated, employment is measured on a full-time equivalent (FTE) basis. A part-time worker, defined here as someone working less than 30 hours a week, is counted as 0.5 FTE.

II. The survey

This study is based on a survey of 121 firms which met the following conditions:

I.   They were all registered for VAT in March / April 1993
II. They were all located in the Northern Region[3] in the UK
III. They all remained in business in the region throughout the survey period
IV. They maintained their co-operation throughout the survey period

The common VAT registration period was utilised in order to provide standardisation in the economic environment faced by firms in the early part of their lives. The firms were identified via VAT records held by Customs and Excise. The limitations of these records, particularly with respect to their ability to identify very small firms are well known (Daly, 1990; Storey, 1994, pp. 50–51; Johnson and Conway, 1997). However they provide comprehensive coverage within their own terms of reference, and for the purpose of this study, are the best available, given the constraints on research resources.

For legal reasons Customs and Excise are unable to divulge the names and addresses of VAT registrants. However they did agree to send out a letter from the authors asking registrants to contact the authors direct. A stamped addressed envelope and response form was enclosed for this purpose. There are no obvious grounds for supposing that self-selection by co-operating respondents has generated any bias in relation to the characteristics of either the firms or the respondents involved. Each respondent was either the sole

owner of his firm, or had a significant ownership stake in it. The broad industrial breakdown of the sample is not significantly different from that of the
business population as a whole (see section III below).

The response rate that the 121 firms represent may be variously calculated
(see Appendix). However, a realistic estimate would be 16 per cent. This
compares favourably with the response rates of 13 and 7 per cent from postal
surveys of rural and urban small firms respectively, reported in Keeble et al.,
1992, and with the 10 per cent response rate – again in a postal survey of
small firms – reported in Mason and Harrison (1993).

The exclusion of non-survivors in this study may be justified on at least two
grounds. First one of the questions we wished to address was whether firms
experienced any learning over the reference period. To achieve this, it was
necessary to focus exclusively on survivors. Second, the recording of zero
out-turn employment for all non-survivors would have ignored any variation
that may exist in the severity of business failure.[4]

As shown later, most of the firms were in the services sector. Eighty-four
per cent employed five or fewer FTEs at the start of the survey. Nearly
73 per cent were unincorporated, and 64 per cent of respondents described
their main market as 'local' or 'regional'. On average, respondents had been
operating in their current firm for 1.4 years by the start of the survey, although
where they had taken over a firm (26 per cent of cases), the age of the firm
was sometimes significantly greater.

III. Data collection and some summary statistics

Data collection

Respondents were interviewed three times: in the winter of 1993/94, the
summer of 1994, and the winter of 1994/95. The first and last of these interviews were face to face, the middle one was undertaken by telephone. The second and third interviews were conducted six and twelve months respectively
after the first interview.

In all three interviews, respondents were asked about their current position,
the recent past, and how they saw their prospects for the future. In addition,
the first interview was used to collect data on a range of respondent, firm
and environmental characteristics. In all three interviews, respondents were
asked for their current part- and full-time employment so that FTEs could be
calculated. They were also asked to provide forecasts of their 'most likely'
employment in the future.[5]

The employment forecasts relevant for this paper are as follows. In the first
interview, respondents provided forecasts for six and twelve months ahead. In
the second interview, they were asked about employment six and eighteen
months ahead. It is possible therefore to compare forecast and out-turn
employment for dates six and twelve months after the first interview, and for a
date six months after the second interview. It is also possible, by comparing

the six month forecast made at the time of the first interview with the six month forecast made at the second interview, to examine whether FTE employment forecasts for six months ahead are changing and if so, whether they are becoming more or less accurate over time.

The employment forecasts are of course informal, in the sense that they do not derive from a structured business plan, but as Risseeuw and Masurel (1994) have pointed out in their empirical study of planning in small firms, there is not much need anyway for very small businesses to have a written business plan. Informal forecasts are nevertheless important as they provide an indication of how the owner perceives future development.

Some summary statistics

Nearly three-quarters of the firms are in services (Wholesaling, Retailing/ Dealing, and Other Services). Another 15 per cent are in Manufacturing. This breakdown is not significantly different from that for all VAT registrations in the North and in the UK as a whole.[6] The headcount and FTE methods of calculating employment yield similar distributions of employment across sectors. These employment distributions broadly reflect the sectoral spread in the numbers of firms.

Table 11.1 gives the mean and standard deviations for actual and forecast FTEs (actual is in bold). Not surprisingly given the relative youth of the firms involved, there was some employment growth over the year, although mean FTEs flattened out in the second six months. While it is true that mean forecasts in all cases exceeded mean out-turns, the large spread in the data implies that we cannot conclude from Table 11.1 alone that the firms are optimistic forecasters. The standard deviations of the forecasts were greater than those of the out-turns, although in no case was the difference (in variances) found to be significant, using the standard F test.[7]

Table 11.1 Actual and forecast employment

	Mean	SD	N
Actual employment, winter 1993/94	**3.09**	**2.94**	**121**
Actual employment, summer 1994	**3.47**	**3.36**	**121**
Forecast of employment, summer 1994, made 6 months earlier	3.80	3.51	121
Actual employment, winter 1994/5	**3.46**	**3.24**	**121**
Forecast of employment, winter 1994/5, made 12 months earlier	4.17	3.83	120[1]
Forecast of employment, winter 1994/5, made 6 months earlier	3.88	3.68	120[1]

Note
[1] One respondent declined to provide this forecast.

Table 11.2 provides some data on the proportionate forecast error. The table distinguishes between firms on the basis of whether their forecasts turned out to be correct, under-estimates, or over-estimates. It can be seen that those respondents who made over-estimates tended on average to make a bigger error than those who made under-estimates. Those respondents who made accurate forecasts mostly consisted of firms whose employment was static (see notes 2–4 to the table). It should also be noted that taking all the firms together, the longer term forecasts tend on average to be less accurate than the shorter term ones. There is no clear evidence of widespread learning between the two successive sub-periods.[8]

The large standard deviations recorded in Table 11.2 imply that in all three periods, the average forecast errors are not significantly different from zero, suggesting that it is not possible to reject the hypothesis that on average, the survey firms are on target. Clearly it is necessary to go beyond the kind of descriptive table so far presented, if further progress is to be made in analysing the relationship between out-turn and forecast employment. The issue is therefore further explored in section V.

Table 11.2 Proportionate forecast error[1]

Time period	Mean	SD	Number of firms
Winter 1993/94 to summer 1994			
Firms with negative error	−0.25	0.16	24
Firms with no error			53[2]
Firms with positive error	0.68	0.75	44
All firms	0.20	0.60	121
All firms, ignoring sign of error	0.30	0.55	121
Winter 1993/94 to winter 1994/95			
Firms with negative error	−0.26	0.17	25
Firms with no error			37[3]
Firms with positive error	0.93	1.18	58
All firms	0.40	0.98	120
All firms, ignoring sign of error	0.50	0.93	120
Summer 1994 to winter 1994/95			
Firms with negative error	−0.27	0.12	25
Firms with no error			50[4]
Firms with positive error	0.59	0.47	45
All firms	0.17	0.45	120
All firms, ignoring sign of error	0.28	0.39	120

Notes
1 Defined as the difference between the forecast of employment for the end of the period, and the actual employment at the end of the period, expressed as a proportion of the actual employment at the end of the period.
2 40 of these businesses did not change their employment over the period.
3 25 of these businesses did not change their employment over the period.
4 33 of these businesses did not change their employment over the period.

IV. Possible sources of forecast error

Before the econometric relationship between forecasts and out-turns is considered, it may be helpful briefly to consider some possible sources of forecast
error. The following are likely to be among the most important sources.

Interview bias

Such bias may arise where respondents wish to impress the interviewer, or
believe that they have something to gain from providing a particular response.
The possibility of such bias was reduced in this study by the interviewer
stressing that (s)he had no interest in any particular outcome, and that the
individual results would not be disclosed to a third party. It should also be
noted that respondents knew, at the time of each forecast, that there would be
a follow-up interview, when forecasts would be set against out-turns.

Over-optimism bias

Madsen (1994) has argued that firms are often committed to higher production (which usually implies higher employment), and that they then search for
information which provides support for their preferred outcome. In this
way, expectations are likely to be biased upwards. Madsen argues, with some
empirical support, that such over-optimism is likely to be an increasing function of uncertainty. The level of uncertainty in a market is likely to be positively related to the level of innovativeness, the intensity of competition, and
the extent of market turbulence. Furthermore, the level of uncertainty is
likely to be higher where the business is more dependent on a limited number
of customers and suppliers, since even a single decision by a customer or a
supplier may have a major effect on the business. In addition, a growing market may stimulate more uncertainty than a static one. Business motivation
will also play a role, with more ambitious respondents more likely to generate
over-optimism bias.

An incomplete or inaccurate information set

Future employment will be affected by a range of factors, including the present state of the respondent's business and its capacity to grow; the current
and future behaviour of competitors; market prospects; and general economic conditions. The availability of good information in each of these areas
will tend to be positively related to the degree to which the owner and any
staff have accumulated knowledge and experience. The size of the business
may itself embody information on past performance and on the location of
the firm on its expansion path.

   The information set available to the owner at the time he makes the forecast
inevitably excludes information on events that occur after that time, but

which could not be accurately foreseen. A forecast error may result from such unanticipated events, even though the information set at the time of the forecast may have been otherwise complete, and been interpreted correctly. However, we are not aware of any unexpected shocks that occurred during any of the forecast periods (see also note 8).

Poor interpretation of information

How well the information that is available is interpreted will influence the forecast error. Owners are likely to vary in the time and effort that they put into evaluating information, and in the skill they have in doing so. One factor influencing the inputs into forecasts will be the consequences that flow from it. A request for a forecast at an interview inevitably restricts these inputs, although it should be noted that in this study the forecasts were only made after some discussion of the business and its plans, and the environment in which it operates.

V. The divergence between actual and forecast employment: statistical analysis

The notation in this section is as follows. E_t is FTE employment at time t. $F_t E_{t+i}$ is the forecast, at time t, of FTE employment at $t + i$, where i is the number of time periods after the date at which the forecast is made. At winter 1993/94, $t = 0$; at summer 1994, $t = 1$; and at winter 1994/95, $t = 2$. Thus one time period covers a six month period. Using this notation $F_0 F_2$, for example, is the FTE forecast for twelve months ahead made at the time of the first interview, ie during the winter 1993/94.

As a starting point for our analysis, actual employment was regressed on forecast weighted employment, for the three available periods, for the 119 firms who provided a complete set of data, that is,

$$E_{t+i} = \alpha + \beta F_t E_{t+i} + u_{t+i}$$

where the notation is as before and where u_{t+i} is the usual white noise random error term. The results are given in Table 11.3. They demonstrate that even over a period as short as six months, there is evidence of systematic over-estimation; the coefficient on forecast employment in all three periods is significantly less than unity.[9] Whilst the intercept is not significantly different from zero by a standard t test, the hypothesis of unbiasedness (column 6) is clearly rejected. Furthermore the evidence of heteroscedasticity in the equation (column 7) also violates the clear requirement for a 'good' prediction that there should be white noise error.[10] There is little evidence of a sectoral or time period component to these results.[11] Nor do the results appear to be affected by measurement error.[12]

Table 11.3 Regressions of actual on forecast employment

(1) Dependent variable	(2) Independent variable	(3) α	(4) ß	(5) R^2	(6) F*	(7) BP(1)
E_1	F_0E_1	0.24 (0.21)	0.85 (0.04)	0.79	9.50	42.00
E_2	F_0E_2	0.49 (0.23)	0.72 (0.04)	0.72	32.48	18.04
E_3	F_1E_2	0.49 (0.21)	0.77 (0.04)	0.76	20.70	7.94

Notes
F* is the test of unbiasedness, i.e. no intercept and unity slope parameter, with 2 degrees of freedom in the numerator, 117 degrees of freedom in the denominator. The critical value is 3.07 at 5% significance.

BP(1) is the Breusch-Pagan Test of Heteroscedasticity based on the regression of the squared residuals on the squared fitted values, with one degree of freedom.

The next stage was to consider the determinants of the forecast error (measured here by $E_{t+i} - F_tE_{t+i}$). On the basis of the discussion in section IV, the effects of a range of respondent, business and environmental character-istics on the error were first examined, using multiple regression.[13] Given the small size of the error, and the short time periods covered, it was not surprising to find that for most of the characteristics considered, it was not possible to detect a systematic influence. They are not therefore discussed further here. However, as can be seen from Table 11.4, it was possible to identify some factors which have a systematic effect on the errors. These factors are: employment in the business at the time of the forecast (E_f); the length of time the firm has been in business (BUSAGE); and the growth of the market (MKTGRWTH), measured here as the proportionate change in employment between 1992 and 1993.

Table 11.4 The divergence between actual and forecast employment: some results

Dependent variables	Equation (1) $E_1 - F_0E_1$	Equation (2) $E_2 - F_0E_2$	Equation (3) $E_2 - F_1E_2$	Equation (4) $E_2 - F_1E_2$
Independent variables				
INTERCEPT	−0.26 (0.22)	−0.23 (0.27)	0.16 (0.25)	0.11 (0.25)
$\ln E_f$	−0.42 (0.22)**	−1.00 (0.27)*	−0.69 (0.23)*	−0.56 (0.21)*
$\Delta \ln E_f$				−1.03 (0.47)*
MKTGRWTH				−0.05 (0.03)**
BUSAGE	0.18 (0.09)*	0.26 (0.10)*	0.04 (0.09)	
R^2	0.05	0.11	0.08	0.10
F	3.31*	7.16*	5.05*	4.32*
RR(1)	3.27	1.56	4.22	2.66
BP(1)	0.07	0.24	0.19	0.93

Notes: RR is the Ramsey-RESET test of functional form; * indicates significant at 5%; ** indicates significant at 10%.

The "best" specification – Equation (4) in Table 11.4 – includes not only the log of employment ($\ln E_f$) but also its proportionate rate of change over the preceding period ($\Delta \ln E_f$). The latter variable is of course only available for the second six month period, and is not therefore incorporated into Equations (1) and (2), both of which relate only to the first round of forecasting. Equation (3) provides a direct comparison for the second six month period with the results presented in Equations (1) and (2).

One plausible, though tentative, interpretation of the results is that respondents may in some way be incorrectly interpreting the information embodied in their own employment figures, including the rate of employment change. For example, if a respondent believes that the expansion path he is on is linear, when it is in fact logarithmic,[14] then he will make systematic errors. Prediction over short periods will appear superficially good, due to the approximation of the logarithmic to the linear path, but it will deteriorate over a longer period. If this interpretation is correct, it will have important implications for long term planning, which may sometimes involve substantial capital investment, by small businesses. This point is highlighted by the smaller ß coefficient (in absolute terms) on the employment term in the second equation in Table 11.3, suggesting that the effects of misinterpreting the signals from current employment are exacerbated over time.

There is some limited evidence from Equation (4) in Table 11.4 that market growth (MKTGRWTH) – which does of course partially capture an industry effect – may temper any error generated by the firm's misperception of the data on its own employment. The systematic, rather than random, effect of market growth on forecast error suggests that firms may not be predicting developments in their own markets well enough and this in turn may have consequences for the accuracy of their employment forecasts.

There is also some suggestion from the positive sign on BUSAGE in Equations (1) and (2) in Table 11.4 that misinterpretation of the employment data may be mitigated by the length of time the firm has been in business. One explanation for this finding may be that firms which are further along their expansion path are more likely to have approached the limits of their expansion, and thus be at a fairly static and predictable employment level. It may also be the case, that as the business grows older, the collective wisdom it embodies increases and enables a truer assessment to be made.

It is important to note that there is no significant intercept in any of the four equations. The absence of such an intercept is consistent with there being no unexpected shocks affecting all the sample firms identically during the forecast period.

VI. Discussion and conclusions

This paper has provided a preliminary examination of the relationship between forecast and out-turn employment for a sample of very small firms over a short time horizon. Our tentative finding is that very small firms tend to systematically over-estimate their prospects. We have no grounds for supposing that the results are caused by unexpected shocks during the forecast periods.[15] Table 11.2 shows that on average the two six month forecasts exceed the out-turn by between 17 and 20 per cent, and by about 40 per cent for the twelve month period. The larger average error for the longer period is not surprising given the greater uncertainty associated with this period. Any interpretation of these data must bear in mind the methods used to obtain the forecast, and in particular, the absence of any penalties for wrong forecasts. It is difficult however to envisage any practical situation in which *all* possibilities for bias are absent. And, as indicated in section IV, every effort was made in this study to reduce any distortion that might arise as a result of the survey method used.

The conclusion of this paper that small firms tend to over-estimate future employment is consistent with the very high failure rate[16] among small young firms. Ganguly (1985, p. 140) for example has shown that over 50 per cent of firms registering for VAT in the U.K. have deregistered by the sixth year. Data on U.K. company registrations HMSO (1994) indicate that only 40 per cent of those incorporated in 1988 were still active in March 1994. It is possible that some of the owners of these firms may have *planned* to leave business within six years. It is however more likely that most started out with longer term intentions, i.e. they over-estimated their prospects.

Further support for this view comes from data collected in the study on the 21 respondents who left business in the year between the first and last interviews, but who are not included in this analysis. In the first interview, only two of these respondents forecast that their 'most likely' employment level in twelve months time would be zero. When the 'failed' respondents were asked in the first interview to predict the likelihood of their being in business in twelve months time on a five point scale – from zero ('will definitely not be in business') to four ('will definitely be in business') – sixteen gave scores of three or four.

Our results suggest that one plausible reason for the over-estimation of future prospects is that firms may not be correctly interpreting the information embodied in data on their own employment record when they make their forecasts, although greater business age and (windfall) market growth may temper the inaccuracy of the estimates. If this interpretation of the results is correct, then one policy option might be to stimulate a greater awareness (and realism), on the part of those involved in very small firms, of business development patterns. Such a policy would however involve public funding. It would thus be necessary to argue that the social net returns from an initiative of this kind are positive. This may not be the case: it may be socially more efficient to let businesses find out their mistakes from experience, notwithstanding the high personal costs that are often involved.

We would be the first to acknowledge the very tentative nature of our results and the interpretation we have given to them. Clearly further work is required. At least two avenues of future research may be suggested. First, it would be useful to explore precisely how forecasts are formed.[17] For example, do very small firms use any rules of thumb in making judgements about the future? Second, it would be helpful to examine any learning in forecasting that takes place over time. We hope to continue monitoring the forecasting performance of the present sample. This monitoring should be able to identify and explain changes over time.

Appendix on response rate

The Customs and Excise letter was mailed to 1014 individuals who registered for VAT in March/April 1993 at offices in Carlisle, Middlesbrough and Washington. Registrations resulting from a change of name or business reorganisation were excluded from this mailing. In total 305 responses were obtained. Of these, 47 (15.4 per cent) were ineligible, either because they were not independent private sector firms, or because they were not located in the Northern Region. (The geographical coverage of the VAT offices identified above sometimes extends outside the Region.) A further 89 (29.2 per cent) respondents replied but refused to cooperate, leaving 169 willing to participate. Of this 169, 24 (7.9 per cent of the original 305) left business after the initial mailing. A further 24 were excluded from consideration in this paper because although they remained in business, they did not participate throughout the survey period. The reasons for this non-participation varied and included illness, migration from the region, and a withdrawal of cooperation, usually because of other commitments.

If it is assumed that the ineligibility rate (15.4 per cent) is applicable to the *whole* sample of 1014, the number of firms who might in principle have been eligible to participate was 858. If it is then assumed that the "death rate" applicable to the 169 (14.2 per cent) applied to this 858, then the total number of respondents eligible to participate and not ruled out on the grounds that they died during the survey period was 736. The response rate in the text is obtained by expressing the number of actual participants as a percentage of this figure of 736. The assumptions in this calculation are not subject to direct test. However the *a priori* arguments for and against their validity are fairly evenly balanced.

Notes

1 This paper is based on research financed by the ESRC (ref R000234670). The support of the ESRC, and of the University of Durham, which provided some subsequent funding, are gratefully acknowledged. HM Customs and Excise also provided much appreciated and valuable assistance at the beginning of the project. In addition, thanks are due to Paul Kattuman, Simon Parker and Jonathan Rougier, of the Department of Economics, Durham University, and to three anonymous referees for providing helpful comments which significantly improved the exposition. All errors and omissions however remain the sole responsibility of the authors.
2 Hakim (1989) however briefly discusses the issue. She refers to (but does not present) the results of a quarterly survey of small businesses conducted by the

Small Business Research Trust, to argue that 'plans tend to be realistic and closely parallel actual growth'. It should be noted however that the methodology used in the survey and the size distribution of the survey firms are not comparable with those presented in this paper.

3 Defined here as the areas covered by the Carlisle, Middlesbrough, Newcastle and Washington VAT offices.

4 When the non-survivors who did not predict their own departure from business are included, all the regressions in Table 11.4 continue to show systematic bias, with the estimates of ß lower than those reported in the table, but with no discernible change in the standard errors. The predictive failure test shows that there is a significant difference between survivors and non-survivors. The relevant results are available from the authors.

5 More complex questions – involving, for example, a probability distribution of possible future employment outcomes – were considered, but rejected on the grounds that respondents might have difficulty in giving meaningful responses. It should also be noted that forecasts relating to other aspects of business, e.g. turn-over, and to other time periods, were also provided by respondents, but these are not considered in this paper.

6 Using data from DTI (1993), chi-squared tests for homogeneity of the distribution of firms between different sectors in the North and the sample, and the UK and the sample, were run. In neither case was the distribution significantly different at the 5 per cent. Details are available from the authors.

7 It has been suggested (see Lovell, 1986) that the influence of events unforeseen at the time of the forecast would ensure greater variation in out-turn employment than in forecast employment. The data in Table 11.1 do not show such greater variation.

8 We compared the proportionate error, ignoring the sign, in the two periods for each firm. 39 per cent showed some improvement, and 31 per cent a deterioration. The rest of the sample showed neither an improvement nor a deterioration.

9 Even if a White adjustment for heteroscedasticity is made, the coefficient is still significantly less than one. (Technically of course the appropriate test of unbias-edness is that reported in column 6 of Table 11.3 *together with* the presence of white noise error.)

10 The tests used here for unbiasedness and non systematic errors are directly analo-gous to those used for rational expectations in the macroeconomics literature. For a good survey, see Holden et al. (1985) and Sheffrin (1983).

11 The classification of very small firms of the kind covered in this study into separ-ate sectors is somewhat problematic. However, when the sample was subdivided into the three broad categories of distribution, other services and production, and each of these sectors was examined separately for each of the three time periods, we found that in seven of the nine cases the null hypothesis was rejected at a significance level of less than one thousandth of one per cent.

12 To test for the presence of such error, we followed Beach et al. (1995) using the procedure proposed by Wald (1940) and Bartlett (1949). The results from the grouping exercises reinforce those presented in Table 11.4 where unbiasedness is clearly rejected. Full results are available from the authors.

13 These characteristics, measures of which were all obtained from the interview sur-vey, are as follows. *Respondent characteristics*: age; education; motivation; own and family's experience in business; period in business; perceived prospects of survival; and previous employment. *Business characteristics:* age; employment; employ-ment of professionals/managers in labour force; importance of larger customers; innovativeness; level of competition; geographical nature of the markets served; method of contacting largest customer; and sources of supply. *Environmental vari-ables:* market growth; and market turbulence. Full details of the way in which these variables are measured and regression results are available from the authors.

14 There is some limited evidence for this: see for example the profile depicted in Johnson (1986, p. 86).
15 In the light of our findings, it is interesting to note the results of the study by Beach et al. (1995) on price expectations by vegetable growers in the U.S. These authors found that such growers typically over-estimated future prices for their produce. They also argued that such over-estimation was not due to unexpected shocks in the forecast period.
16 The term 'failure' is used here as a catch-all phrase covering all forms of movement out of business. Not all such movement implies that the business involved was financially unsuccessful. However, as the text suggests, withdrawal from business activity in the early stages is often not intended, and in this sense can be regarded as an expression of failure.
17 Some results of a preliminary exploration of this issue are available from the authors.

References

Bartlett, M. S., 'Fitting of Straight Lines When Both Variables are Subject to Error', *Biometrics* 5, 207–212.
Beach, E. D., J. Fernandez-Cornejo and N. D. Uri, 1995, 'Testing the Rational Expectations Hypothesis Using Survey Data from Vegetable Growers in the U.S.A.', *Journal of Economic Studies* 22, 46–59.
Brown, C., J. Hamilton and J. Medoff, 1990, *Employers Large and Small*, Cambridge, Mass.: Harvard UP.
Curran, J., J. Kitching, B. Abbott and V. Mills, 1993, *Employment and Employment Relations in the Small Service Sector Enterprise: A Report*, ESRC Centre for Research on Small Service Sector Enterprises, Kingston Hill: Kingston Business School, Kingston University.
Daly, M., 1990, 'The 1980s – A Decade of Growth of Enterprise', *Employment Gazette* 98, 553–565.
Daly, M., M. Campbell, G. Robson and G. Gallagher, 1991, 'Job Creation 1987–89: The Contributions of Large and Small Firms', *Employment Gazette* (November) 589–596.
DTI, 1993, *VAT Registrations and Deregistrations in the U.K. (1980–1991)*, mimeo, London: DTI.
Ganguly, P., 1985, *Small Business Statistics and International Comparisons*, edited by Graham Bannock, and published on behalf of the Small Business Trust, London: Harper and Row.
Hakim, C., 1989, 'Identifying Fast Growth Firms', *Employment Gazette* 97, 29–41.
HMSO, 1994, *Companies in 1993/94*, London: DTI.
Holden, K., D. Peel and J. L. Thompson, 1985, *Expectations: Theory and Evidence*, Basingstoke: Macmillan.
Johnson, P. S., 1986, *New Firms: An Economic Perspective*, London: Unwin Hyman.
Johnson, P. S., and C. Conway, 1997, 'How Good are the U.K. VAT Registration Data at Measuring Firm Births?', *Small Business Economics*, forthcoming.
Keeble, D. P., P. Tyler, G. Broom and J. Lewis, 1992, *Business Success in the Countryside*, London: Department of the Environment.
Lovell, M., 1986, 'Tests of the Rational Expectations Hypothesis', *American Economic Review* 74, 99–110.

Madson, J. B., 1994, 'Tests of Rationality Versus An "Over Optimist" Bias', *Journal of Economic Psychology* **15**, 587–599.

Mason, C. and C. Harrison, 1993, 'Spatial Variations in The Role of Equity Investments in the Financing of SMEs', in J. Curran and D. Storey (eds.), *Small Firms in Urban and Rural Locations*, London: Routledge.

Morissette, R., 1993, 'Canadian Jobs and Firm Size: Do Smaller Firms Pay Less?', *Canadian Journal of Economics* **26**(1) 159–174.

Reilly, K.T., 1955, 'Human Capital and Information: The Employer Size – Wage Effect', *Journal of Human Resources* **XXX** (1), 1–18.

Risseeuw, P. and E. Masurel, 1994, 'The Role of Planning in Small Firms: Empirical Evidence from a Service Industry', *Small Business Economics* **6**, 313–322.

Scott, M., I. Roberts, G. Holroyd and D. Sawbridge, 1989, *Management and Industrial Relations in Small Firms*, Research Paper 70, Department of Employment: London.

Sheffrin, S. M. 1983, *Rational Expectations*, Cambridge: CUP.

Storey, D., 1994, *Understanding the Small Business Sector*, London: Routledge.

Storey, D. and S. Johnson, 1987, *Job Generation and Labour Market Change*, Basingstoke: Macmillan.

Wald, A., 1940, 'The Fitting of Straight Lines if both Variables are Subject to Error', *Annals of Mathematical Statistics* **11**, 284–300.

12 Small business growth in the short run [1]

Peter Johnson, Cheryl Conway, Paul Kattuman

Source: *Small Business Economics*, 1999, 12 (2), 103–112.

This paper examines the determinants of short run employment growth in very small firms in the Services sector. The study shows evidence of non linearities in the growth–size relationship, and it is argued that these non linearities reflect the short run constraints that small firms face in adjusting to demand shocks. The paper also suggests that there are other systematic influences on growth apart from size. The paper draws on survey evidence from the Northern Region of the United Kingdom.

1. Introduction

This paper examines the determinants of short run employment growth in small firms in the Services sector. Small firm growth has of course been the subject of extensive research[2] (for a good survey, see Storey, 1994, ch. 5). Some justification for yet another study is therefore necessary. Such justification may be found in four features of this paper. First, we explore an important and interesting question that has not been investigated sufficiently in empirical work to date: the way in which short run constraints, embodied in the firm's short run cost function, influence the dynamics of the growth process of small firms. Our results are consistent with such constraints 'anchoring' short run firm growth. Second, we focus on firms in the Services sector,[3] whereas, as Variyam and Kraybill (1992) have pointed out, most firm growth studies have been concerned with Manufacturing.[4]

Third, we consider growth over a twelve month period, a time span that is shorter than that of many other small firm studies (Mata's work (1994) is an exception).[5] This focus is appropriate from both a managerial and policy viewpoint. Most owner managers in the kind of very small firm considered here are unlikely to have a planning horizon, even of an informal kind, beyond twelve months,[6] and policy initiatives will need to reflect that fact. There is also evidence to suggest that a twelve month planning horizon is a major concern of bank managers when assessing funding requests from new small firms (Deakins and Hussain, 1993).[7] For these reasons, insights into the determinants of growth over the period of a year are likely to be important.

This will be particularly true for the newest firms which may be able to survive for a short initial 'honeymoon' period, but which need to grow beyond their initial size if they are to survive once this period is over.[8]

Finally, our study largely concentrates on micro businesses, most of them with less than five employees (see section 3 below). A number of studies of firm growth are of course based on coverage of the full size range, including small size bands,[9] but these studies do not provide the kind of focus on very small firms that is provided here. Reid's study (1995) of 73 'small entrepreneurial' firms in Scotland, in which 78 per cent of the sample had between one and ten employees (Reid, 1993, p. 192), is more relevant for our purposes, but it is an exception.

The plan of this paper is as follows. In section 2 we discuss considerations that underlie the growth equation that we estimate. Section 3 describes the data and variables which come from a survey of firms in the North of England. Some empirical results are presented in section 4.

The final section discusses the results of the study, and makes some suggestions for further work.

2. The growth equation

Our approach is to model the short term growth of small firms as a function of firm size, and of a number of underlying economic influences, thus

$$\dot{S}_{i,t} = f(S_{i,t-1}, \mathbf{X}_{i,t-1}) \qquad (1)$$

where

$\dot{S}_{i,t}$ = firm i's proportionate growth between $t-1$ and t;
$S_{i,t-1}$ = the size of the ith firm at time $t-1$;
$\mathbf{X}_{i,t-1}$ = a vector of variables relating to characteristics of the owner, the firm and its market environment at time $t-1$.

Much has been written about the dynamics of firm growth,[10] and in particular the relationship between firm growth and size. Most empirical work on this relationship has focused on testing Gibrat's Law which posits that the growth rates of firms are random, and are independent of their sizes.[11] This simple stochastic process, with modifications and suitable boundary conditions, generates positively skewed size distributions of firms.[12]

Gibrat's Law is consistent with the assumption that no size of firm is more or less favoured than any other: costs are constant over all output levels (Ijiri and Simon, 1977, p. 141). While this assumption may be appropriate over the longer term, it may have less validity in the short run, where firms are likely to be significantly constrained in their freedom to alter their size. We set out below how these short run constraints may affect the growth–size relationship.

Consider a profit maximising firm operating in a market for a relatively homogeneous service. At any give time, the technology of the firm – embodied in its installed physical capital – is relatively fixed; in other words, there is a specific short run cost function associated with the firm under observation. We assume that this short run average cost function is u-shaped, so that there is a unique short run profit maximising output $(Q_{\pi\max})$.[13] We also assume that demand varies stochastically over time. These random demand variations may be thought of in terms of changes in orders placed with particular firms, which nevertheless operate in competitive markets, where prices are broadly 'given'. The observed growth behaviour of the firm will depend on (a) the nature of stochastic demand, and (b) the way in which the firm changes its output rate optimally in response to shocks to demand.

If we limit attention to a single short run cost function, the conditional mean of the firm growth rate under the above assumptions will be negatively related to size, with zero growth expected at $Q_{\pi\max}$. We first establish that in the face of positive and negative shocks, responses of firms operating away from $Q_{\pi\max}$ will be asymmetric. We need to show that positive shocks will induce larger responses than negative shocks for firms operating at scales less than $Q_{\pi\max}$ and that positive shocks will induce smaller responses than negative shocks for firms operating at scales higher than $Q_{\pi\max}$.

This is not difficult. Consider first, a firm on the left of $Q_{\pi\max}$. Responding to a negative shock will lower short run profits, while responding to a positive shock will raise them. Given a relatively sticky price, the firm will be eager to respond to positive shocks up to $Q_{\pi\max}$. Faced with a negative demand shock, however, a firm will try to reduce the severity of this shock by strenuously deploying non-price competitive measures, for instance, by offering better customer service. It is reasonable to conclude that positive shocks will induce larger responses than negative shocks for firms operating at scales less than $Q_{\pi\max}$.

Now consider a firm operating to the right of $Q_{\pi\max}$. Responding to a positive shock will lower its short run profits, while responding to a negative shock will raise them. Given price, the firm will benefit by responding as fully as it can to negative shocks up to $Q_{\pi\max}$. Faced with a positive shock, the firm can and will exercise its choice of not responding to it fully. It can be concluded that negative shocks will induce larger responses than positive shocks for firms operating at scales greater than $Q_{\pi\max}$.

As the cost function is u-shaped, these arguments will apply with even greater force the further away the firm is from $Q_{\pi\max}$. With a positively sloped short run marginal cost curve, and a constant market price, the further to the left of $Q_{\pi\max}$ the firm is located, the bigger the addition (reduction) to profit that a given positive (negative) shock will generate. Thus the smaller the firm is, the more likely it is to respond to positive shocks, and the less likely it is to respond to negative shocks.

For firms located to the right of $Q_{\pi\,max}$, the reverse argument holds: for a given positive (negative) shock, the greater the reduction (addition) to profit. Thus the larger the firm is, the less likely it is to respond to positive shocks, and the more likely it is to respond to negative ones.

The implication of the above analysis is that over the output range relevant to a given short run cost function, the conditional mean of the observed growth rate of the firm can be expected to be negatively related to its size with zero growth expected at $Q_{\pi\,max}$.[14]

While, at any given time, a number of firms in the sample may be located on the same short run cost function, though at different points, other firms will be on different functions. The growth–size relationship discussed above will be repeated for each short run cost function represented by the firms in the sample. Some firms may of course respond to a shock to their size by moving to a new cost function. However such a move, which will typically involve sunk costs, is likely to occur only as the result of a large shock. Since small shocks are more probable than large shocks there are likely to be relatively few cases of transit to a different cost function.

The above discussion has implications for what we would expect to observe in a cross section sample of the kind examined in this paper. Given that a number of distinct short run cost functions are likely to be covered by the sample, we would expect to see a non-linear growth–size relationship[15] with the degree of non-linearity being dependent on the number of cost functions spanned by the sample. Within the range of each cost function we expect to see a negatively sloped growth–size relation; between each pair of successive costs functions, will lie regions where size is unstable, populated only by the relatively few firms 'in transit'. Clearly, the growth equation should not be restricted to a prespecified degree of non-linearity in size. A non-parametric regression can help in determining this specification. The appropriate parametric specification will thus be a polynomial regression with the highest order determined by data.

We have included a number of additional variables to control for influences on growth apart from size. These are considered in the next section.

3. The data and variables

Data sources

This empirical part of our study draws on data from a previous study undertaken by two of the authors (Johnson and Conway, 1995). These data cover the growth record of 75 businesses in Services over the period winter 1993/1994 to winter 1994/1995. *[The data sources used to identify these businesses are discussed on pp. 148–9.]*

There are no obvious grounds for supposing that self-selection by co-operating respondents has generated any serious bias in relation to the characteristics of either the businesses or the respondents involved. All the firms are however by definition *survivors*. Since non survivors are more likely to have experienced negative growth, their exclusion could induce some bias into the results. Furthermore, for a given negative growth rate, the smallest of the firms may be less likely to survive, and hence be more likely to be eliminated from the sample. This in turn will tend to bias upwards the growth of the smallest firms in the sample. While we have been unable to correct for these selection biases, we note that Dunne and Hughes (1994) in their analysis of the growth–size relationship for over 2000 U.K. companies, found that their efforts to incorporate adjustment for sample selection bias did not affect the substance of their results (see also Reid, 1993, p. 199).

The data used in this paper were collected via interviews in the winter of 1993/94, and the winter of 1994/95.

No firm in our study had more than 18 full time equivalent (FTE) employees.[16] Eighty five per cent had five FTEs or less. Employment in the full sample grew by 5.5 per cent over the year.

Measuring growth and size

Growth is measured here in FTEs. Following Barkham et al. (1996), employment is chosen as it is the most robust of the measures available to us. Other measures, e.g. profits, assets or turnover, may of course yield different results. It is also true that firms are unlikely to have employment per se as a goal. Nevertheless employment provides one important indicator of business development, and it is of course relevant for policy.

The particular measure of growth[17] used is

$$(\log E_{94/5} - \log E_{93/4})$$

where E is FTE employment, and the subscripts refer to the winter for which the employment data were obtained. Although the precise date in the winter of 1993/94 on which each firm was initially interviewed varied, the second interview in the winter of 1994/95 was carried out as near as possible to the first anniversary of that initial interview.

Initial size (labelled SIZE hereafter) is also measured in terms of FTEs.

Some underlying determinants of growth

In equation (1), we included, alongside initial size, a vector of variables relating to characteristics of the owner, the firm and its market. Variable selection has been determined by the choice of factors examined in previous studies and by the availability of data. The latter consideration means that our study omits some potentially important influences on growth (e.g. financial variables). At the same time however we have been able to incorporate some potentially relevant variables not considered in previous studies. We now deal with each set of characteristics in turn.

Characteristics of owners

Education (EDUC)

In the 17 studies recently reviewed by Storey (1994, p. 127), the influence of education (variously measured) was either insignificant (9), or positive and significant (8). There are no grounds from this work for suggesting that education has a negative effect on growth.

One plausible interpretation of the results of these studies is that although in some cases education may do little to enhance entrepreneurial drive and ambition, in others it may provide an important source of human capital relevant for business activity. This is likely to be particularly true where the business is involved in highly technical fields. In this study EDUC is a dummy variable with the value zero when the respondent has no A levels, and 1 when he has obtained one or more.[18]

Experience (AGE; TIMTR)

Numerous firm growth studies have incorporated a business age variable. The *a priori* arguments for such a variable are however mixed. On the one hand the framework of entrepreneurial learning provided by Jovanovic (1982) may be used to argue that older businesses are better at growing, ie they gain in experience. On the other hand an ageing business may run out of corporate energy. (These arguments can of course be reconciled by a nonlinear relationship between age and growth, with the relationship being positive in the early years, and negative in later years.) A number of studies (e.g. Dunne and Hughes, 1994 and Evans, 1987) have reported a negative effect of age on growth. Dobson and Gerrard's study (1989) however – which concentrates on rather smaller firms – shows a positive effect.

Here, we focus on the age and experience of the business *owner*, rather than of the business itself. This is a more satisfactory approach in a study where most firms are very small, and where the driving force behind the growth of the business is its owner.

We used two measures of the owner's experience, each representing a different level of generality. The first is the age of the respondent (AGE). As with business age, the *a priori* arguments here are conflicting. On the one hand, general experience increases with age, and this may enhance growth opportunities. On the other hand it may be argued that owners become more set in their ways as they age. Their experience then hinders rather than helps their business. Furthermore, the energy that they have to devote to business interests declines with age. Like the trees in Marshall's (1920, p. 263) forest, ". . . sooner or later age tells on them all." As a result the business eventually disappears. Empirical studies of the effect of age on growth have generated mixed results (Storey 1994, p. 134), with a number of studies unable to identify a significant effect of age either way.[19]

Age captures the general experience of the business owner. It might however be expected – again following Jovanovic's (1982) analysis of entrepreneurial learning – that the length of experience in the business (TIMTR) would have an impact on business growth. A key argument here is that actual participation in business discloses to its owner – in a way which is not possible by other means – whether or not he/she has the necessary skills to engage in such activity. The more efficient operators remain in business; the less efficient exit. Thus the individual who has already been in business, and who has therefore tested his skills, is more likely to make a success of the current venture than someone who is in business for the first time. However, Storey et al. (1989, p. 29) were unable to detect any impact of previous 'own account' experience on growth.

TIMTR is the number of years spent by the respondent as owner of the business.

Characteristics of the business

The entry process (METHENT)

We distinguished between those respondents who entered business by setting up from scratch, and those who bought an existing business. The choice of entry method may have a variety of implications for subsequent growth. First, business energy may be greater in a newly established operation. The founder needs to get established as quickly as possible, and this may entail faster growth. Someone taking over a business may encounter opposition from existing staff who already have established working procedures. At the same time a new owner of an existing business does not face the teething problems arising from setting up *ab initio* and may be able to treat the business taken over as an established base for growth. The dummy variable used here is METHENT, which takes the value zero for businesses set up from scratch, and 1 for those which were already going concerns. The expected sign on this variable is ambiguous.

Legal status (STATUS)

Unincorporated businesses have less access to the funds necessary to finance growth than incorporated businesses. The personal liability associated with sole proprietorships and partnerships is likely to act as an inhibitor of fund raising by the owner(s), as well as making the business less attractive to institutional investors. Unincorporated status may also provide a signal that owners are reluctant to expand via incorporation either because they do not wish to contemplate losing control, or because they find the greater disclosure required uncongenial. Some empirical support for these arguments comes from Hakim's (1989) study of fast growth firms. Reid (1993, pp. 201–203) however included legal status in his analysis of net asset growth in small businesses in Scotland, but found it insignificant.[20] The dummy variable used here (STATUS) takes the value zero for unincorporated businesses and 1 for incorporated businesses.

Customers (IMPCUST; TYPCUST)

The inclusion of a variable (IMPCUST) which measures the proportion of sales accounted for by the three biggest customers provided an opportunity to examine whether customer dominance affects growth. Adams and Hall (1993) included a similar variable in their study, but were agnostic about whether its effect on growth would be positive or negative. Too much reliance on one customer may curtail opportunities for growth, and limit the firm's learning about the market place.[21] However if the biggest customer is growing relatively rapidly, with the supplying firm sharing in that growth, then it may make sense for the firm to focus its attention on that customer, especially where a strong relationship is established.

Our data set also makes it possible to explore whether the sector – public or private – in which the firm's biggest customer is located has any impact on the firm's growth. One reason for thinking that this variable might be important is that there may be differences in the continuity of orders from customers in the two sectors, with the private sector more likely to change suppliers than their public sector counterparts. Once a firm is on the 'preferred' list of public sector contractors, it is relatively more likely to receive a steady stream of orders, and in this way growth may be encouraged. The two sectors are however subject to different financial constraints which may in turn affect ordering patterns and hence growth. The variable used here is TYPCUST which takes the value zero where the most important customer is the public sector and one where that customer is in the private sector.

Staffing (PPROF)

The measure used to capture the character of the firm's employment which in turn might have implications for growth, is PPROF, the number of 'professionals' expressed as a proportion of the labour force. This variable is included on the grounds that the more 'high powered' the firm's labour force, the more growth potential it has. Against this, is the argument that growth may be impeded where highly qualified staff are required because of the recruitment and salary costs involved.

The characteristics of the market

A single market characteristic – turbulence (TURB) – is utilised. Following Beesley and Hamilton (1984), turbulence is measured here as the *sum* of the birth and death rates. VAT registration and deregistrations, both deflated by the stock of VAT registered businesses, are used as proxies for birth and death rates respectively. Turbulence is included here as a measure of the vibrancy of the market. High levels of turbulence tend to reflect considerable dynamism in economic activity, and hence more opportunities for growth; both Beesley and Hamilton (1984) and Audretsch and Acs (1990) find turbulence positively related to industry growth.

4. Results

The results of our econometric analysis of the determinants of firm growth are reported in Tables 12.1 and 12.2. Following the analysis in section 2, we

Table 12.1 Some results

	Equation 1	*Equation 2*
CONSTANT	0.42	0.66***
EDUC	−0.29**	−0.28**
AGE	−0.51 E-3	
TIMTR	0.00	0.46E-4
METHENT	0.01	
STATUS	0.01	0.30
SIZE	−0.14***	−0.43***
SIZESQ	0.01**	0.06***
SIZECUB		−0.002***
IMPCUST	0.00	
TYPCUST	0.00	
PPROF	−0.33**	−0.37***
TURB	0.00	0.00
EDUCxPPROF	0.31	0.33*

Notes
*** Significant at 1 per cent.
** Significant at 5 per cent.
* Significant at 10 per cent.

The variables are as follows:

EDUC (Education): no A levels = 0; A levels = 1.

AGE (Age): age of respondent (years).

TIMTR (Time traded): period respondent in business (years).

METHENT (Method of entry): set up from scratch = 0; purchased business = 1.

STATUS (Status): unincorporated = 0; incorporated = 1.

SIZE Opening FTEs

SIZESQ SIZE squared.

SIZECUB SIZE cubed.

IMPCUST (Important customers): % of turnover sold to 3 most important customers.

TYPCUST (Type of customer): most important customer in public sector = 0; most important customer in private sector = 1.

PPROF % of employment accounted for by professionals.

TURB (Turbulence): sum of birth and death rates.

Note: Full details of the precise measures used are available from the authors.

Table 12.2 Fit and diagnostic statistic

	Equation 1	Equation 2
R^2	0.07	0.22
F	F (12,62) = 1.47	F(9,65) = 3.36***
Functional form	χ^2 (1) = 0.09 (0.76)	χ^2 (1) = 0.34 (0.56)
Normality	χ^2 (2) = 0.43 (0.81)	χ^2 (2) = 2.20 (0.33)
Heteroscedasticity	χ^2 (1) = 0.20 (0.66)	χ^2 (1) = 0.02 (0.89)
n	75	75

Notes
P values in brackets.
*** Significant at 1 per cent.
** Significant at 5 per cent.
* Significant at 10 per cent.
F( ) tests the significance of the regression. The functional form test is Ramsey's RESET using the square of the fitted values; the normality test is the Jarque-Bera test based on a test of skewness and kurtosis of the residuals; and the heteroscedasticity test is a composite test based on the regression of squared residuals and squared fitted values.

ran regressions with SIZE entered in progressively higher powers, alongside all the other variables outlined in the previous section. Non linear formulations, including a variety of interaction effects involving the latter were examined, following a systematic protocol.

Our first equation, Equation 1 still fails the F test, and is not therefore considered further here. We then proceeded in accord with section 2 by entering SIZE in higher powers, and by dropping variables that appeared irrelevant. Equation 2, which passes all the diagnostic tests, is the result. It incorporates SIZE, its square (SIZESQ), and its cube (SIZECUB).

All three size variables are highly significant. Figure 12.1 plots out the growth–size relationship implied by Equation 2. This figure suggests *two* short run profit maximising employment levels at around two and seventeen employees.

Equation 2 omits a number of the variables listed in section 2 and included in Equation 1. These are AGE, METHENT, IMPCUST and TYPCUST. Both EDUC and PPROF have negative signs – although both variables are now significant – and the interaction term is positive and significant. The significant negative signs on EDUC and PPROF are at first sight a little puzzling. They may however hint that for the very small Services businesses covered in this study, it is possible for the owners and employees to be overqualified in a way which generates a level of frustration that is inimical to growth. There is however some evidence from the interaction term that

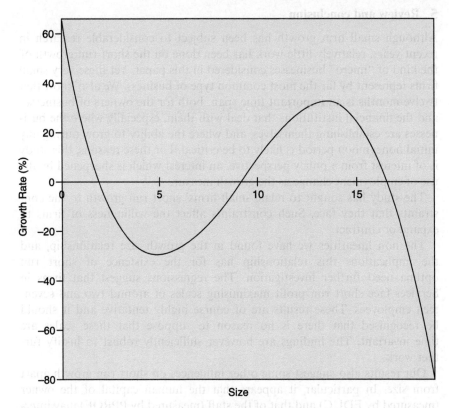

Figure 12.1 The growth–size relationship: firms in services.

complementarities between the human capital of the owner and his work-force may generate a positive effect on growth.

Perhaps the most interesting aspect of the results reported in Tables 12.1 and 12.2 relates to their implications for short run size. Figure 12.1 suggests that Services firms are either best kept very small or are expanded significantly. It is interesting that the higher profit maximising scale of around seventeen employees is in the middle of the range at which salaried managerial appointments tend to be made by small firms (Storey, 1994, p. 13). This scale thus implies a significantly different managerial style. Expansion beyond a very small size may thus require a discrete jump to a significantly larger operation. One potential explanation for this finding is that beyond a very small scale, the typical owner of a Services firm finds himself badly stretched, especially where he is relying on the quality of personalised customer service to maintain his business. Only by introducing some formal management structure can this problem be overcome, but significantly greater scale is necessary to support such a development.

5. Review and conclusion

Although small firm growth has been subject to considerable research in recent years, relatively little work has been done on the short run growth of the kind of "micro" businesses considered in this paper. Yet these very small firms represent by far the most common type of business. We also know that twelve months is an important time span, both for the owners of businesses and the financial institutions that deal with them, especially where the businesses are establishing themselves, and where the ability to grow during any initial honeymoon period is likely to be critical. For these reasons, this study is of interest from a policy perspective, an interest which is sharpened by the use of employment change as the growth measure.

The study has sought to relate small firms' short run growth to the constraints that they face. Such constraints affect the willingness of firms to expand or contract.

The non linearities we have found in the growth–size relationship, and the implications this relationship has for the existence of short run optima need further investigation. The regressions suggest that firms in Services face short run profit maximising scales of around two and seventeen employees. These results are of course highly tentative and it should be recognised that there is no reason to suppose that these scales are time invariant. The findings are however sufficiently robust to justify further work.

Our results also suggest some other influences on short run growth apart from size. In particular, it appears that the human capital of the owner (measured by EDUC) and that of the staff (measured by PPROF) may interact to have a positive effect on growth.

There is clearly much scope for further work, particularly in the analysis of the growth–size relationship in the short run, and in the impact technological constraints may have. Differences between sectors also need exploration.[22] Refinement in the measurement of the variables used, and extension to other time periods and geographical areas, would similarly repay further investigation.

An awareness of the growth–size relationship, and of which output levels are likely to be most profitable, is likely to be of importance in formulating small firms policy, since there is little point in encouraging firms via training or other means to produce at scales which generate lower returns. This study also suggests that contraction may sometimes be an appropriate response to demand shocks.

Notes

1 This paper is based on work carried out under ESRC Research Grant R00234670. The help of the ESRC, and of the University of Durham which provided some subsequent funding, are gratefully acknowledged. Thanks are also due to HM Customs and Excise who provided invaluable assistance in the early stages of the

project, to the many business owners who co-operated in the survey, and to Denis O'Brien, Suma Athreye, Richard Tiffin and anonymous referees who provided valuable comments on an earlier draft of this paper. Any errors and omissions however remain the sole responsibility of the authors.

2 Examples of recent studies include Dobson and Gerrard (1989), Reid (1993, ch. 11) and Barkham et al. (1996). Audretsch (1995), Mata (1994) and Wagner (1994) have looked at the growth of new firms, the majority of which start off in a small way. As indicated later in the text, there is also an extensive literature on the general relationship between size and growth: see note 11. A number of recent contributions to this literature – for example, Evans (1987), Dunne and Hughes (1994) and Hart and Oulton (1996) – include relatively more firms in the smaller size ranges than most other studies.

3 This sector is defined as Sections G to K in the U.K.'s 1992 Standard Industrial Classification.

4 The emphasis on Manufacturing is also evident from the surveys by Geroski (1995) and Sutton (1997).

5 Apart from Mata's study, the nearest we have been able to get is two years (Woo et al., 1989, quoted in Storey, 1994, p. 125). Dobson and Gerrard (1989), Adams and Hall (1993) and Reid (1995) all use a three year time horizon.

6 In their study of real estate agencies in the Netherlands, Risseeuw and Masurel (1994) show that only 14 per cent of firms had a written plan with a financial paragraph, and that reviews of plans usually occurred on a yearly basis.

7 For the importance of short term (i.e. one year or less) finance for small firms, see Keasey and Watson (1994).

8 We are grateful to an anonymous referee for making this point.

9 See for example the references in note 2.

10 For recent 'stochastic' optimising models, see Hopenhayn (1992) and Ericson and Pakes (1995). Jovanovic (1982) is also relevant and is referred to in the following section.

11 Thus $\dot{S}_{i,t} = u_{i,t}$ where $u_{i,t}$ is a normally distributed error term with a constant variance. For a good review of the theoretical and empirical issues raised by Gibrat's Law, see Hay and Morris (1990, p. 537f), Scherer and Ross (1990, pp. 144–145), Dunne and Hughes (1994) and Sutton (1997). For empirical work in the small firm sector, see Reid (1993) and Dobson and Gerrard (1989).

12 Sutton (1997) has shown that this result still holds even when the Gibrat's Law assumption is significantly relaxed.

13 Defined as the output where (a rising) short run marginal cost equates with price. This output level is not necessarily that at which short run average costs are minimised.

14 See Leonard (1987) for a model that is similar in spirit, but where it is assumed that the process of adjustment to a fixed, desired size is subject to stochastic shocks.

15 Evans (1987), Hall (1987) and Hart and Oulton (1996) have explored non-linearities in the growth–size relationship, but they have not focused on an economic rationale for nonlinearity.

16 One part-time employee working less than 30 hours per week, equals 0.5 FTE.

17 An alternative measure of growth $((E_{94/95} - E_{93/94})/(0.5E_{93/94} + 0.5E_{94/95}))$ was also tried. The use of the mean size in the denominator is suggested by Davis et al. (1996) as one way of ameliorating any regression-to-the-mean bias, although Caree and Klomp (1996) have queried the validity of this approach. The results using this measure did not differ significantly from those reported in section 4.

18 An alternative measure of educational achievement (degree; no degree) was in fact tried, but produced less clear results.

19 Some studies have tested a quadratic relationship, but again most of the results show no significant effect.

176   *Growth and development*

20 However it was significantly positive in his profitability equation.
21 These problems may be further increased if the customer firm is significantly bigger than the supplier, and is able to exploit this size difference.
22 Equations (1) and (2) were also run for thirty firms in the Production sector, but both equations failed the diagnostic tests.

References

Adams, G. and G. Hall, 1993, 'Influences on the Growth of SMEs: An International Comparison', *Entrepreneurship and Regional Development* **5**, 73–84.
Audretsch, D. B., 1995, 'Innovation, Growth and Survival', *International Journal of Industrial Organization* **13**, 441–457.
Audretsch, D. B. and Z. Acs, 1990, 'The Entrepreneurial Regime, Learning and Industry Turbulence', *Small Business Economics* **2**, 119–128.
Barkham, R., G. Gudgin, M. Hart and E. Harvey, 1996, *The Determinants of Small Firm Growth. An Inter-Regional Study in the United Kingdom 1986–90*. Regional Policy and Development Series 12, Regional Studies Association. Jessica Kingsley Publishers, London.
Beesley, M. E. and R. T. Hamilton, 1984, 'Small Firms' Seedbed Role and the Concept of Turbulence', *Journal of Industrial Economics* **XXXIII**, 217–231.
Caree, M. and L. Klomp, 1996, 'Small Business and Job Creation: A Comment', *Small Business Economics* **8**, 317–332.
Davis, S. J., J. Haltiwanger and S. Schuh, 1996, 'Small Business and Job Creation: Dissecting the Myth and Reassessing the Facts', *Small Business Economics* **8**, 297–315.
Deakins, D. and G. Hussain, 1993, 'Overcoming the Adverse Selection Problem: Evidence and Policy Implications from a Study of Bank Managers on the Importance of Different Criteria Used in Making a Lending Decision', in F. M. Chittenden, M. Robertson and D. Watkins (eds.), *Small Firms: Recession and Recovery*, London: Paul Chapman Publishing, pp. 177–187.
Dobson, S. and B. Gerrard, 1989, 'Growth and Profitability in the Leeds Engineering Sector', *Scottish Journal of Political Economy* **36**, 334–349.
Dunne, P. and A. Hughes, 1994, 'Age, Size, Growth and Survival: U.K. Companies in the 1980s', *Journal of Industrial Economics* **XLII**, 115–140.
Ericson, R. and A. Pakes, 1995, 'Markov-perfect Industry Dynamics: A Framework for Empirical Work', *Review of Economic Studies* **62**, 53–82.
Evans, D. S., 1987, 'The Relationship between Firm Growth, Size, and Age: Estimates for 100 Manufacturing Industries', *Journal of Industrial Economics* **XXXV**, 567–581.
Geroski, P. A., 1995, 'What Do We Know about Entry?', *International Journal of Industrial Organization* **13**, 421–440.
Hakim, C., 1989, 'Identifying Fast Growth Small Firms', *Employment Gazette* **97**, 29–41.
Hall, B. H., 1987, 'The Relationship between Size and Firm Growth in the U.S. Manufacturing Sector', *Journal of Industrial Economics* **XXXV**, 583–606.
Hart, P. E. and N. Oulton, 1996, 'Growth and Size of Firms', *Economic Journal* **106**, 1242–1252.
Hay, D. and D. Morris, 1990, *Industrial Economics and Organization*, Oxford: Oxford University Press.

Hopenhayn, H. A., 1992, 'Entry, Exit and Firm Dynamics in Long Run Equilibrium', *Econometrica* **60**, 1127–1150.

Ijiri, Y. and H. A. Simon, 1977, *Skew Distributions and Sizes of Business Firms*, Amsterdam, North-Holland.

Johnson, P. S. and V. Conway, 1995, *End of Award Report to the ESRC (R000234670): A Cohort Study of Recently Formed Businesses: the First Stage*, mimeo.

Jovanovic, B., 1982, 'Selection and Evolution of Industry', *Econometrica* **50**, 649–670.

Keasey, K. and R. Watson, 1994, 'The Bank Financing of Small Firms in the U.K.: Issues and Evidence', *Small Business Economics* **6**, 349–362.

Marshall, A., 1920, *The Principles of Economics*, 8th edn., reset 1949. London: Macmillan.

Mata, J., 1994, 'Firm Growth during Infancy', *Small Business Economics* **6**, 27–39.

Reid, G. C., 1993, *Small Business Enterprise. An Economic Analysis*, London: Routledge.

Reid, G. C., 1995, 'Early Life-cycle Behaviour of Micro-firms in Scotland', *Small Business Economics* **7**, 89–95.

Risseeuw, P. and E. Masurel, 1994, 'The Role of Planning in Small Firms: Empirical Evidence from a Service Industry', *Small Business Economics* **6**, 313–322.

Scherer, F. M. and D. Ross, 1990, *Industrial Market Structure and Economic Performance*, Boston: Houghton Mifflin Company.

Storey, D. J., R. Watson and P. Wynarczyk, 1989, *Fast Growth Businesses: Case Studies of 40 Firms in Northern England*, Department of Employment, Research paper No 67, (1989), London.

Storey, D., 1994, *Understanding The Small Business Sector*, London: Routledge.

Sutton, J., 1997, 'Gibrat's Legacy', *Journal of Economic Literature* **35**, 40–59.

Variyam, J. N. and D. S. Kraybill, 1992, 'Empirical Evidence on Determinants of Firm Growth', *Economic Letters* **38**, 31–36.

Wagner, J., 1994, 'The Post-entry Performance of New Small Firms in German Manufacturing Industries', *Journal of Industrial Economics* **42**, 141–154.

Woo, C. Y., A. C. Cooper, W. C. Dunkelberg, U. Daellenwach and W. J. Dennis, 1989, 'Determinants of Growth for Small and Large Entrepreneurial Start-ups', paper presented at Babson Entrepreneurship Conference.

13 The size–age–growth relationship in not-for-profit tourist attractions

Evidence from UK museums [1]

Peter Johnson

Source: *Tourism Economics*, 2000, 6 (3), 221–232.

The size–age–growth relationship in private-sector firms has been very widely studied. This paper examines the same relationship in not-for-profit tourist attractions, focusing attention on UK museums. The current scale and structure of the UK museums sector, including the extent of entry and exit, are described. The author then briefly discusses the nature of the size–age–growth relationship in the for-profit sector, and assesses the relevance of this relationship for museums. He then presents empirical findings for UK museums. The evidence suggests that, outside the government sector, both the mean growth and the standard deviation of growth tend to decline with size, a finding consistent with evidence for the for-profit sector. No significant effect of age was detected. Finally, there is evidence – again, outside the government sector – that the net impact of charging is negative. The closing section of the paper concludes the study and suggests avenues for further work.

The size–age–growth relationship in private-sector firms has been very widely studied. (For a summary of the empirical evidence, see the review by Caves;[2] for a comprehensive analysis of UK data, see the study by Dunne and Hughes.[3]) In contrast (to the author's knowledge), there has been no analysis of the issue in not-for-profit organizations, a description that fits many tourist attractions. This paper addresses some of this imbalance by examining the relationship in the UK museums sector.[4] This sector has a significant role to play in determining the UK's attractiveness as a tourist destination: museums account for just under twenty per cent of all visits to attractions in the UK. The evidence on income elasticities of demand for museum visiting – see the studies by Darnell *et al*[5] – also suggests that, *ceteris paribus*, patronage is likely to grow more than proportionately as incomes grow. Insights into museum growth are therefore likely to be important.

The paper is structured as follows. In the next section, the current scale and structure of the UK museums sector are summarized. This section also looks at entry and exit. In the subsequent section, the nature of the size–age–growth relationship in the for-profit sector is briefly discussed, and the relevance of this relationship for museums is assessed. In the fourth section, some empirical findings are presented for UK museums. The final section concludes the study.

For the purposes of this paper, 'museums' includes galleries.

The UK museums sector: its current scale and structure

A measure of scale: visit numbers

The most commonly used measure of the scale of museums – and the one that is used here – is the number of visits.[6] This measure may fail to capture many dimensions of a museum's output, such as the contribution to collection, preservation or scholarship, but it is the one that is both most readily available and most relevant to the current policy emphasis[7] on access.

Visits are counted in a variety of ways: for a review, see Allin.[8] Counts tend to be relatively more accurate when a museum charges. There has been considerable debate about the reliability of those visit figures that are estimated.[9]

Estimates of the number of and visits to UK museums

There are various estimates of the scale of the sector in the UK.[10] The Museums Association, probably the most comprehensive source, listed 2,539 museums for 1997/98.[11] In 1998, the (then) Museums and Galleries Commission (MGC) estimated that about 1,800 museums were eligible for registration under its Registration Scheme.[12] This scheme was established in 1988 to set minimum quality and professional standards.[13] The annual survey of tourist attractions sponsored by the British Tourist Authority (BTA) and the English Tourist Board (ETB)[14] listed 1,745 museums on its 1997 database.[15] Museums on this database are self-defining; no attempt is made to impose a particular definition. Estimated visit numbers vary from 81 to 88 million.[16]

Although the BTA/ETB database is less rigorous, in terms of definitions, than its MGC counterpart, it has a longer run of visit data, and is used later in the paper in a more formal analysis of museum growth.

Types of museum

The MGC source provides a detailed categorization of museum by type. Some summary data are provided in Table 13.1. The diversity of museum types is immediately apparent. Numerically, the independent and local authority museums dwarf the other categories – together they account for over 79 per cent of all museums – but they are responsible for a significantly smaller share (55 per cent) of visits: see the fourth column of Table 13.1. This reflects the fact that the average number of visits to these museums, especially the independents, is dwarfed by that of the nationals.

Table 13.1 Visitors to UK museums, 1997

Museum category	No of museums on data base (% of total in brackets)	No of museums for whom visit numbers are available	Estimated total number of visits (000s) (% of total in brackets)[a]	% founded: Before 1900	% founded: After 1980	Average number of visits (000s)	% of museums with visit numbers <5000	% of museums with visit numbers >100000
Armed Services	109 (6.2)	88	5,842.4 (6.6)	0.9	21.5	53.6	22.7	14.8
English Heritage	25 (1.4)	12	944.9 (1.1)	0.0	20.0	37.8	8.3	16.7
Independent	679 (38.6)	556	17,054.4 (19.4)	8.5	39.3	25.1	44.2	5.1
Local authority	721 (40.9)	640	30,937.4 (35.2)	18.1	22.3	42.9	14.1	9.0
National	48 (2.7)	43	25,400.4 (28.9)	34.8	19.6	529.2	0.0	74.5
National Trust	88 (5.0)	28	4,559.0 (5.2)	0.0	18.6	51.8	3.6	10.7
University	91 (5.0)	70	3,266.5 (3.7)	48.8	5.8	35.9	38.7	12.9
All	1761 (100.0)	1437	88,005.1 (100.0)	14.4	27.8	50.0	26.8	10.0

Note
a Obtained by multiplying the total number of museums in each category by the average size of those providing visitor data.

Source: MGC data base.

Two other features of the museums sector may also be noted from Table 13.1. First, museums vary enormously in their visit numbers. Over a quarter of museums are very small, attracting fewer than five thousand visits per year. Small independent and university museums are particularly prevalent. In contrast, three-quarters of the national museums have annual visits of over 100,000. Second, new and very old museums exist side by side. The national, university and, to a lesser extent, local authority museums all have significant roots in the nineteenth century. At the same time, the sector has experienced considerable formation activity in recent years: at least 18 per cent of museums in each category apart from one (university museums) were formed after 1980. Nearly 40 per cent of the independents come into this category.[17]

Entry and exit

Nearly all museums start with low levels of patronage. For example, of the 123 museums formed between 1989 and 1997 for which visit data in the year of opening are available from the BTA/ETB database, 61 per cent had under 10,000 visits. Only 11 per cent – nearly all in the public sector – had over 50,000 visits. Comprehensive data on museum exits are not available. However, information supplied to the author from the BTA/ETB data set[18] identifies 232 museums which have closed since 1978, and provides their last recorded visit numbers. About 54 per cent had under 5,000 visits per year, and 72 per cent under 10,000 visits per year. Less than 5 per cent had over 50,000 visits per year. These figures on entry and exit may be related to the size distribution of museums. For example, in the mid-1980s 46 per cent of museums on the BTA/ETB database[19] had under 10,000 visits per year while 17 per cent had over 50,000 visits.[20] Thus both the entry and exit rates are very much higher at the bottom end of the size distribution. These findings are consistent with the literature on the births and deaths of commercial firms.[21]

The size–age–growth relationship

In this section the relationship between the size, age and growth of firms in the for-profit sector is examined. At the end of the section we examine how far similar arguments might apply to museums.

Size

Much of the work on the relationship between growth and size in the for-profit sector has been devoted to testing the Law of Proportionate Effect (LPE) – or Gibrat's Law[22] as it is sometimes known – which postulates that growth in firm size in any time period is a stochastic phenomenon. If LPE holds, size has no impact, positive or negative, on growth. Two implications of LPE are that: (a) the mean growth of firms is the same for different size bands; and (b) the standard deviation of growth rates is also the same in all size bands.[23]

The recent empirical evidence[24] suggests that both mean growth and the standard deviation of growth rates decline with firm size, although the study by Dunne and Hughes[25] suggests that, at least for UK firms, this may occur only up to a threshold size, after which LPE may operate.[26]

Age

The age of a firm may have both positive and negative effects on its growth. On the positive side, age provides an indicator of the accumulated learning experience 'embodied' in a firm's management.[27] Managers become better able to identify growth opportunities and the most effective way of taking advantage of those opportunities. They may also become more adept at dealing with 'shocks'. The possibility of a negative impact of age arises because there may a Marshallian-type loss of institutional energy, and commitment to innovation.

Various studies have found a negative effect of firm age on growth although, significantly, Dobson and Gerrard's study[28] of small firms found a positive effect, a reflection perhaps of the vigour of youth.

Do these arguments apply to museums?

The above paragraphs relate to private-sector firms. Not-for-profit museums face different constraints, for example in terms of public policy, and, by definition, have different objectives. However, like private-sector firms, they face a very wide variety of influences on their growth, including management skills, access to public funding, the economic environment in which they operate, consumer tastes, and the presence of competing attractions, the combined impact of which may lead to growth appearing to be a stochastic phenomenon. LPE is therefore an appropriate hypothesis to explore. And, as with private-sector firms, both negative and positive effects of age on growth may be postulated.

The evidence for the museums sector

Table 13.2 presents some data on growth experience between 1989 and 1997 by visit numbers, and by broad museum category which help to throw light on whether the implications discussed in the previous section hold for museums. The categorization of museums broadly reflects different funding regimes. The BTA/ETB database is used here (and in Table 13.3) because it provides a longer run. The 'local authority' category in this database is common to both the BTA/ ETB and MGC data. The 'government' and 'private' BTA/ETB categories are not so easily mapped on to the MGC categories, but, very roughly, the former corresponds to the MGC 'national' category, while the latter covers the other MGC categories.[29]

Table 13.2 Growth and size in UK museums

Visitor numbers in 1989	Local authority museums			Government museums			Private museums[a]		
	Number	Mean growth, 1989–97	Standard deviation: growth	Number	Mean growth, 1989–97	Standard deviation: growth	Number	Mean growth, 1989–97	Standard deviation: growth
1–5,000	35	0.87	2.03	5	3.87	4.31	92	0.45	1.41
5,001–10,000	24	0.70	1.10	3	−0.09	0.28	65	0.19	1.14
10,001–25,000	82	0.23	1.01	7	0.24	0.50	74	0.14	1.04
25,001–50,000	71	0.08	0.54	6	0.24	0.57	41	0.07	0.80
50,001–100,000	44	−0.01	0.55	2	1.13	Na	24	−0.03	0.36
100,001–250000	27	−0.18	0.52	9	0.30	0.46	14	−0.11	0.36
250,001–500,000	10	−0.44	0.32	8	0.16	0.18	7	−0.06	0.33
More than 500,000	6	−0.31	0.20	9	0.17	0.32	2	−0.16	0.35
TOTAL	299	0.20	1.04	49	0.61	1.73	319	0.20	1.10

Note
a Excludes three museums with a growth rate over the period of over 1,900 per cent.
Source: BTA/ETB data base analysed by the author.

Table 13.3 Size and growth of UK museums, by year of opening

Period	Local authority			Government			Private		
	Mean size, 1997 (000s) (n in brackets)	Mean growth, 1987–97 (n in brackets)	Standard deviation: growth, 1987–97 (n in brackets)	Mean size, 1997 (000s) (n in brackets)	Mean growth, 1987–97 (n in brackets)	Standard deviation: growth, 1987–97 (n in brackets)	Mean size, 1997 (000s) (n in brackets)	Mean growth, 1987–97 (n in brackets)	Standard deviation: growth, 1987–97 (n in brackets)
Pre 1901	77.9 (72)	0.05 (56)	0.57 (56)	1,244.7 (16)	0.16 (15)	0.42 (15)	68.2 (31)	0.36 (23)	1.46 (23)
1901–1920	66.7 (41)	0.26 (31)	0.76 (31)	518.9 (1)	0.46 (1)	–	27.1 (17)	0.34 (10)	0.65 (10)
1921–1940	39.3 (50)	0.03 (33)	0.50 (33)	163.2 (10)	2.04 (9)	3.4 (9)	20.6 (35)	–0.08 (24)	0.74 (24)
1941–1960	31.8 (42)	0.40 (33)	1.81 (33)	100.7 (7)	0.20 (5)	0.46 (5)	20.1 (46)	0.46 (27)	1.86 (27)
1961–1980	30.1 (125)	0.08 (86)	0.93 (86)	137.7 (18)	0.07 (15)	0.34 (15)	28.2 (125)	–0.11 (148)	0.93 (148)
Post 1980	41.8 (137)	0.52 (59)	1.22 (59)	62.1 (18)	1.66 (4)	1.94 (4)	22.6 (137)	0.28 (83)	1.08 (83)
TOTAL	45.4 (469)	0.20 (299)	1.04 (299)	376.7 (70)	0.61 (49)	1.73 (49)	26.3 (677)	0.20 (319)	1.10 (319)

Source: BTA/ETB database analysed by the author.

Before the data are examined, two potentially important sources of bias, frequently discussed in the analysis of the growth of private-sector firms, should be considered, as they may influence any analysis of the size–growth relationship. The first, attrition bias, arises because, inevitably, only survivors are included in the table. The argument here is that small, slow growing organizations are more likely to disappear altogether than their larger counterparts, who will tend, instead of closing, to slide down the size distribution. If this argument holds, surviving small organizations will tend to be those whose growth record is good – the poor growers have disappeared – whereas the larger survivors will have a much more mixed record. Fortunately, the limited evidence available suggests that selection bias may not be a major problem, certainly in the for-profit sector.[30] It is also evident from the MGC and BTA/ETB data sets that large numbers of museums are able to survive on very small visit flows.

The second potential source of bias arises from what is known as 'regression to the mean'.[31] Essentially such a problem arises if there are transitory changes in scale, with these changes occurring around some constant long-run scale. Museums may be 'large' at the beginning of the period under study because they have experienced a transitory increase in size in the previous period. 'Small' museums, conversely, may have experienced a decline in the previous period. An implication of this hypothesis is that, on average, low-patronage museums will grow, and high-patronage museums will decline as they revert back to their long-run size. There is, however, much debate in the firm growth literature about the validity of such a scenario, with some authors[32] arguing that it is inappropriate to assume that there is some constant long-run size to which a firm tends. Certainly there is no evidence of such a size in the museums field.

Table 13.2 suggests a number of interesting features of the museum size–growth relationship. First, it is the smallest size band in each category that has, by a margin, the highest average growth and the largest standard deviation. Second, in both the private and local authority categories, the mean growth and standard deviation of visit growth generally decline with size. No clear picture emerges, however, in the government category. The preliminary conclusion that might be drawn from Table 13.2 is that there is no evidence to support the application of LPE in the museums sector. If anything, the mean growth rate and its variability decline with visit numbers.

Table 13.3 examines the links between age and visit numbers by setting out the relationship between the year of opening, and current size and growth over the period 1989–97 by type of museum. There is no clear pattern in the mean or standard deviation of visit growth rates 1989–97; for example, the highest mean growth in each category is in museums opened in different periods. It is, however, clear that the museums formed before 1900 have on average the highest patronage in all three categories. Average size also consistently declines (at least) up to 1960 across all three categories.

Some regression results

Ordinary least squares regression was used to supplement the descriptive statistics presented above.

Adapting Dunne and Hughes's approach,[33] the estimated model is a multiplicative one of the following form:

$$\left(\frac{V97}{V89}\right)_i = \alpha(V89_i)^{\beta-1}(A_i)^{\gamma}(C_i)^{\delta}\,\varepsilon_{it} \tag{1}$$

where
$V89_i$ = number of visits to museum i in 1989
$V97_i$ = number of visits to museum i in 1997
A_i = the age of museum i
C_i = a dummy indicating whether a museum charges $(C_i = e)$ or is free $(C_i = 0)$.

The rationale for including $V89_i$ and A_i has been given above. It should be noted that where $\beta > 1$, larger museums grow faster than their smaller counterparts; and that where $\beta < 1$, the reverse is the case. LPE postulates that $\beta = 1$; hence size has no effect on growth. C_i is included as it might be expected that the existence of an admission charge would affect visit growth. There is, however, some ambiguity over the expected sign. On the one hand, a charging museum might tend to grow more slowly than one that is free, since newcomers to museum visiting are likely to choose a free-admission museum over a charging one. On the other hand, charging may provide additional revenues that can be ploughed back to improve the quality of the visitor experience, and hence the number of visits. The coefficient will thus pick up the net effect of these influences.[34] A constant growth rate, α, is assumed to affect all museums.

Equation 1 may be rewritten:

$$\ln V97_i = \ln\alpha + \beta\ln V89_i + \gamma\ln A_i + \delta\ln C_i + \ln\varepsilon_{it} \tag{2}$$

Equation 2 was estimated for the period 1987–97 for each of the three museum categories on the BTA/ETB database. Use of the full samples results in equations that all fail the Jarque–Bera test for normality, and in the case of private museums, also the tests for functional form and heteroscedasticity. We then proceeded pragmatically by excluding, on the basis of the OLS residuals, the most extreme outliers from each category.[35] This procedure generated more satisfactory results in terms of the diagnostic tests, although it should be noted that there was no change in the signs, and little adjustment in the magnitude and reported significance of the coefficients.[36]

The results of the estimations are given in Table 13.4. We examine first the museums in the public sector. Equations 1 and 2 relate, respectively, to local

Table 13.4 The growth of UK museums: some regressions

(i) RESULTS

	Equation 1 Local authority	Equation 2 Government	Equation 3 Private
Constant	1.52*** (0.24)	0.48 (0.38)	0.68*** (0.22)
$\ln V_{it}$	0.87††† (0.02)	0.99 (0.04)	0.94††† (0.02)
$\ln A_i$	−0.03 (0.04)	−0.03 (0.09)	−0.01 (0.04)
$\ln C_i$	−0.33*** (0.07)	−0.18 (0.12)	−0.18** (0.7)

(ii) FIT AND DIAGNOSTIC STATISTICS

	Equation 1 Local authority	Equation 2 Government	Equation 3 Private
N	286	44	302
R^2	0.84	0.97	0.88
F Statistic	(3, 282) 499.16 [0.00]	(3, 40) 385.42 [0.00]	(3, 298) 710.46 [0.00]
Functional form[a]	1.74 [0.19]	0.00 [0.95]	4.93 [0.03]
Normality[b]	0.91 [0.63]	3.40 [0.18]	3.13 [0.21]
Heteroscedasticity[c]	2.95 [0.09]	1.72 [0.19]	13.87 [0.00]

Notes
***　Significantly different from zero at one per cent
**　Significantly different from zero at five per cent
†††　Significantly different from one at one per cent
[a]　Ramsey's RESET test using the square of the fitted values
[b]　Based on the test of skewness and kurtosis of residuals
[c]　Based on the regression of squared residuals on squared fitted values
Figures in round brackets in the top half of the table are standard errors; figures in square brackets in the bottom half of the table are p values

authority museums and government museums. Both equations have an excellent fit and satisfy the diagnostic tests.

The reported coefficients suggest that smaller museums tend to grow faster (ie $\beta < 1$) in the local authority category, although there is no evidence that this is so with government museums. These findings are, of course, consistent with the evidence in Table 13.2. In both equations, age has a negative sign, but is not significant, a result in line with Table 13.3. The coefficient on the charging dummy is significant for local authority museums, but it is insignificant for the government museums. One possible explanation for this difference is that the prestigious status of many nationals – a status not typically shared by local authority museums – and the swamping of admission charges by all the other costs (eg travel) of visiting such museums, most of which are located in the capital, make charging of very little consequence.

The results for private museums in Equation 3 mirror the local authority results. However although this equation has a good fit, it fails the test for heteroscedasticity. Examination of the residuals in this equation suggests that the explanatory power of the equation is at its highest at the bottom and top of the size distribution.[37] Further work is required to assess why this should be so.

Review and conclusions

This paper provides an exploratory review of the size–age–growth relationship in the UK museums sector. It suggests that, outside the government category, the mean growth in visits, and the variation in visit growth, tend to decline with size. Little support for LPE was therefore obtained from the data. This finding is consistent with recent evidence from the for-profit sector. No significant effect of museum age on growth was identified. Finally, there is some suggestion that charging has a negative impact on visits to local authority museums, although this does not appear to be the case with government museums.

These results raise a number of issues. For example, *why* do the more highly patronized museums tend to grow more slowly? Do they, for example, find it relatively more difficult to respond to new ideas and developments? Do they tend to be less responsive to changing visitor needs? If the answer to either or both these questions is 'yes', how might responsiveness be increased? The greater instability in growth rates found among the smaller museums highlights the greater risks they face – a characteristic confirmed by the exit data – and poses the question of whether anything can be done to reduce the risk, for example by better training or planning.

The evidence on charging suggests that some care should be taken over proposals to raise admission prices in local museums, especially where access is a policy objective.

Clearly there is plenty of scope for further work on museum growth. Such work is likely to need a combination of formal statistical analysis based on a richer data set than is currently available, and detailed case study work.

Notes

1   The author is grateful to Bethan Hurst at the Museums and Galleries Commission and to Max Hanna for supplying much of the data on which this paper is based.

He is also grateful to Adrian Darnell for his comments on earlier drafts and to Prudence Cox who provided research assistance. The author is, however, solely responsible for the interpretation of the data and for all errors and omissions.

2 R.E. Caves, 'Industrial organization and new findings on the turnover and mobility of firms', *Journal of Economic Literature*, Vol 36, No 4, December 1998, pp 1947–1982.

3 P. Dunne and A. Hughes, 'Age, size, growth and survival: UK companies in the 1980s', *Journal of Industrial Economics*, Vol 42, No 2, 1994, pp 115–140.

4 Some institutions classified as museums may operate as commercial enterprises. They are, however, a small minority. There is a growing economics and business literature on museums. See, for example, B. Frey and W.W. Pommerehne, *Muses and Markets, Explorations in the Economics of the Arts*, Blackwell, Oxford, 1989; M. Feldstein, ed, *The Economics of Art Museums*, University of Chicago Press, Chicago, 1991; P.S. Johnson and R.B. Thomas, *Tourism, Museums and the Local Economy*, Edward Elgar, Aldershot, 1992; J. Heilbrun and M. Gray, *The Economics of Art and Culture*, Cambridge University Press, Cambridge, 1993; B. Frey, 'Cultural economics and museum behaviour', *Scottish Journal of Political Economy*, Vol 41, No 4, August 1994, pp 325–355; and A. Peacock, 'A future for the past; the political economy of heritage', *Proceedings of the British Academy*, Vol 87, 1995, pp 189–243. For some recent studies, see P.S. Johnson and R.B. Thomas, Special Issue on the Economics of Museums, *Journal of Cultural Economics*, Vol 22, Nos 2–3, 1998, pp 73–207. There is, however, little on the analysis of museum growth.

5 A.C. Darnell, P.S. Johnson and R.B. Thomas, 'Beamish Museum – modelling visitor flows', *Tourism Management*, Vol 11, 1990, pp 251–257; and A.C. Darnell, P.S. Johnson and R.B. Thomas, 'The demand for local government authority museums: management issues and hard evidence', *Local Government Studies*, Vol 24, No 4, Winter 1998, pp 77–94.

6 The number of visits to a museum is not, of course, equivalent to the number of (different) visitors, since many visits are repeats. Repeat visits are an important element in total visitor demand, particularly in well established museums. For a discussion of repeat visiting, see A.C. Darnell and P.S. Johnson, 'Repeat visits to attractions: a preliminary economic analysis', *Tourism Management*, forthcoming.

7 *A New Approach to Investment in Culture*, Department for Culture, Media and Sport, London, 1998.

8 P. Allin, Recording Visitor Numbers at National Museums and Galleries, unpublished paper, Department for Culture, Media and Sport, London, 1996, quoted in S.W. Creigh-Tyte and S. Selwood, 'Museums in the UK: some evidence on scale and activities', *Journal of Cultural Economics*, Vol 22, Nos 2–3, 1998, pp 151–165.

9 Creigh-Tyte and Selwood, *op cit*, Ref 8.

10 One of the reasons for this variation is that estimates use different definitions. For example, heritage attractions are included in the museums estimate in *Museum Workforce Survey: an Analysis of the Workforce in the Museum, Gallery and Heritage Sector in the United Kingdom*, a report prepared for the Museum Training Institute by M. Scott, M. Klemm and N. Wilson, Management Centre, Bradford University, MTI, Bradford, 1993.

11 *Museum Yearbook 1997/8*, Museums Association, London, 1997.

12 *Museum Focus*, Museums and Galleries Commission, London, 1998.

13 *Registration Scheme for Museums and Galleries in the United Kingdom*, Museums and Galleries Commission, London, 1995.

14 Now the English Tourism *Council*.

15 *Sightseeing in the UK 1997*, BTA/ETB Research Services, London, 1998.

16 These estimates are based on the figures provided by the MGC and BTA/ETB surveys, adjusted for those museums not providing visit numbers.

17 The importance of recent entry in the UK museums sector is mirrored in the US data: see J. Blau, 'Art museums', in G.R. Carroll and M.T. Hannon, eds, *Organizations in Industry: Strategy, Structure and Selection*, Oxford University Press, Oxford, 1995, pp 87–114.

18 The author is grateful to Max Hanna for supplying this material. All errors and omissions in the interpretation of the data are, however, the sole responsibility of the author.

19 *Sightseeing in the UK 1987*, BTA/ETB Research Services, London, 1987, p 22.

20 These figures on size distribution are taken from the BTA/ETB database and are not directly comparable with the MGC data given in Table 13.1 It is likely that the BTA/ETB survey picks up relatively more smaller museums. The BTA/ETB figures have remained fairly static over time. Hence, although the entry and exit data cover different periods, the size distribution of existing museums has been fairly constant.

21 Caves, *op cit*, Ref 2.

22 R. Gibrat, *Les Inégalités économiques*, Receuil Sirey, Paris, 1931.

23 For a useful exposition of LPE, see D.A. Hay and D.J. Morris, *Industrial Economics and Organization*, 2nd ed, Oxford University Press, Oxford, 1991, pp 537–541. There are other implications of LPE that are not considered here.

24 F.M. Scherer and D. Ross, *Industrial Market Structure and Economic Performance*, 3rd ed, Houghton Mifflin, Boston, MA, 1990, pp 144–145; and Caves, *op cit*, Ref 2.

25 Dunne and Hughes, *op cit*, Ref 3.

26 There may have been some changes in the size–growth relationship over time (see Dunne and Hughes, *op cit*, Ref 3), with studies in the 1950s showing an advantage for the larger firm. It should also be noted that a number of earlier studies (eg P.E. Hart and S.J. Prais, 'The analysis of business concentration: a statistical approach', *Journal of the Royal Statistical Society*, Series A, No 119, Part 2, 1956, pp 150–181; and H.A. Simon and C.P. Bonini, 'The size distribution of business firms', *American Economic Review*, Vol 48, No 4, September 1958, pp 607–617, did not find that the variation in growth declined with size.

27 P. Geroski, 'What do we know about entry?' *International Journal of Industrial Organization*, Vol 13, No 4, December 1995, pp 421–440.

28 S. Dobson and B. Gerrard, 'Growth and profitability in the Leeds engineering sector', *Scottish Journal of Political Economy*, Vol 36, No 4, November 1989, pp 334–352.

29 Respondents to the BTA/ETB survey self-classify their museums. One of the most significant classification problems arises over the allocation of museums relating to the Armed Services. The BTA/ETB 'government' category includes some of these museums, while others are listed under 'private'.

30 Dunne and Hughes, *op cit*, Ref 3; and G. Reid, *Small Business Enterprise: an Economic Analysis*, Routledge, London, 1993, p 199.

31 See, for example, S.J. Davis, J. Haltiwanger and S. Schuh, *Small Business and Job Creation: Dissecting the Myth and Reassessing the Facts*, NBER Working Paper Series 4492, National Bureau of Economic Research, Cambridge, MA, 1993.

32 For example, M. Carree and L. Klomp, 'Small business and job creation: a comment', *Small Business Economics*, Vol 8, No 4, August 1996, pp 317–322.

33 Dunne and Hughes, *op cit*, Ref 2.

34 The effects of charging on visitor numbers has been subject to a good deal of debate: see, for example, S. Bailey and P. Falconer, 'Charging for admission to museums and galleries: a framework for analysing the impact on access', *Journal of Cultural Economics*, Vol 22, Nos 2–3, 1998, pp 167–177, and J. O'Hagan,

'National museums: to charge or not to charge?', *Journal of Cultural Economics*, Vol 19, No 1, 1995, pp 33–47.
35 Twelve, five and fifteen outliers were excluded, respectively, from the local authority, government and private categories.
36 Results are available from the author.
37 Details are available from the author.

Part V
Policy

14 Government policies towards business formation

An economic appraisal of a training scheme[1]

P. S. Johnson and R. B. Thomas

Source: *Scottish Journal of Political* Economy, 1984, 31 (2), 131–46.

In recent years there has been a very substantial increase in public support for new and small businesses. The present government sees the small firm sector as a "source of enterprise, innovation and growth" (Department of Industry, 1982b). It aims to "stimulate the development of small businesses and create an economic climate which will promote growth" (*loc cit*). Over 90 policy measures have been introduced by the present government in support of this objective.

Despite this enthusiasm, and despite the commitment of substantial resources in this area, relatively little attention has been given to the serious economic evaluation of the impact of these measures.[2] This paper represents a step towards remedying this omission by reporting a social cost benefit analysis of a government financed training scheme for people who intend to set up in business. It is likely that the basic approach adopted in this paper can be applied with the necessary adaptation to the economic appraisal of other forms of public support for small and new businesses and their owners.

There is of course already a substantial literature on the economic evaluation of manpower training and retraining in industry (see the survey in Ziderman, 1978). Both private and social cost benefit evaluations have been undertaken and considerable attention has been paid to the underlying theoretical issues (Somers and Wood, 1969). However, virtually all of this effort has been focused on the (re)training of employ*ees*, i.e. people who are in paid employment; little or no attention has been given to evaluating the training of people who wish to go into, or are already in, self-employment. ("Self-employment" is used here in a broad non-technical sense, and includes anyone who sets up in business, either by himself or with others; the business concerned may or may not have employees.

The paper is in three parts. The first examines the effects of self-employment training on the output of the economy since these effects are likely to constitute the most important element in both the social costs and benefits of such training (Output effects also figure prominently in most evaluations of conventional training.) The second presents the results of the case study appraisal. The final section presents a conclusion.

I THE EFFECTS OF SELF-EMPLOYMENT TRAINING ON OUTPUT

In this section, two issues are examined: first, the nature of output effects; and, second, the valuation of these effects. We limit our consideration to training which is off-the-job, i.e. where the trainee produces no output during training. The case study in Section II deals with training which is mainly of this type.

The nature of output effects

Costs and benefits

(i) Costs

A key question on the costs side is whether output in the economy is foregone as a result of a person going on the training programme. If the trainee would otherwise have been unemployed then the economy does not suffer loss of output when he enrols. Even if the trainee would have been in paid employment or self-employment, there may still be no output foregone if (for example) the remaining workers in the firm in which the trainee was employed can be persuaded to increase their productivity to a level which is sufficient to compensate for the trainee's absence, or if the trainee is replaced by someone of equal efficiency from the unemployed labour force. This replacement may occur after a process of "bumping". Replacement need not necessarily occur in the firm from which the trainee has come, but in other firms in the same industry. For example, if the trainee is already self-employed at the commencement of the training and closes his business in order to go on the course, his competitors may be able to expand their output by taking on additional workers. Of course if there are no increases in productivity and no unemployed resources available to permit replacement, then output must be foregone.

Such foregone output arising from the trainee's attendance on a course may also induce additional output losses among suppliers of goods and services both "upstream" and "downstream" in the production process.

(ii) Benefits

The measurement of the benefits of training requires some assessment of output changes that result from the training. Possible output changes may be separated into those in the trainee's firm(s) and those in other firms. These are summarised in Table 14.1. For the moment we assume that if additional labour is required for any output expansion, it is available and forthcoming and is drawn, directly or indirectly, from the unemployed pool, i.e. replacement is equal to one. (We look more closely at the replacement issue in the next sub-section.) The term "trainee's firm(s)" in the table covers the one or more firms that are relevant for the with/without training comparison. Without the training he might have been in paid or self-employment. After the training he still faces those two options. Even where the appropriate comparison is between the same type of employment, a change of firm may still nevertheless be involved.[3] The most typical with/without training comparison for our purposes is between "without-training self-employment" and "with-training self-employment", since most of the trainees would have set up anyway, but the analysis can be extended to other combinations.

The increase in the output of the trainee (1(i)), in each period, will be due to improvements in his performance and/or to an increase in his hours of work. The output of employees in the trainee's firm(s) may also be enhanced (1(ii)). This may be due to changes in productivity, for example if the ex-trainee has acquired greater skills at motivating others to achieve higher performance, or is able to organise them in more productive ways.[4] The training may also make participants more expansion orientated and therefore more willing to take on additional workers. Firm founders may, for example, become less hesitant about raising external finance. The combined effects of the training on the output of the trainee and of his employees may be usefully illustrated by the output profile given in Figure 14.1. A "with training" profile may start earlier than a "without training" profile (the training course may persuade someone to set up in business earlier than he would otherwise have done); or it may raise the profile while keeping the start and death dates the same; or it may increase the life of the business; or it may combine some or all of these effects.

Table 14.1 Output changes resulting from the training of an individual

---

1 Output changes in the trainee's firm(s)
   (i)   Increases in output of the trainee[a]
           by increased productivity
           by increased input (hours per week)
   (ii) Increases in output of employees[a]
           by increased productivity
           by increased input (hours per week or number of workers)

---

2 Output changes in other firms
     Increases in output
        (e.g. due to forward or backward links or to imitation of cost reductions in
        the trainee's firm)
     Decreases in output
        (e.g. due to lower costs in the trainee's firm)

Note
a Decreases in output are possible but most unlikely in this category

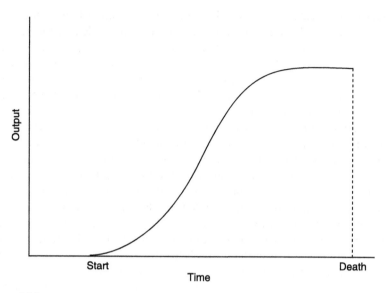

Figure 14.1

These output effects may arise whatever the appropriate pre/post training comparison (paid employment to paid employment; paid employment to self-employment; self-employment to paid employment). For example, even where the trainee returns to paid employment he may still generate output effects for other employees in the firm.

The output effects on other firms are shown in section 2 of Table 14.1. These may be positive or negative. The positive changes may arise from two quite different sources. First, increased output in the trainee's firm will generate consequential increased output of goods and services elsewhere in the production chain. Second, the output of competitors (i.e. firms at the same stage in the production chain) may be raised following the training. The ex-trainee's firm may, for example, introduce a cost-reducing innovation that other firms can imitate. Output in other industries may also increase if the ex-trainee, as a result of the training, develops an innovation that makes possible the production of other goods and services for the first time. Any change in the output of competitors will have "knock-on" implications for the output of goods and services supplied to the industry in question.

The negative output effects are those falls in output of competitors, resulting, for example, from the ex-trainee being able to produce at lower costs as a result of training. If he were able to stop other firms from imitating, however, he may force competitors out of business or at least to reduce their output. Training may also enable someone whose costs would otherwise be above the competitive level to bring them down in line with those of other firms. In such cases there may be no net increase in industry output in the long run. A further possibility is that the introduction of an innovation as the result of training[5] may have adverse effects on output in other industries whose goods become obsolescent.

Replacement and displacement

We now turn to a closer examination of the replacement issue. (Replacement is of course only relevant where increases in output require increased input.) Consider first the case of a trainee who, as a result of the training, changes jobs. It is then necessary to assess whether the job that he would have done, had he not been trained, is filled by someone, perhaps after a chain of bumping, from the pool of unemployed. If it is not, i.e. the replacement rate $R = 0$, then the trainee's *additional* output resulting from the training is all that is counted. Where there is replacement and the job the trainee would have done is done (directly or indirectly) by someone from the unemployed pool, i.e. $R = 1$, then the additional output is the *whole* of the trainee's output in his post-training activity.

So far we have discussed replacement effects in relation to the individual trainee. They may also be relevant in the case of any additional labour,[6] in the trainee's firm or in other firms, which results from increases in output caused by the training. If, following training, an increase in labour input of employees is planned, it is important to know where these extra workers are to come from. If they come from other firms and are then replaced by people from the unemployed pool then $R = 1$ and the relevant benefits are the whole of the addition to output in the trainee's firm that is made by the extra employees. In cases where $R = 0$, workers attracted from other firms are not replaced so there will be a fall in the output of other firms which must be offset against the gain in output of the trainee's firm. Such a reduction in the output of other firms occurs because of constraints on the supply of labour: with zero replacement, any expansion achieved in the trainee's firm necessarily entails a reduction in the output in the firms from which the extra labour has been transferred. However, as indicated in Table 14.1 (under 2) other firms' output may also be reduced because of the effects of the trainee's firm in the product market. Such "product market displacement" will in turn lead to the laying off of workers and a rise in unemployment.[7]

The relationship between the training programme and its ultimate effects on output in the economy are clearly extremely complex. Output-reducing and output-creating effects are likely to be combined. Calculation of the net output effects which is crucial for a cost benefit appraisal, is likely to become more difficult as the time period under consideration lengthens.[8] In estimating output effects, the case study evaluation in Section II makes some attempt to look at output changes in other firms as well as the trainee's firm, but the scope for precise estimation is inevitably limited. In this context it is worth noting that few, if any, conventional training evaluations incorporate estimates of the more indirect effects that such training may have beyond the trainee's own performance narrowly defined.

The valuation of output changes

In a perfectly competitive world in which there is no uncertainty, workers (and other factors) are paid the value of their marginal product. Many social cost benefit appraisals of conventional training programmes have assumed that such a world exists and have therefore used wage changes as a basis for valuing any change in output that is attributable to training. Thus, "with training" and "without training" wage profiles are estimated and the difference is identified as the value of the output effect of the training.

On similar assumptions, the profits of the self-employed worker can be regarded as the competitive return to his co-ordinating and administrative functions. Profits thus measure the value of the founder's contribution to the business. Some of the profit may, of course, represent a "wage" for ordinary productive activities and some may be a return to capital.

Taking wages plus profits as value added, gives a measure of the value of output. Changes in this value added which are attributable to training thus provide a measure of the training effect.

This approach is subject to a number of severe limitations. Not the least is the difficulty that arises over the interpretation of profits, and indeed, wages, when Knightian uncertainty is present.[9] However this approach is probably still the best practical procedure and has been used as the basis for estimating benefits in the case study.

II THE CASE STUDY

The course studied

The self-employment training course with which our cost benefit analysis was concerned was one of the New Enterprise Programmes (NEP) financed by the Manpower Services Commission (MSC). In its publicity material, the MSC has specified the objectives of the NEPs as getting people into business "quicker, with fewer mistakes, and surviving longer".

Normally, participants on an NEP programme must be unemployed at the time they go on the course. Each programme lasts 16 weeks. The first four weeks usually consist of a residential period at a business school and cover class and tutorial work on topics such as marketing and finance. The remaining 12 weeks are non-residential and are spent in starting to put a business proposal into practice, e.g. by undertaking market research. Some participants may even commence trading. During this project period, trainees maintain close contact with the business school. Throughout the course, the trainee is paid a Training Opportunities Scheme (TOPS) allowance, and the MSC agrees a fee with the institution to cover tuition, accommodation and administrative costs. Many of the expenses incurred by the trainee during the project phase (e.g. travel, market research, typing costs) are also met by the MSC on the basis of a project "budget" agreed between the MSC, the institution and the trainee. About eight NEPS at four university centres are run each year. The courses are largely administered from MSC headquarters, although the regional offices play some part in recruitment and subsequent management. The NEPs started in 1977 and by the end of 1981 about 350 people had been trained. There was a very low drop-out rate. About 300 businesses were known to have been set up. These employed approximately 2000 employees. In 1981 the government spent, in exchequer terms, over £500,000 on NEPs.

Up to the date at which the research contract was agreed 20 NEPs had been run. The particular NEP chosen for the appraisal was selected in the following way. First, the first two courses at each of the four providing institutions were eliminated on the grounds that they were largely experimental. Second, two further NEPs were excluded because they had special characteristics (for example one of these courses was restricted to people who were considering entering the hotel and catering trade). Third, it was felt that it would be optimal, both for recall of past events and for forecasting to the end of the five year time horizon, for the interviews to take place two to three years after the end of the course. A further six NEPs were eliminated on the grounds that the time between the end of the programme and the interviews would have been either less than two years or more than three years. There was little to choose between the remaining four courses in terms of how typical they were in relation to a "standard" NEP. The NEP with the best data was therefore selected. Suitable records were available on the fifteen people who went on the course.

The analytical framework

The decision criterion

The net present value (NPV) is taken as the decision criterion although some reference to the Internal Rate of Return (IRR) is also made.

Costs and benefits

The NPV of a course is $B-C$ where B is the present value of the benefits and C is the present value of the costs. In the light of our previous discussion these costs and benefits are now specified more rigorously. For simplicity the framework outlined below assumes no uncertainty although it would not be difficult to incorporate probabilities into it. Furthermore, in our empirical results we do provide both "least likely" and "most likely" estimates.[10]

In the following discussion we take a time horizon of T periods. Each period is given the subscript t where,

$$t = 0, 1, 2, \ldots, T$$

Period zero is when the training occurs. All the costs occur in this period. The benefits may occur in any period. (There may be some trading during training.) We assume there are n trainees. Each trainee is given the subscript i where

$$i = 1, 2, \ldots, n$$

(i) Costs

The total costs of the training, C, can be broken down into costs of attendance C_1, the costs of provision, C_2 and the costs of administration C_3. (The time subscript for period zero is omitted.) Thus the present value of costs is

$$C = (C_1 + C_2 + C_3) \tag{1}$$

The attendance costs, C_1, consists of two elements. The first is the additional living and other expenses (e.g. travel, subsistence, books) which would not have been incurred if the trainee had not gone on the course. We call these costs, for trainee i, L_i. The second element is the cost of the output foregone by trainees while attending the course. Thus,

$$C_1 = \sum_{i=1}^{n} L_i + \sum_{i=1}^{n} (1 + R_i) W_i^N \tag{2}$$

where
$\quad W_i^N =$ the wage (or self-employment income) that trainee i would have received if he had not gone on the course.
$\quad R_i =$ the appropriate replacement rate for trainee i.

The costs of provision, C_2, comprise those real resource costs of providing the course at the institution concerned. These consist of teaching and other staff costs (including staff time sent on the selection of trainees and travel costs of staff in the course of their contact with students). Office costs (telephone, stationery, etc), costs of providing residential accommodation for trainees which are additional to accommodation costs that would have been incurred anyway, costs of marketing the course, costs of undertaking any project work in the course, and an appropriate portion of the institution's overhead costs. The costs of administration, C_3, are the various staff, travel, office and overhead costs incurred by the headquarters and regional staff of the agency (e.g. Manpower Services Commission) sponsoring the course.

(ii) Benefits

It is helpful to subdivide the benefits of the course in any period into (i) the output changes enumerated in Table 14.1; and (ii) "other" benefits. These effects may be further subdivided in to B_{1t}, increases in output of the trainees themselves (shown as 1(i) in Table 14.1); B_{2t}, increases in the output of the employees in the trainee's firms (shown as 1(ii) in Table 14.1); and B_{3t}, output changes in *other* firms (shown as 2 in Table 14.1). Such changes may be positive or negative. Where B_{3t} are negative, they may or may not be sufficient to offset the combined positive contribution of B_{1t} and B_{2t}. Other benefits which include psychic benefits are labelled B_{4t}, thus the present value of benefits is calculated as follows

$$B = \sum_{t=0}^{T} (B_{1t} + B_{2t} + B_{3t} + B_{4t})(1 + r)^{-t} \tag{3}$$

where the notation is as before, and r is the appropriate rate of discount.

The first benefit, B_{1t}, is defined as follows,

$$B_{1t} = \sum_{i=1}^{n} [W_{it}^{T} - (1 - R_{it}) W_{it}^{N}] \tag{4}$$

where W_{it}^{T} is the wage (or self-employment income) that the ex- trainee i can earn in period t, and W_{it}^{N} is the wage (or self-employment income) that trainee i would have received in the period t if he had not gone on the course. The rest of the notation is as before.

The second benefit, B_{2t} is given by the change in the wage bill in the firms associated with the trainees. This change may come about in the form of an increase in the number of employees or a higher wage for existing employees (if they are more productive) or a combination of the two.

The change in the number of employees in period t resulting from the training of trainee i can be written as the difference between the number of employees actually employed in the period by the ex-trainee N_{it}^{T} and the number that the ex-trainee would have employed had there been no training, N_{it}^{N}. If there is a change in productivity of existing employees as a result of the firm's founder being trained, this can be represented as a change in the skill level, thus

$$B_{2t} = \sum_{i=1}^{n} \sum_{j=1}^{m} (N_{ijt}^{T} - N_{ijt}^{N}) W_{jt} R_{jt} \tag{5}$$

where

N_{ijt}^{T} = the number of employees actually employed by trainee i with skill j in period t

N_{ijt}^{N} = the number that would have been employed by trainee i with skill j in period t

W_{jt} = the wage attached to skill j in period t
R_{jt} = the appropriate replacement rate for skill j in period t
   j = the skill level $j = 1,2, \ldots, m$

The rest of the notation is as before.

The output effects in other firms in period t can be incorporated into total benefits by applying an appropriate adjustment factor $(1 + A_{it})$ to both B_{1t} and B_{2t}. A_{it} is the balance of the output increasing and decreasing effects. Its sign may be positive or negative. Thus from equations (4) and (5) B_{3t} itself is calculated as follows

$$B_{3t} = \sum_{i=1}^{n} A_{it} \{[W_{it}^T - (1 - R_{it})W_{it}^N] + \sum_{j=1}^{m} [(N_{ijt}^T - N_{ijt}^N)W_{jt}R_{jt}]\} \tag{6}$$

B_{4t} may include consumption benefits which the trainee derives from the course. These are often real enough to individuals but they may not have any subsequent effect on the performance of the business. B_{4t} may also include benefits which arise when government is seen to be supportive of small business and entrepreneurship. Such effects may have beneficial consequences far beyond the influence of those who go on the NEPs. Some of these benefits may be substantial, but measurement presents such formidable problems that we have been forced to ignore them.

Data sources

Cost data were relatively straightforward to calculate. The Manpower Services Commission provided fairly precise information on direct resource costs. Estimates of the value of foregone output were based on an assessment of each trainee's qualifications and experience in employment. This assessment was made in the context of the general state of the particular labour market involved. Where the trainee did not provide information on his own wages immediately prior to going on the training, *New Earnings Survey* data were used instead. In all cases adjustments were made to allow for additional labour costs, e.g. insurance and pension contributions.

The benefits side was not quite so straightforward. Our first step was to build up both "with training" and "without training" employment profiles for each trainee's firm in as much detail as possible. These profiles were then used in conjunction with wages, and sometimes profits data, obtained either direct from the trainee or the *New Earnings Survey*, as a basis for estimating the NEP effects on output.[11]

We considered two possible approaches to the building up of a "without training" employment profile. One relied on the use of a control group of individuals who were identical in all relevant economic characteristics except that they had not been through the training. The difficulties of achieving a control group with no exact matching of individuals in terms of such factors as age, experience, drive, and the nature of their business, would have been formidable. The second approach, used here, was to rely on trainees' own assessment of what employment would have been like in the absence of the training. The principal source of such information was extended in-depth interviews. On the basis of data obtained in these interviews we were able to construct "with" and "without training" profiles for the five year period following training.

There are of course difficulties associated with this approach. However we feel that some confidence may be placed in our results for the following reasons. First, it was stressed at the outset of the interview, that we had no interest whatsoever in obtaining any particular result. By this means the pos-sibilities for interview bias were reduced. Second, most trainees had a fairly *clear* view of the "without" profile and of the future "with" profile. Profiles were sketched out in the interview itself and discussed at some length with the interviewee against the background of any pre-NEP experience of business and in the light of his or her answers to questions on the impact of the NEP itself. Third, in follow-up contact a year after the initial interviews, inter-viewees were asked again about the hypothetical profiles without any prompt-ing on what their views had been. No significant changes were suggested. Finally, we have been encouraged by our experience in an exercise with an identical approach where we discussed the profiles we had obtained with an independent management consultant who knew each of the businesses. In all cases he thought they reflected reasonable judgements. Thus, although there are clearly difficulties with this approach, we nevertheless feel the profiles are meaningful. A similar view of the value of the subjective with/without approach is taken in a recent study of the small business loan guarantee scheme (Department of Industry 1982a).

Some interviewees suggested a range of possible outcomes. In such cases high and low estimates of employment attributable to the NEP and thus a "most favourable" and a "least favourable" benefits profile were constructed. On the basis of all the available evidence to them the authors then made a judgement of the "most likely" outcome.

The adjustment factor which allows for the output effects in other firms was estimated on the basis of our knowledge of the likely extent of product market displacement.[12] In much previous research the displacement effect has either been ignored (or assumed to be zero) or arbitrary assumptions has been made. Sometimes a range of alternatives is presented from which the reader is invited to choose. It is widely agreed that the estimation of dis-placement is a formidable task[13] but we took the view that the provision of some estimates, albeit based on subjective assessments, was much superior to sidestepping the issue.

Our estimates of displacement were based on our interpretation of a series of interview questions about matters such as the innovatory aspects of the business, the nature of the product market competition, the amount of sales drawn from competitors and the likelihood of other businesses taking up the firm's sales if the firm suddenly ceased trading. Our examination was confined to first round effects in (what the interviewee perceived as) the same product market. Since most of the firms interviewed only competed within a restricted geographical area, attention was usually confined to effects in that area. The estimates of displacement are prone to error though in many cases it was possible to be reasonably confident about the size. Nevertheless a range of estimates was used from which a "most likely" outcome was assessed.

The results

The "most likely" outcome

Quarterly time periods (beginning March–May 1980) have been used in the calculation of the present values of costs and benefits. The mid-point of quarter zero (April 1980) was taken as the base date and all values are in April 1980 prices. The time horizon was 20 quarters (five years). The Treasury's test discount rate of 5 per cent[14] per annum in real terms was used for discounting. We also calculated NPVs using a 7 per cent discount rate, i.e. 5 per cent plus a 2 per cent premium to offset appraisal optimism.

The estimated present value of costs and of "most likely" benefits, together with the NPV of the NEP, are shown in Table 14.2.

Our estimates of the output changes in other firms led to a major reduction in the benefits, a reflection of the fact that few of the businesses covered in this study were important innovators. The NPV based on the Treasury's test rate of discount of 5 per cent was £61,381. The internal rate of return is 19.5 per cent. This result suggests that the NEP is worthwhile over the five year period.

The pattern of benefits

The firms set up by the trainees were very diverse in nature and covered both manufacturing (for example, food products, surgical footwear, horse boxes) and services (for example, computer consultancy, trombone design and repair, water sealant treatment). There was also considerable diversity in the nature of the impact of the training. Three principal types of benefit may however be detected: (i) the provision of an opportunity during the twelve month project period to stand back and develop thorough business plans in a critical but supportive environment; (ii) crucial specific help on technical aspects of business operation, for example on the completion of VAT returns, bookkeeping and cash flow projections; (iii) more general assistance such as the provision of the confidence and ability to develop and profit from business contacts with financial and other institutions. These varied modes of the impact of training were a result of differences in the personal characteristics

Table 14.2 NPV of the NEP. April 1980 prices: five year time horizon (£s)

	5% discount rate	7% discount rate
Benefits (using "most likely" profiles)[a]		
Increases in output of trainees themselves $\left(\sum_{t=0}^{T} B_{1t}\,(1+r)^{-t}\right)$		
Increases in output of employees in trainees' firms $\left(\sum_{t=0}^{T} B_{2t}\,(1+r)^{-t}\right)$	458,560	428,159
Changes in output in other firms $\left(\sum_{t=0}^{T} B_{3t}\,(1+r)^{-t}\right)$	− 302,224	−282,310
Other benefits $\left(\sum_{t=0}^{T} B_{4t}\,(1+r)^{-t}\right)$	n.a.	n.a.
Total benefits *(B)*	156,336	145,849
***Costs*[b]**		
Attendance costs[c] (C_1)	43,347	43,454
Provision costs (C_2)	35,146	35,232
Administration costs (C_3)	16,462	16,503
Total costs *(C)*	<u>94,955</u>	<u>95,189</u>
Net present value	61,381	50,660

Notes

a Benefits estimates assume a replacement rate of 1 so that employees in newly founded firms are assumed to be replaced. Thus *all* additional earnings are included.

b The course studied ran from January to early May 1980. All the costs have, therefore, been assumed to fall at the mid-point of the course, i.e. the beginning of March. This is the beginning of quarter zero (March, April, May 1980). To put them on the base date (mid quarter zero) they have therefore, been compounded by $(1 + r/4)^{\frac{1}{2}}$. As in the text the time script zero has been omitted.

c The attendance cost included £39,901 as an estate of the value of output foregone. This was calculated on the assumption of a zero replacement rate so that all foregone earnings were taken as a measure of the output foregone.

n.a. Not available.

of the trainees and in their businesses. Inevitably there was also a marked variation in the size of this impact. In some cases a seemingly large effect on output was offset, sometimes totally, by the displacement effect. This may be illustrated by the case of one trainee who set up a small engineering firm. He benefited very substantially from the course: the employment profiles worked out with the trainee during the interview suggested that the training had more than doubled his employment. However, the nature of this firm – a fairly "standard" sub-contracting business in the same (local market) – meant that his gains were largely reflected in the losses of others.

Two features of the overall pattern of benefits are particularly worth noting. First, the businesses we have observed have a slow build up. This is reflected in Figure 14.2, which shows that the payback period (i.e. the point at which the line crosses the horizontal axis) is about four years (16 quarters).

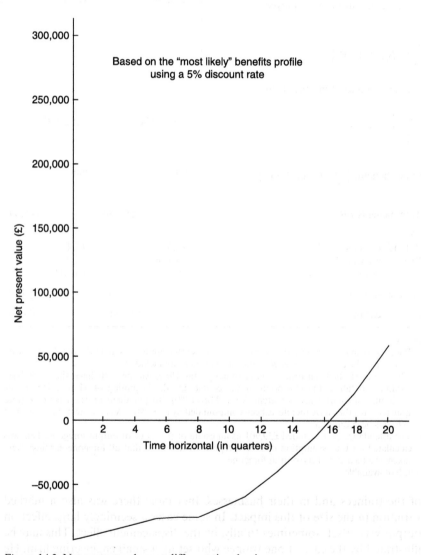

Figure 14.2 Net present values at different time horizons.

Even on the "most favourable" estimates of benefits the pay-back period is almost three years.

Second, a substantial part of the present value of benefits was contributed by just a small number of businesses. Taking a 5 per cent discount rate, 50 per cent of the estimated present value of benefits was contributed by the "most successful" businesses, 70 per cent by the "most successful" two businesses, and 80 per cent by the "most successful" three businesses. This suggests very strongly that one or two "high fliers" may justify the course, with the great majority of businesses yielding little or no social benefit. If such "high fliers" can be spotted in advance of training there may be important implications for selection.

Alternative outcomes

As noted earlier, in cases where interviewees suggested a range of possible outcomes we considered the "least favourable" and "most favourable" benefit profiles. On the "least favourable" assumptions about benefits the NPV using a 5 per cent discount rate is negative (–£33,641) and on the "most favourable" it is very strongly positive (£341,175). The wide range results from the fact that many of the data represent forecasts of future employment.

We have also examined some possible implications of errors in costs by looking at the way the NPV based on our "most likely" benefits profile would alter if costs were 15 per cent higher or lower than our estimate. The results do not change significantly. If for example we underestimated costs by 15 per cent there would still be a positive NPV (£47,138) over a five year time horizon using a 5 per cent discount rate. We also examined the implications of counting foregone output as a cost. If no output were foregone during the training – a possibility in times of high unemployment – the NPV would be substantially higher. Taking the original cost estimates in Table 14.2, and deducting our estimate of the value of foregone output, the NPV would rise to £101,282 (on a 5 per cent discount rate).

III CONCLUSIONS

This study has shown that taking a five-year time horizon, the self-employment training course we studied yielded a positive net present value. Our analysis suggests that it is crucially important to look beyond the direct effects of self-employment training and recognition was therefore given to the effect on the output of other firms. This was done by estimating the effect of increases in output in the trainee's business in displacing output in other firms. This effect proved to be substantial.

In interpreting our results it is necessary to bear in mind a number of qualifications. The estimates of benefits are based on certain assumptions, e.g. that it is appropriate to measure benefits in terms of employment valued on the basis of marginal productivity theory. Furthermore some benefits have not been counted (such as consumption benefits enjoyed by trainees undergoing the course) and the five-year time horizon ignores subsequent benefits. Errors may also arise because of the subjective element in the assessment of "without training" positions and of the displacement effects. However, a follow-up contact a year after the interviews on which the present results are based, strongly confirmed the broad picture given here and gave us confidence that our approach was an advance on ignoring or arbitrarily specifying certain elements in the benefit calculation. Provided these limitations are taken into account the results do provide a useful indication of the social value of entrepreneurial training.

The results of the case study suggest that the current level of provision of NEPs is "justifiable" and that some expansion may be appropriate in the scale of provision. This of course assumes that the particular course we studied was "typical". It is worth stressing, however, that the economic criterion is only one element in the decision process, and that the analysis reported here took the NEP as given and made no attempt to assess the internal efficiency of the course.

Notes

1 Part of this paper is based on work undertaken by the authors for the Manpower Services Commission. The help of the Commission is gratefully acknowledged. It does not, however, necessarily support the conclusions reached in this study. The authors have benefited from comments by seminar participants at the University of Glasgow and the SSRC Labour Economics Study Group at the London School of Economics where earlier version of this paper were presented. All errors and omissions are the sole responsibility of the authors.
2 There are exceptions – see for example Department of Industry (1981).
3 The training may itself cause the trainee to change firms. Even if the trainee remains in paid employment, this may occur. Where the trainee moves from paid employment to self-employment (or vice-versa), a change in firms is of course inevitable.
4 These output changes may be considered as part of the returns to entrepreneurs and therefore should be counted under 1(i). Where exactly they are classified makes little difference for the present purposes as long as they are counted somewhere.
5 Training may make a founder more confident about introducing an innovation; it may even provide him, either directly or indirectly, through contacts, with the necessary technical skills.
6 Hughes and Brinkley (1980) refer to this as induced employment.
7 In some cases, product market displacement may directly affect the replacement rate and hence the extent to which output can expand. Where the output expansion attributable to the formation of a new firm is constrained by the availability of unemployed resources, product market displacement may reduce or eliminate this constraint. There may of course be a problem of timing here: such displacement may only occur as a direct *result* of output expansion, but such expansion may only be possible if displacement occurs! However, it is not difficult to envisage circumstances in which such difficulties can be overcome. For the purposes of this paper the replacement and product market displacement effects are treated as if they were independent.

8 Conventional multiplier effects are ignored on the grounds that if resources were not being spent on the training course, they would be allocated to other projects which would also have similar multiplier effects.

9 "Pure profits", the difference between the businessman's total revenue and his contractual payments – the latter includes any returns to the businessman which might properly be regarded as rewards for "routine services performed by the entrepreneur personally for the business (wages or earned by property which belongs to him (rent or capital return)" (Knight, 1921, p. 277) – are a residual. Such a residual, which may be negative or positive, does not represent a return to a particular factor but arises as a windfall gain solely because of the existence of uncertainty. Positive pure profits imply that the anticipated marginal products of the hired factors on which contractual payments to them are based are less than the *actual* marginal products. In this sense, pure profits come from the productive factors themselves. Training cannot by definition increase the ability of the business man to generate pure profits. (If it made him consistently more "lucky" this fact would in the long run, be reflected in his transfer earnings.)

10 On the costs side, we also attach probabilities to the wage that the trainee would have obtained had he not gone on the course. In all cases except one, however, we set this probability equal to one.

11 Full details of the cost and benefit calculations are given in Johnson and Thomas (1982). It is interesting to note that the "with NEP" profiles have sometimes been used by commentators as if they represented the NEP effect, i.e. they assume implicitly that the *whole* of a business's output is attributable to the NEP, and that no output would have occurred without the NEP. See, for example, the *Employment Gazette* (December 1981, vol. 89 (12), p. 502. Such is very unlikely to be the case.

12 No attempt has been made to estimate the possible *positive* output effects which were mentioned earlier. Their measurement would be extremely difficult and they are likely to be small in the case of our sample because few of the firms had substantial forward or backward links.

13 See, for example, Mackay *et al.* (1980).

14 This figure is recommended in H.M. Treasury's *Investment Appraisal in the Public Sector* (1982) and the government Economic Service Working Paper, no. 22, *The Test Discount Rate and the Required Rate of Return on Investment* (H.M. Treasury 1979). The discount factor for quarterly discounting has been taken as $1/(1 + r/4)^t$ where r is the annual rate of interest.

References

DEPARTMENT OF INDUSTRY (1981). *The Value of the Counselling Activity of the Small Firms Service*. A report by Research Associates Ltd, Department of Industry.

DEPARTMENT OF INDUSTRY (1982a). *Interim Assessment of the Small Business Loan Guarantee Scheme*. Department of Industry, London.

DEPARTMENT OF INDUSTRY (1982b). "Background to the U.K. Government's Small Firms Policy", Internal document, Department of Industry, London.

HUGHES, J. J. and BRINKLEY, I. (1980). "The Measurement of Secondary Labour Market Effects Associated with Government Training", *Scottish Journal of Political Economy*, vol. 27, no. 1, pp. 63–79.

JOHNSON, P. S. and THOMAS, R. B. (1982). *A Cost-Benefit Analysis of a New Enterprise Programme*. A report prepared for the Manpower Services Commission (Mimeo). Department of Economics, Durham University.

KNIGHT, F. H. (1921). *Risk, Uncertainty and Profit*. Houghton Mifflin, Boston.

MACKAY, D. I., MACKAY, R., McVEAN, P. and EDWARDS, R. (1980). *Redundancy and Displacement*. Research Paper no. 16. Department of Employment.

SOMERS, G. C. and WOOD, W. D. (1969). *Cost–Benefit Analysis of Manpower Policies: Proceedings of a North American Conference*. Industrial Relations Centre, Queen's University Kingston, Ontario.

ZIDERMAN, A. (1978). *Manpower Training: Theory and Policy*. Macmillan, London.

15 Targeting firm births and economic regeneration in a lagging region[1]

Peter Johnson

Source: *Small Business Economics*, 2005, 24, (5), 451–464.

This paper provides a critical evaluation of the practice of targeting the firm birth rate as part of a regional regeneration policy. It raises some fundamental questions about the appropriateness of such a practice and shows that different specifications of the birth rate generate very different implications for policy intervention, as measured by the number of births required. It also demonstrates that even when the specification is agreed, the translation of the target into actual number of births is far from straightforward, especially where the target aspires to match a region's performance with what is going on elsewhere and where the survival rate of businesses is also being targeted in parallel. The North East of England is used as the particular context for the evaluation, although the discussion has much wider applicability.

1 Introduction

This paper provides a critical evaluation of the practice of targeting the firm birth rate as part of a regional regeneration policy. It raises some fundamental questions about the appropriateness of such a practice and shows that different specifications of the birth rate generate very different implications for policy intervention, as measured by the number of births required. It also demonstrates that even when the specification is agreed, the translation of the target into actual numbers of births is far from straightforward, especially where the target aspires to match a region's performance with what is going on elsewhere and where the survival rate of businesses is also being targeted in parallel.

The North East (NE) of England is used as the particular context for this evaluation. This region is an especially appropriate focus for our discussion for two reasons. First, the Regional Development Agency (RDA) for the NE, One NorthEast, hereafter ONE, has targeted the birth rate. Second, a top policy priority for the region is economic regeneration. The NE has had a relatively poor economic performance over the longer term (Evans et al., 1995), its economy is currently rather weak (ONE, 1999, p. 18; Fothergill, 2001) – notwithstanding the very substantial restructuring that has occurred

(Hudson, 1998, ch. 3) – and question marks hang over its prospects (see for example, Cambridge Econometrics, 2000, p. 182).

Although the focus here is on the NE, the discussion has much wider applicability. The North West, Scotland and Wales for example are all regions where problems of economic decline have also been considerable. Furthermore, as indicated later, the development agencies in a number of English regions specified the birth rate as a policy objective in their initial strategy documents which were published in 1999. The discussion is also directly relevant to regional agencies in other countries where regeneration policies are focused on stimulating entrepreneurial activity.

The plan for this paper is as follows. In the next section, we consider the underlying economic basis for using the birth rate as a target and point to some of the issues that such a target raises. Then in section 3, we examine the measurement of the birth rate. As we show later in the paper, how the birth rate is measured has important implications for policy. Section 4 outlines the context for ONE's birth rate policy, comparing the NE's birth rate record, both over time and across industries, with that of the Rest of the United Kingdom (RUK). In section 5, ONE's birth rate target for the NE is considered. The development of this policy is outlined and the particular way in which the target was specified by ONE in its 1999 strategy document (ONE, 1999) is examined. Section 6 then explores some key issues relating to this target and its interpretation, paying particular attention to the way in which different targets may imply different numbers of births and to the interrelationship between birth and survival rates. The latter uses a simulation. Section 7 concludes the paper. Appendix I sets out, for comparative purposes, the business birth and survival objectives set by each RDA in their original strategy documents. Appendix II outlines the methodological basis for the simulation of the impact of different birth and survival rate policies that is presented in section 6.

2 The economic basis for targeting the birth rate

As section 5 indicates, ONE set itself the task of raising the NE birth rate to the RUK level, on the grounds that it would contribute to the elimination of the economically disadvantaged position of the region. Empirical work has highlighted the role of firm formation as a mechanism for employment generation (e.g. Ashcroft and Love, 1996; Gallagher et al., 1996; Hart and Oulton, 2001), innovation (e.g. Audretsch, 1999, esp. 8–10), economic growth (e.g. Schmitz, 1989) and the reduction in unemployment (e.g. Thurik, 1999). Central government policy statements (DTI, 1998; DTI/DfEE, 2001) have emphasised the importance of encouraging an entrepreneurial culture in which start-ups can flourish as a mechanism for maintaining competitiveness and a dynamic economy. It is therefore not surprising to find – see Appendix I – that the encouragement of business births is an objective that most of the RDAs, including ONE, set themselves in their initial strategy documents.

How far is it appropriate to target the birth rate in order to stimulate regeneration? A number of issues need to be highlighted here. The first is the potential interrelationship between birth and death rates. We know that substantial numbers of new businesses exit fairly early on in life: the evidence from VAT data for the NE suggests that about 60 per cent of new registrations in the NE exit within five years.[2] Policy measures designed to encourage births may simply raise this exit rate, if the capacity of the region, in terms of the market opportunities available for the new businesses, remains unchanged. Thus the new firms themselves may fail earlier than previous cohorts. They may also displace (or reduce the scale of) existing businesses. There may of course be some welfare advantages from such displacement, if more efficient firms are dislodging less efficient ones. However displacement may only be occurring as the result of policy measures which happen to favour new businesses over existing ones, and not as a result of some efficiency advantage inherent in the newcomers' operations.

A second issue relates to the complex set of determinants that lie behind birth and self-employment rates. There is now an extensive literature on these determinants over time (e.g. Evans and Leighton, 1989; Black et al., 1996) and across people (e.g. Blanchflower and Oswald, 1991), regions (e.g. Keeble and Walker, 1994; Johnson and Parker, 1996; Armington and Acs, 2002) and countries (e.g. Acs et al., 1992).[3] Policy initiatives may succeed in compensating for factors in the economic environment that are less favourable to firm formation – although even here the evidence is mixed – but there is likely to be a limit on the extent to which such compensation can be made. ONE of course is aware of the need for an altogether broader approach to the economic needs of the NE, but there are dangers that the identification of a specific birth rate objective may potentially distort policy priorities.

Third, it should be noted that while comparability with the RUK is an understandable aim, there may be little reason to suppose that the NE's optimal rate, given its industrial structure, the available opportunities, the way those opportunities are perceived and the supply of would-be founders, should all be the same as elsewhere. In the absence of this similarity, the appropriate mix of new and existing business activity is likely to vary across regions. This variation will apply to both new births generally, and to new high-tech businesses specifically.

Finally, the underlying economic or other justification for public policy designed to support business formation needs to be articulated. There are fundamental issues that need to be addressed here: for example, Holtz-Eakin (2000) has argued that standard efficiency and equity arguments provide little foundation for small firms' policies. There are also concerns relating to the effectiveness of current policies aimed at small businesses. Again, some recent studies have raised doubts on this score: see for example Robson and Bennett (2000) and Bennett et al. (2001). Thus even if it was appropriate in principle to target the birth rate, there is no guarantee that effective policies to achieve the target could be devised and implemented.

3 Measuring the birth rate

Throughout this paper VAT registrations are used as proxies for the number of births and the number of 'live' registrations is treated as a proxy for the business stock. *[The usefulness and limitations of VAT data are discussed in chapter 4.]*

Birth rates may be measured in different ways. A common measure is the number of births as a proportion of the business stock, designated here as *BRS*. More formally, *BRS* for the NE in this case may be defined as follows (ignoring time subscripts)

$$BRS_{NE} = \sum_{i=1}^{n} \frac{R_{NE}^i}{S_{NE}^i}$$

And for the RUK as

$$BRS_{RUK} = \sum_{i=1}^{n} \frac{R_{RUK}^i}{S_{RUK}^i}$$

where

R_{NE}^i = the number of new registrations in sector i in the NE in the period

S_{NE}^i = the stock of registered businesses in sector i in the NE at the beginning of the period

R_{RUK}^i = the number of new registrations in sector i in the RUK in the period

S_{RUK}^i = the stock of registered businesses in sector i in the RUK at the beginning of the period

n = the number of sectors

In its original (1999) strategy document ONE used the *BRS* measure for its quantitative target. An alternative measure (here *BRP*) utilises population (or work force) as the denominator. *BRS* is particularly appropriate for analysing the extent to which the business sector is being rejuvenated, while *BRP*, which was used by both the North West and East Midlands RDAs – the only other RDAs to set quantitative formation targets in their original strategy documents (see East Midlands Development Agency, 1999; and Northwest Development Agency, 1999, respectively)[4] – is more relevant for examining how 'entrepreneurial' a region's people are. It is perhaps surprising, given its interest in stimulating the entrepreneurial culture of the region, that ONE did not make use of the *BRP* in its 1999 strategy, although it has since used this measure in later discussions (ONE, 2002a, p. 11). The two measures are of course related, even though their focus is different. Table 15.1 provides data on the two birth rates for the U.K regions/countries. It is clear that the

Table 15.1 BRS and BRP: U.K. regions/countries, 1999

Region/country	BRS[a]	BRP[b]
NE	0.10	0.21
NW	0.11	0.33
Yorks and Humber	0.10	0.29
E. Midlands	0.10	0.34
W. Midlands	0.11	0.34
E. of England	0.10	0.40
London	0.14	0.66
SE	0.11	0.45
SW	0.10	0.38
Wales	0.08	0.26
Scotland	0.10	0.28
N. Ireland	0.07	0.28
U.K.	0.11	0.38

Notes

a Number of registrations in 1999 as a proportion of the registered stock of businesses at the beginning of 1999.

b Number of registrations in 1999 per 100 of the population.

Source: Small Business Service (2000).

variation in *BRS* is much less than that in *BRP*. The NE has the lowest *BRP*
in the U.K (0.55 of the U.K. figure); Wales and Northern Ireland have lower
BRS scores. (The NE's figure is 0.91 of the U.K.'s.)

Empirical work on the determinants of formation suggests that how the
birth rate is measured can have an important influence on the results. For
example, Keeble and Walker (1994) show that the factors explaining variations in formation rates across the U.K. regions differ depending on how
these rates are measured. In the case of some significant independent variables, the sign of the coefficient differs, depending on which birth rate measure is used.[5]

Death rates, based on deregistration data, can be similarly defined with
respect to either the business stock (*DRS*) or to the population (*DRP*). The
rest of this paper uses only *BRS* and *DRS*, as it is these measures that are the
most relevant for ONE's targets.

In the next section, we examine the behaviour of the birth rate and death
rate *relatives* over time. The Birth Rate Relative, comparing the birth rate in
the NE with that in the RUK may be defined as

$$BRELS_{NE, RUK} = \frac{BRS_{NE}}{BRS_{RUK}}$$

Similarly, the comparable Death Rate Relative may be defined as

$$DRELS_{NE, RUK} = \frac{DRS_{NE}}{DRS_{RUK}}$$

4 The context for the NE's birth rate policy: the NE and RUK compared

Before the actual policy in the NE is examined, we provide the context for the birth objective by examining the behaviour of $BRELS_{NE,RUK}$ in the two decades up to the publication of ONE's 1999 strategy document: see Figure 15.1. $DRELS_{NE,RUK}$ is also included in the figure as it is relevant for analysing the impact of $BRELS_{NE,RUK}$.

$BRELS_{NE,RUK}$ shows a clear downward trend. In 1997, this relative was at its lowest level since 1980. Thus ONE faced a particular challenge over its region's birth rate when it drew up its strategy document in 1999. The overall trend in the Death Rate Relative is also downward but has a somewhat shallower slope. Thus the fall in the death relative has not been enough to compensate (in terms of the effect on the stock of businesses) for the fall in the birth relative. It is worth noting that the death relative has become more volatile since the beginning of the 1990s, although the reasons for this are unclear. These factors gave a further edge to the challenge faced by ONE in devising an appropriate strategy.

We now explore the behaviour of the $BRELS_{NE,RUK}$ in more detail. From an accounting viewpoint, a distinction may be made between (i) the effects on the relatives of differences between the NE and RUK in industrial structure (the 'structural effect'), and (ii) the effects of differences in the NE's and RUK's formation rates in individual industries (the 'formation effect'). The structural effect picks up the extent to which the NE's industrial structure is biased towards or against sectors that have higher formation rates. To identify this effect we may recalculate the relatives on the assumption that the NE has the same structure as RUK and then apply the NE's birth rate to this revised structure. Structure here is defined in terms of the distribution of the stock of businesses across sectors. In this particular exercise, we are able to work with

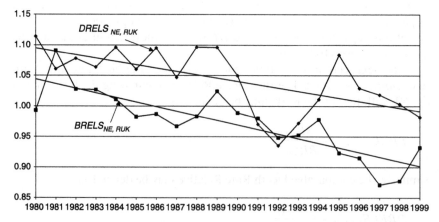

Figure 15.1 Birth and death relatives: NE/RUK.

eleven sectors. The birth rate for the NE allowing for structural effects, BRS_{NE}^{STR}, reflects the extent to which the NE has a sectoral structure which is biased towards or against sectors that have higher formation rates. More formally, and ignoring time subscripts

$$BRS_{NE}^{STR} = \frac{\displaystyle\sum_{i=1}^{n}\left[\left(\sum_{i=1}^{n} S_{NE}^{i} \times \frac{S_{RUK}^{i}}{\displaystyle\sum_{i=1}^{n} S_{RUK}^{i}}\right) \times \frac{R_{NE}^{i}}{S_{NE}^{i}}\right]}{\displaystyle\sum_{i=1}^{n} S_{NE}^{i}}$$

where the notation is as before.

The formation effect arises because *for given sectors* the NE formation rate may be higher or lower than that in the RUK. Table 15.2 shows $BRELS_{NE, RUK}$ by broad industrial sector for the period 1994–8. The relevant birth rates are calculated as the total number of births, 1994–1998, divided by the sum of the stock at the start of each year, 1994–1998. This procedure provides a "weighted" birth rate.

In only two sectors, "Hotels and restaurants", and "Public administration; Other community, social and personal services", is the ratio greater than one. Thus if the NE does have a relative advantage in formation terms, it is not in areas which would be generally regarded as being at the forefront of economic progress.

Table 15.2 $BRELS_{NE, RUK}$ by sector, 1994–1998

Sector	$BRELS_{NE, RUK}$
Agriculture; forestry and fishing	0.77
Mining and quarrying; Electricity, gas and water supply	0.87
Manufacturing	0.90
Construction	0.93
Wholesale, retail and repairs	0.89
Hotels and restaurants	1.10
Transport, storage and communication	0.91
Financial intermediation	0.80
Real estate, renting and business activities	0.83
Public administration; Other community, social and personal services	1.08
Education, health and social work.	0.95
TOTAL	0.91

Source: based on DTI data.

A birth rate for the NE allowing for formation effects, BRS_{NE}^{FORM} may be calculated as follows (again ignoring time subscripts):

$$BRS_{NE}^{FORM} = \frac{\sum_{i=1}^{n}\left[S_{NE}^{i} \times \frac{R_{RUK}^{i}}{S_{RUK}^{i}}\right]}{\sum_{i=1}^{n} S_{NE}^{i}}$$

where the notation is as previously.

Figure 15.2 recalculates the birth relatives using BRS_{NE}^{STR} ($BRELS_{NE,RUK}^{STR}$) and BRS_{NE}^{FORM} ($BRELS_{NE,RUK}^{FORM}$). The figure shows that allowance for different sectoral structures ($BRELS_{NE,RUK}^{STR}$) makes little difference to the NE/RUK relative, except perhaps between 1989 and 1993. Thus Figure 15.2 indicates that the NE's relatively lower birth rate does not reflect a regional sectoral structure that is biased against sectors with low birth rates. When however allowance is made for differences between the NE and the RUK in the birth rate in individual sectors, via $BRELS_{NE}^{FORM}$, the change in the relative is much more noticeable. It levels out the relative, though the latter still retains a slight downward trend. It is clear from Figure 15.2 that the NE's relatively lower performance reflects its lower birth rate in individual sectors, rather than a sectoral structure that emphasises sectors with low birth rates. This finding is consistent with the results of earlier studies (Johnson 1983; Storey and Johnson 1987).

The approach adopted above has some obvious limitations. First, it is essentially an accounting exercise; it tells us nothing about the *causes* that lie behind the trends shown in Figure 15.2. Second, it may not be appropriate to treat the effects of differences in sectoral structure and those of differences

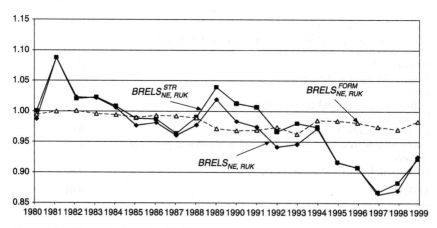

Figure 15.2 Birth relatives: NE/RUK.

in birth rates in individual industries as independent influences. For example, the NE's lower birth rate in particular sectors may lead to a sectoral structure that is less congenial to formation activity. Third, the results are likely to be sensitive to the level of sectoral aggregation. Nonetheless, the approach does provide some initial pointers to the nature of the differences between the NE and the RUK. The results suggest that the region's lower birth rate does not derive so much from its structure but from a more widespread reluctance (for whatever reason) to set up in business that is present across the board.

5 A birth rate target for the NE

Each of the eight English RDAs established in 1999 was charged with drawing up an economic development strategy for its region.[6] In its statutory guidance to the RDAs[7] on what to include in this strategy, the then Department for the Environment, Transport and the Regions (DETR)[8] asked each of them to include "business *formations* and survival *rates*" as one of its core "state of the region" indicators,[9] and the "*number* of business start-ups and survival *rates*" (our italics) as an indicator of its activity. It is however puzzling why *numbers* should be used for business start-ups and *rates* for measuring survival.

In its Regional Economic Strategy, ONE pointed out that in the NE "The rate of new VAT registrations . . . is lower than every U.K region except Wales and Northern Ireland . . ." (ONE, 1999, p. 19). This statement is based on the *BRS* measure. As we have seen however, if the *BRP* measure is used (see Table 15.1), the NE is the lowest performer of all. This difference demonstrates that the precise choice of measure is important in terms of any assessment of regional ranking.

The same Strategy accepted an explicit target to "increase business start-ups to [the] U.K. average by 2010" (ONE, 1999, p. 103). Such a target, implicitly couched here by ONE in terms of *numbers*, is nevertheless only meaningful in terms of birth *rates*. In terms of the latter, the target is of course the equivalent of the NE's rate equalling the aggregate rate for the rest of the U.K. (RUK). In 1999, the base year for this study, the (percentage) rates were, respectively, 0.1007 and 0.1082 and it is these rates that are assumed in the rest of this paper.

The birth rate target for the NE was an expression of the Strategy's wider commitment to building a 'new' entrepreneurial culture' in the region, and its assessment that

> The key to strengthening the Region's wealth creating capacity is to provide an environment in which entrepreneurs can run successful businesses . . . New businesses will be essential elements of the Region's clusters because they are often visionary and flexible in their thinking, management and marketing. They provide the mechanisms

that create whole new industries. The Region must rediscover the spirit of enterprise . . .

   To do this, we must motivate those already in the Region to start new businesses and equip them with the skills to do so. . . .

(ONE, 1999, p. 44)

Alongside the target of raising the overall birth rate, ONE also set itself a further target of increasing the number of new *high technology* businesses to the U.K average by 2010 (ONE, 1999, p.103). It is not immediately clear what this target means – again there seems to be the potential for some confusion between *numbers* and *rates* – nor it is clear how it relates precisely to the target of creating 200 "high growth" companies by 2010 (ONE, 1999, p. 45). (Does high growth always mean high technology?) Furthermore no U.K. wide data are cited (it is unclear whether such data are available) and there is a certain arbitrariness about the figure:[10] no indication is given about how the figure of 200 was arrived at. Specific targets on high growth/high tech companies have been set by a number of RDAs (see Appendix I). This paper however is concerned only with the overall birth rate.

   When ONE's strategy for encouraging a more entrepreneurial culture was published in 2001 (ONE 2001), it did not specify the target of reaching equivalence with the rest of the U.K. Again, in the revised overall economic strategy published a year later (2002b) the parity goal was not alluded to, although the supporting economic and technical report, supporting this revised strategy, *did* spell out the task in the following terms: "There is now a clear aim to generate new and growing companies [sic] by a least the same rate as other U.K. regions." (ONE, 2002a, p.3). The report gives both BRS and BRP measures but does not say which one it would use in analysing parity.

6 The target formation rate: some issues

In this section we examine some of the detailed issues associated with the use by ONE of BRS_{NE} as a policy target. The following may be noted. First, the choice of birth rate measure carries very different implications for the number of registrations required to ensure equality between the NE and RUK. For BRS_{NE} to equal BRS_{RUK}, in 1999, the NE would have needed another 315 registrations.[11] With *BRP* however, 3787 additional registrations would have been required.[12] Clearly the financial implications of providing support for business births is likely to vary hugely with the precise specification of the target. It so happens that ONE chose the indicator with the more modest numbers target, although there is no evidence that this was done deliberately.

   Second, the implications of the target BRS_{NE} for numbers of births, and hence for policy intervention, will be affected by other regions' policies. We have already drawn attention to the birth rate aspirations of some other RDAs (see Appendix I). Even the South East Development Agency (SEDA), the region with one of the highest formation rates already, sought a "step change" in that rate (SEDA, p. 15).

Finally, predictions about the future time path of *BRS* are complicated by the direct effect of an increase in the numerator on the denominator – more births imply an immediate increase in stock – and by any changes in the survival rate, of both new and existing firms, on the denominator. Births and deaths may not of course be independent. The former may for example stimulate deaths among the existing business stock, through a "competition" effect. Alternatively, births may reduce deaths through a "multiplier" effect. Births (deaths) may also affect births (deaths) in a subsequent period. The evidence on these relationships is mixed (Johnson and Parker, 1996). It should be noted that where the DRS_{NE} exceeds the BRS_{NE}, a target BRS_{NE} may be achievable without increasing the number of births, or even by letting it fall. The reason for this is that where DRS_{NE} exceeds BRS_{NE} the stock, the denominator for BRS_{NE}, must be falling and hence a lower number of births may achieve the BRS_{NE} target. This is not merely an academic point: between 1992 and 1998, DRS_{NE} was higher than BRS_{NE} in all but one year: see Figure 15.2.

Interestingly, as we have seen, ONE committed itself to raising the survival rate of new businesses to the U.K average (ONE 1999, p. 103). Paradoxically, an increased survival rate, which lowers the rate at which the stock is depleted, does of course make the attainment of a BRS_{NE} target more challenging (see below).

Some of the relationships between the birth rate and the survival rate may be seen from the results of some simulations: see Table 15.3. This table assumes that the birth rate and the survival rate operate independently and that policy makers can alter either or both. It also assumes that a single birth rate, once it is chosen, and the *same* survival function – again once it is chosen – prevail throughout the period between 1999 and 2010 (the target year specified in ONE's strategy document (ONE 1999, p.103)). The further assumption is made that that the target rate is the *current* RUK rate (0.1082). Appendix II sets out the basis of the simulations.

Although the calculations in Table 15.3 are based on highly simplified assumptions – not least that the birth rate and survival function are unrelated – they do serve to highlight the wide variation in the number of births required to achieve the target rate, given different survival functions. On the assumptions in the table and in the simulation, this number varies from −376 to +603. The figures in Table 15.3 are intended to be no more than illustrative; they do however demonstrate the important point that the additional number of births required in 2010 to achieve the formation target in that year vary substantially depending on what happens to the survival rate.

Table 15.3 Some simulations

Assumptions		Additional number of births required in 2010	Implied DRS_{NE} in 2010
BRS_{NE} *(assumed to be the same throughout the period up to 2010)*	*Survival rate (assumed to be the same throughout the period up to 2010)*		
Actual BRS_{NE} *in* 1999 (=0.1007)	As estimated on current data	−512	0.1123
Target BRS_{NE} (=0.1082)*	As estimated on current data	88	0.1127
Target BRS_{NE} (=0.1082)*	5 per cent improvement on estimated current rate**	339	0.1076
Target BRS_{NE} (=0.1082)*	10 per cent improvement on estimated current rate**	603	0.1024
Target BRS_{NE} (=0.1082)*	5 per cent reduction on estimated current rate**	−150	0.1178
Target BRS_{NE} (=0.1082)*	10 percent reduction on estimated current rate**	−376	0.1229

* The 'target' rate is assumed to be the current rate for the RUK.
** The percentage change is applied to the survival rate in each year following registration.

7 Conclusion

This paper has examined some key issues relating to the targeting of the birth rate as part of a regional regeneration policy, a practice that is widespread among RDAs in England. The paper has raised some important questions over the appropriateness of targeting the birth rate, arguing that formation activity cannot be seen in isolation from other aspects of the regional economy and that it may simply not be possible to devise effective policies to raise such activity, even if such a goal were desirable. It has shown that precisely how the rate is defined may have important implications for policy intervention. It has also shown that however this target rate is defined, attempts by a particular region to identify that rate with the rate existing elsewhere in the country may generate considerable uncertainty in terms of the implications for numbers of births, as other regions may at the same time also be trying to influence their own birth rates. Further uncertainties over the number of births necessary to achieve the target rate arise when the survival rate is a parallel target and account is taken of the economic interrelationships between births and deaths.

Irrespective of whether or not it makes sense to target the birth rate, it is nevertheless possible to enhance our knowledge of regional differences in birth rates in a way that assists policy formulation. An "accounting" decomposition of the birth rate along the lines suggested in this paper may for example help to identify the source of the differences between a particular region and the rest of the country. Certainly for the NE, our preliminary analysis suggests that the source of these differences lies more in differences between the NE and RUK in the birth rate in the same industry rather than in the NE having an industrial structure that is less favourable to formation activity. Some detailed consideration by policymakers of why this is the case might be a helpful starting point for determining strategy on births.

Notes

1 The author is most grateful to the Department of Trade and Industry for providing the data that forms the basis of this paper. He would also like to thank colleagues at the Durham Business School and the British Academy of Management Annual Meeting, London, September 2002, for helpful comments on earlier drafts. The usual disclaimer applies.
2 Data kindly supplied to the author by the DTI. The data relate to the 1993 and 1994 cohort of new registrations in the region. It should be noted that exit is not synonymous with failure.
3 For a good recent survey, see Le (1999).
4 Yorkshire and Humberside promised such targets.
5 Two variables for which this is true are the size structure of industry and the political complexion of local government.
6 For a discussion of some of the challenges faced by the RDAs in undertaking this task, see Roberts and Benneworth (2001).
7 Under the Regional Development Agencies Act 1998.
8 Lead responsibility for sponsorship of the RDAs is now with the Department of Trade and Industry, although the Department of Transport, Local Government and the Regions (DTLR) remains responsible for the regeneration programmes – Single Regeneration Budget, Land and Property – which are administered by RDAs on behalf of DTLR.
9 See the old DETR's website: http://www.local-regions.detr.gov.uk/rda/indicators/index.htm, still available at the time of writing, 21 January 2001. The same information may also be accessed through the DTI website.
10 The criticism of arbitrariness was acknowledged in the evaluation of the strategy commissioned by ONE (SQW Limited 2002, p. 24).
11 This figure is the difference between the actual number of registrations in 1999 in the North East and what that figure would have been if the BRS_{RUK} had been applied to the stock of registered businesses in the North East at the beginning of 1999.
12 This figure is the difference between the actual number of registrations in 1999 in the North East and what that figure would have been if the BRP_{RUK} had been applied to the population of the North East at the beginning of 1999.

Appendix I RDA Policies towards business formation

(Unless otherwise stated, page numbers refer to the relevant Strategy document)

Name of RDA (1999 Strategy document in brackets)	Targets on overall level of business formation		Targets on survival		Targets on high growth businesses	
	Non quantitative	*Quantitative*	*Non quantitative*	*Quantitative*	*Non quantitative*	*Quantitative*
1	*2*	*3*	*4*	*5*	*6*	*7*
One North East (*Unlocking Our Potential*)	"We must motivate those already in the Region to start new businesses and equip them with the skills to do so. We must encourage entrepreneurs to move to the North East from elsewhere" (p. 44)	Increase business formation rate (births as % of opening business stock) to U.K average by 2010 (p. 103)	None specified	Increase small firms survival to U.K. average by 2010 (p. 103)	"The region will encourage start-ups of fast growth businesses." (p. 9) "The North East must become a natural home for fast-growth businesses." (p. 45)	Increase number of new high technology businesses to U.K average by 2010 (p. 103) Create 200 high growth companies by 2010 (p. 45)
East Midlands Development Agency (*East Midlands Prosperity through East Midlands People*)	"Develop a strong culture of enterprise and innovation . . . and creating a climate within which entrepreneurs and	38 business starts per 10K of adult population by 2005; 40 by 2010 (*Regional Delivery Plan, 2000–2003*, May 2000, p. 60)	See Column 2	62% of businesses surviving 3 years by 2005; 65% by 2010 (*Regional Delivery Plan*, May 2000)	See Column 2	50 entrepreneurial spin-offs secured within 5 years (p. 39). [It is hoped that in the main, these spin-offs will be in the knowledge

	world class businesses can prosper" (p.18) "Marked improvement in business formation and survival rates" (p. 39)	None specified, but targets promised for 2005 and 2010 (p. 39). [Target in terms of VAT registrations as % of business stock.]	See Column 2	None, but targets promised for 2005 and 2010 (p. 39). [Target in terms of three year business survival rates.]	See Column 2	knowledge intensive industries and use new technologies.] None specified
Yorkshire Forward (*Regional Economic Strategy for Yorkshire and Humber*)	"To achieve higher business birth and survival rates to create a radical improvement in the number of new, competitive businesses that last" (p. 6) "We have a vision of a world class region ... that has a culture of enterprise and creativity ..." (p. 11)				

Continued

Appendix I *continued*

Name of RDA (1999 Strategy document in brackets)	Targets on overall level of business formation		Targets on survival		Targets on high growth businesses	
	Non quantitative	Quantitative	Non quantitative	Quantitative	Non quantitative	Quantitative
1	*2*	*3*	*4*	*5*	*6*	*7*
East of England Development Agency (*Moving Forward A Strategy for the East of England*)	"Increase the number of business start-ups, especially those with high growth potential and help existing SMEs grow" (p.12) "A key priority will be to ensure that the region meets the target set by government for creating new high growth potential start ups." (p.14) Fostering an "entrepreneurial culture" (p. 14)	None specified		None specified	See Column 2	Meet or exceed target of 1135 new high growth businesses. (p. 48) [Ongoing time scale]

Advantage West Midlands (*Creating Advantage*)	"... there will be improved access to ... support for business start-ups." (p.6) "As a region we need to develop these links [between new ideas and business] by ... increasing ... entrepreneur-ship." (p. 23; see also p. 42)	None specified	None as yet, though the development of various targets is promised	None specified	None as yet, though the development of various targets is promised
South East England Development Agency (*Building a World Class Region*)	[The Region] "needs to secure a step change increase in the business birth rate and in the number of businesses achieving significant rates of growth... There is also a critical need to create an environment in which entrepreneurs can thrive" (p. 15)	None specified	None specified	See Column 2 "Establish new and effective support systems to increase the rate of start-ups with high growth potential" (p.13) "Facilitate spin-outs from universities, research establishments and large business" (p.13)	None specified

Continued

Appendix I *continued*

Name of RDA (1999 Strategy document in brackets) *1*	Targets on overall level of business formation		Targets on survival		Targets on high growth businesses	
	Non quantitative *2*	Quantitative *3*	Non quantitative *4*	Quantitative *5*	Non quantitative *6*	Quantitative *7*
South West of England Development Agency (*Regional Strategy for the South West of England*)	"The region also needs to encourage new businesses to start, existing businesses to grow and diversify and companies from other parts of the U.K and overseas to relocate and invest in the South West" (Section 2: Strategy, p. 7)	None specified	None specified	None specified	None specified	None specified
Northwest Development Agency (*England's North West: A Strategy towards 2020*)	"To accelerate the creation of successful businesses, the NWDA together with partners will therefore promote entrepreneurial activity . . . to increase business creation, survival and growth . . ." (p. 25)	No of new business start ups per 10K adult residents raised to 36 by 2003 and 38 by 2006 (p. 63) Proportion of work force in self employment raised to 11 per cent by 2003 and 11.5 per cent by 2006 (p. 63)	See Column 2	None specified	To create the right conditions for spinouts in . . . targeted growth areas (p. 25)	None specified

Appendix II Formation rate simulations in the NE

This appendix gives the derivation of the data in Table 15.3. The starting point for the simulations on which that table was based was the assumption that the same birth rate, once chosen, would prevail in each of the years up to 2010. In order to examine the behaviour of the stock figure, it was necessary to estimate a survival function for registered businesses by their age from registration. This survival function was then applied both to the existing stock at the beginning of 1999 and to each annual cohort of newcomers up to 2010.

The survival function was based on survival data provided to the author by the Department of Trade and Industry for each new annual cohort of registrations, 1993–1998. The relevant data are reproduced below.

Table A1 Survival rates of new registrations, NE: 1993–1998

Cohort year	1993	1994	1995	1996	1997	1998
No of regns.	5010	4450	4090	4085	4165	4215
% surviving after:						
6 months	92	92	92	94	95	97
12 months	82	82	84	86	88	93
18 months	73	72	76	78	80	
24 months	65	65	69	71	77	
30 months	58	59	62	65		
36 months	53	54	57	63		
42 months	48	49	53			
48 months	44	45	51			
54 months	41	43				
60 months	39	41				
66 months	37					
72 months	35					

It should be noted that there is evidence of increasing survival rates though time. It was assumed therefore that the estimated survival function for the 1998 cohort, for whom only two periods of actual data were available, provided the most appropriate survival function post 1999 for both new registrations and for the existing stock. The survival data for cohorts registering in the five years prior to 1998 were used to estimate a function for 72 months after registration for the 1998 cohort in the following way. Let V_t^c be the actual survival rate at time t (measured in months) of cohort c (defined in terms of the year of registration) and $V_{t,est}^c$ an estimate of that rate. Then

$$V_{18,est}^{1998} = (V_{18}^{1997}/V_{12}^{1997}) \times V_{12}^{1998}$$

$$V_{24,est}^{1998} = (V_{24}^{1997}/V_{18}^{1997}) \times V_{18,est}^{1998}$$

$$V_{30,est}^{1998} = (V_{30}^{1996}/V_{24}^{1996}) \times V_{24,est}^{1998}$$

and so on. This procedure gives the following survival function for the 1998 cohort.

Table A2 Survival function for 1998 cohort

No of regns.	4215
% surviving after:	
6 months	97
12 months	93
18 months	85
24 months	81
30 months	74
36 months	71
42 months	64
48 months	60
54 months	56
60 months	54
66 months	51
72 months	49

An exponential function was then fitted to the estimated values for the 1998 cohort to provide estimates of survival rates after 72 months over the period up to 2010. This function ($V_{t,est}^{1998} = 106.7e^{-0.0567t}$) was used to calculate the survival of the stock already existing at the beginning of 1998, and the survival of new registrations entering in each of the years up to 2010. An age breakdown of the existing stock enabled the survival function to be applied appropriately.

The assumptions on the birth and survival rates does of course automatically generate the death rate. The simulation thus assumes that policy makers can only affect the birth and survival function; they do not influence directly the death rate.

References

Acs, Z. J., D. B. Audretsch and D. S. Evans, 1992, *The Determinants of Variations in Self-Employment Rates across Countries and over Time*, mimeo, second draft. Cambridge, MA: National Economic Research Associates, Inc.

Armington, C. and Z. J. Acs, 2002, 'The Determinants of Regional Variation in New Firm Formation', *Regional Studies*, **36**, 33–45.

Ashcroft, B. and J. H. Love, 1996, 'Employment Change and New Firm Formation in UK Counties, 1981–9', in M. W. Danson (ed.), *Small Firm Formation and Regional Economic Development*, London: Routledge, pp. 17–35.

Audretsch, D. B., 1999, 'Linking Entrepreneurship to Economic Growth', in G. D. Libecap (ed.), *The Sources of Entrepreneurial Activity. Advances in the Study of Entrepreneurship and Economic Growth*, Vol 11, Stamford, CT: JAI Press, pp. 1–28.

Bennett, R. J., P. J. A. Robson and W. J. A. Bratton, 2001, 'Government Advice Networks for SMEs: an Assessment of the Influence of Local Context on Business Link Use, Impact and Satisfaction', *Applied Economics*, **33**, 871–885.

Black, J., D. de Meza and D. Jeffreys, 1996, 'House Prices, the Supply of Collateral and the Enterprise Economy', *Economic Journal*, **106**, 60–75.

Blanchflower, D. G. and A. Oswald, 1991, *What Makes an Entrepreneur?* National Bureau of Economic Research Working Paper 3252, revised. Cambridge, MA: NBER.

Cambridge Econometrics, 2000, *Regional Economic Prospects. Volume 1: Main Report*, Cambridge: Cambridge Econometrics.

DTI, 1998, *Our Competitive Future: Building the Knowledge Driven Economy*, CM 4176, London: Stationery Office.

DTI/DfEE, 2001, *Opportunity for All in a World of Change: a White Paper on Skills Enterprise and Innovation*, URN01/538C, London: DTI.

East Midlands Development Agency, 1999, *Economic Development Strategy for the East Midlands. Regional Delivery Plan 2000–2003*. Nottingham: East Midlands Development Agency.

Evans, L. E., P. S. Johnson and R. B. Thomas, 1995, *The Northern Region Economy: Progress and Prospects in the North of England*, London: Mansell.

Evans, D. S. and L. S. Leighton, 1989, 'The Determinants of Changes in US Self-Employment, 1968–1987', *Small Business Economics*, **1**, 111–119.

Fothergill, S., 2001, 'The True Scale of the Regional Problem in the U.K.', *Regional Studies*, **35**, 241–246.

Gallagher, C., J. Kidd and P. Miller, 1996, 'Empirical Research on the Role of New Firms in Scotland', in M. W. Danson (ed.), *Small Firm Formation and Regional Economic Development*, London: Routledge, pp. 65–80.

Hart, P.E. and N. Oulton, 2001, 'Galtonian Regression, Company Age and Job Generation 1986–95', *Scottish Journal of Political Economy*, **48**, 82–98.

Holtz-Eakin, D., 2000, 'Public Policy towards Entrepreneurship', *Small Business Economics*, **15**, 283–291.

Hudson, R., 1998, *Production, Places and Environment*, Harlow: Prentice Hall.

Johnson, P. S., 1983, 'New Manufacturing Firms in the UK Regions', *Scottish Journal of Political Economy*, **30**, 75–79.

Johnson, P. S. and S. Parker, 1996, 'Spatial Variations in the Determinants and Effects of Firm Births and Deaths', *Regional Studies*, **30**, 679–688.

Keeble, D. and S. Walker, 1994, 'New Firms, Small Firms and Dead Firms: Spatial Patterns and Determinants in the United Kingdom', *Regional Studies*, **28**, 411–427.

Le, A. T., 1999, 'Empirical Studies of Self-Employment' *Journal of Economic Surveys*, **13**, 381–417.

Northwest Development Agency, 1999, *England's North West. A Strategy towards 2020*, Warrington: Northwest Development Agency.

One NorthEast, 1999, *Regional Economic Strategy for the North East. Unlocking our Potential*. Newcastle: One North East.

One NorthEast, 2001, *Everybody's Business. The North East of England Enterprise Strategy*. Newcastle: One North East.

One NorthEast, 2002a, *Realising Our Potential: Economic Anaysis and Technical Report*. Newcastle: One North East.

One NorthEast, 2002b, *Realising Our Potential: the Regional Economic Strategy for the North East of England*. Newcastle: One North East.

Roberts, P. and P. Benneworth, 2001, 'Pathways to the Future? An Initial Assessment of RDA Strategies and their Contribution to Integrated Regional Development', *Local Economy*, **16**, 142–159.

Robson, P. J. A and R. J. Bennett, 2000, 'SME Growth: the Relationship with Business Advice and External Collaboration', *Small Business Economics*, **15**, 193–208.

Schmitz, J. A., 1989, 'Entrepreneurship, and Long-Run Growth', *Journal of Political Economy*, **97**, 721–739.

Small Business Service, 2000, *Business Start-Ups and Closures: VAT Registrations and De-Registrations, 1980–99*, URN00/111, Sheffield: Research and Evaluation Unit, Small Business Service, October.

South East Development Agency, 1999, *Building a World Class Region. An Economic Strategy for the South East of England*. Guildford: South East Development Agency.

SQW Limited, 2002 *Regional Economic Strategy Evaluation Study. A Final Report to ONE NorthEast*, Cambridge: SQW.

Storey, D. J. and S. Johnson, 1987, 'Regional Variations in Entrepreneurship in the UK', *Scottish Journal of Political Economy*, **34**, 161–173.

Thurik, A. R., 1999, 'Entrepreneurship, Industrial Transformation and Growth', in G. D. Libecap, (ed), *The Sources of Entrepreneurial Activity. Advances in the Study of Entrepreneurship and Economic Growth*, Vol 11, Stamford, CT: JAI Press, pp. 29–65.

16 Some reflections

The papers in this volume help in a modest way to demonstrate the complexity of small firm activity and development and provide illustrations of some of the methodological and data issues faced by researchers in this area. The nature of these challenges does of course change over time as the result of changes in, for example, the economic, technological and cultural environment in which small firms operate and in research approaches and techniques. However, the preceding papers also raise some research issues and challenges that have a certain timelessness about them. Some of these are sketched out below.

Definitional issues

The discussion of definitional issues rarely fires the imagination. Yet such issues are important in the interpretation of results. The definitions of formation, founder, new firm or small firm in the papers in this volume are largely dictated by the particular data sources employed. However it is important to be aware of their limitations and how they relate to other relevant concepts.

'Newness' for example is multi-dimensional. Using one definition only (based on, say, VAT or company registrations) raises the question of how far research results are specific to the particular definition used. Similarly, 'small' may be variously defined. Different yardsticks (e.g. sales, employment, assets) may be utilised and rank firms differently in terms of their size. Even when the yardstick is agreed, 'small' is not an unambiguous category. As has been pointed out elsewhere (Johnson 2007: 9–10), official definitions have changed over the years, a fact that reflects this ambiguity. Another definitional issue – already alluded too – relates to the firm–establishment distinction. These units of analysis cannot be regarded as identical.

Potentially, these definitional matters have important research implications. One way in which these implications may be explored is by examining the sensitivity of the results to changes in definitions. Unfortunately, this in turn requires a richness in data that is not always available.

The interrelatedness of economic activity

New and small firms are part of a bigger and complex economic system. Research needs to take account of this 'embeddedness', not least through a careful acknowledgement of the ways in which one element of the system may affect another.

Such interrelatedness is expressed in all sorts of ways and at different levels. For example, at the macro level, business formation is influenced by, and influences, economic aggregates (see chapter 6) and industrial structure (chapters 2, 5 and 7). At the micro level, the extent of competition from other firms will affect the survivability and success of a new venture and the impact it makes on economic activity. When it comes to looking at the behaviour and performance of firms in a particular size band, the effect of what is happening in *other* size bands is likely to be an important influence.

Interrelatedness may have a spatial dimension too: the economies of different regions impact on each other. For example, variations in regional prices and in the tightness of the labour market will lead to flows of actual and potential business founders and existing small businesses across boundaries, as individuals search for better economic opportunities. Johnson (2003) provides some preliminary evidence on this phenomenon.

The relevance of economic interrelatedness is also shown in the formation decision, since potential new business founders are affected not only by perceived prospects in own account activity, but also by how they see paid employment opportunities. (Chapters 3 and 8 are relevant here.)

Awareness of the interrelatedness of economic activity is especially important when it comes to the formulation and evaluation of policy measures for new and small firms. As far as policy formulation is concerned, the encouragement of formations and small business activity cannot be viewed in isolation from the current economic context. For example, the opportunities for business formation and the supply of would-be founders are significantly affected by such factors as income levels and industrial structure (see chapter 15).

In policy evaluation, knock-on effects may assume considerable importance. Chapter 14 makes some, albeit modest, attempt to take these effects into account. Policy assistance for one firm will almost certainly have implications for other (non-assisted) firms. These implications may be positive or negative. Positive effects may result, for example where the policy-assisted firm raises the survival and growth rates in other firms. Economies of agglomeration have obvious relevance here. In addition, the policy-assisted new firm may directly encourage other formations, especially if it is innovative in character. In rare cases, major innovations may spawn entirely new industries. Negative effects may arise when the policy-assisted firm forces others out of business, or to contract.

Positive *and* negative knock-on effects may occur simultaneously. For example, an innovative new firm may give rise to a new industry, but the firms that are unable to imitate the innovation may find the demand for their products disappearing. The inclusion of knock-on effects does however raise big problems of measurement. A key issue here is how widely the knock-on effects 'net' is cast in terms both of geographical coverage and of the supply chain.

Formation as a process

In chapter 3 potential founders are portrayed as comparing, at a particular point in time, the likely returns from own-account activity with those from paid employment. This approach makes for simplicity. However, other papers in this volume point to formation activity as a *process*. Chapters 2 and 8 for example highlight the potential relevance of previous labour market experience as a stimulus to formation activity. Individuals usually think about setting up in business long before they actually do so. Chapter 4 gives further modest support to this process view of formation by pointing out, with supporting evidence, that VAT registration and the start of trading may occur at different times. The fairly recent development of the literature on nascent entrepreneurship has of course provided a powerful emphasis on the process nature of starting up. (For an excellent review of this literature see Davidsson 2005.)

It is important, too, to recognise in all this that individuals who have been involved in earlier ventures learn *over time* about own-account business activity. Such 'serial entrepreneurs' are thus likely to approach each successive formation decision in a different way. Thus past and present activity are interrelated. Similarly, someone involved in running a 'portfolio' of business activities is often able to learn in one area in a way that helps in another. (For a recent comprehensive study on serial and portfolio entrepreneurs, see Ucbasaran et al. 2006.)

Reconciling results

One of the features of the empirical work on new and small firms is the mixed results that have been generated on similar topics. For example, well over a decade ago, Storey highlighted the different findings from four investigations seeking to identify the factors influencing self-employment (Storey 1994: 65–67). More recently, Johnson et al. (2006) have drawn attention to some of the seemingly conflicting results coming out of nascent entrepreneurship studies. Again, Johnson (2007: 61; 1988) has highlighted the different findings generated by studies of the determinants of formation activity. A number of the papers in this volume have also referred to differences in research results

Different results are to be expected, given the variety of data sets, time periods and statistical methods used. It would however increase understanding if rather more effort was devoted to identifying more precisely the source of these differences.

A final word: the importance of keeping a broader perspective

The small business sector plays a crucial role in developed economies and the efforts of researchers over the past few decades have led to a greatly enhanced knowledge of that role. Yet it is important that the sector is seen as part of the economic system as a whole. Within a particular sector, newer firms will typically exist alongside older ones, and smaller firms alongside larger ones. Furthermore, sectors differ significantly in their age and size distributions. These variations reflect a complex range of influences, including production technology, the capacities of management and owners, the nature of demand and the policy environment. The research challenge in all this is to see new and small firms as two elements only, albeit often very significant ones, in the overall economic system.

This kind of perspective immediately raises the issue – already alluded to in the Introduction in relation to entrepreneurship (p. 5) – of what constitutes the optimal mix of small and large firms, and new and old firms, in the economic system, a mix that is likely to vary through time and across sectors. It also highlights the question of how the different elements interact with each other. The papers in this volume touch fleetingly and then often only indirectly, on these important issues. A considerable research agenda remains.

References

Davidsson, P. (2005) 'Developments in the study of nascent entrepreneurs', paper given at the Conference on Nascent Entrepreneurship: the Hidden Potential, Durham, UK, September.

Johnson, P.S. (2003) 'A note on the interregional movement of new companies', *Applied Economics Letters* 10: 463–6.

Johnson, P.S., Parker, S.C. and Wijbenga, F. (2006) 'Nascent entrepreneurship research: achievements and opportunities', *Small Business Economics* 27: 1–4.

Johnson, P.S. (2007) *The Economics of Small Firms: An Introduction*, London: Routledge.

Storey, D. (1994) *Understanding the Small Business Sector*, London: Routledge.

Ucbasaran, D., Westhead, P. and Wright, M. (2006) *Habitual Entrepreneurs*, Cheltenham: Edward Elgar.

Index

Page numbers in *italics* refer to tables.

For Product Safety concerns and information please contact our EU representative GPSR@taylorandfrancis.com Taylor & Francis Verlag GmbH, Kaufingerstraße 24, 80331 München, Germany